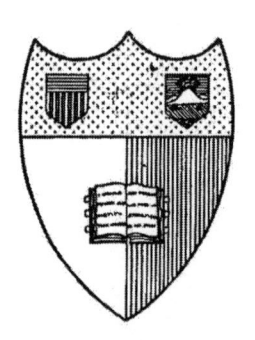

Cornell University Library
Ithaca, New York

FROM

Hispanic Society

Cornell University Library
NA 997.S91A3

George Edmund Street :unpublished notes

PUBLICATIONS OF
THE HISPANIC SOCIETY OF AMERICA
No. 100

ZAMORA ON THE DOURO

GEORGE EDMUND STREET

UNPUBLISHED NOTES
AND
REPRINTED PAPERS

WITH AN ESSAY

BY

GEORGIANA GODDARD KING

QUAM DILECTA TABERNACULA TUA DOMINE VIRTUTUM

THE HISPANIC SOCIETY
OF AMERICA
1916

COPYRIGHT, 1916, BY
THE HISPANIC SOCIETY
OF AMERICA

CONTENTS

I.	1
II. NOTES OF A TOUR IN CENTRAL ITALY . .	59
III. NOTES ON FRENCH CHURCHES	97
SOME FRENCH CHURCHES CHIEFLY IN THE ROYAL DOMAIN	99
ARCHITECTURAL NOTES IN FRANCE	127
SOME CHURCHES OF LE PUY EN VELAY AND AUVERGNE	201
APPENDIX	253
S. MARY'S STONE	255
CHURCHES IN NORTHERN GERMANY	270
INDEX	333

LIST OF ILLUSTRATIONS

Zamora on the Douro . . . . *Frontispiece*

                                                                         PAGE

George Street at about twenty-five 8
In Leon Cathedral 29
The Old Cathedral of Salamanca 46
George Edmund Street in 1877 57
Master Matthew's Porch at Santiago 92
The Ambulatory, Cathedral of Tours 127
The South Transept at Soissons 162
Nave and Transept, Salamanca 196
The Templars' Church at Segovia 227
The Western Porch, Saumur 249
Rood-screen in Lübeck Cathedral 271
The Great S. Martin, Cologne 307

GEORGE EDMUND STREET

I have to thank Arthur Edmund Street, Esq., of London, for the generous loan of some notebooks and drawings, and through these for a more intimate knowledge of his great father's fine temper and manly art.

Bryn Mawr, *Epiphany*, 1915

I

"And he that talked with me had a golden reed to measure the city, and the gates thereof and the walls thereof. And the city lieth foursquare, and the length is as large as the breadth. And the building of the wall of it was of jasper; every several gate was of one pearl."

GEORGE EDMUND STREET

I

I HAVE written the memorial, brief enough and all inadequate, of a man who died more than thirty years ago, who lived a Tory and a High Churchman, who worked to revive Gothic architecture in England. His books are out of print, his occasional papers and pamphlets so entirely dispersed and forgotten that not even a bibliography can be recovered. His name goes unrecognized in general talk; his party is wasted to a wraith or transformed beyond recognition; his Church is menaced by Disestablishment in Wales, and Modernism on the Continent; his strong and sincere architecture is superseded by steel and concrete; yet no man ever less fought a losing fight, no figure ever less evoked regret or toleration. He prospered, but his personality made that a kind of happy consequence; he served God, but his genius made that a kind of crowning grace; he was an Englishman, but was that in no mean or halfway fashion. Rather, George Street embodied and expressed in his own temper the very genius of the northern kind.

His people were substantial, of the strong British stock which is good for grafting on. In the sixteenth century they were respected in and about Worcester; one of the name went to Parliament in 1563, and another had been Mayor in 1535. In the eighteenth century some of them went to Surrey, and early in the nineteenth Thomas Street was a solicitor in London. He had moved into the suburbs, however, before his youngest son, George Edmund Street, was born. This was in 1824. The boy did well enough at school, but at fifteen he was taken away, when his father removed from Camberwell to Crediton. No school was at hand, and a solicitor would not send his son to Eton and Oxford. Instead, he sent him to the London office. This was in 1840. After the father's death, in that year, young Street was anxious to go to college and to prepare for Holy Orders, but want of money made the hope impossible, and the strong vocation proved to be for the Third Order — a layman's part in building up the house of the Lord and making fair the ministry therein.

It seems to have mattered not at all, in the event, that Street was not a University man. In reading the correspondence of Keats, we must deplore that he had not had certain conventions of good taste and good feeling sharply imposed upon him at a great public school; in reading the poetry of Browning we must regret that he missed the tradition of self-criticism and academic stability which would have saved him from the fantasticality of his Greek names and the dullness of his longer *Parleyings;* but Street seems to have got out of his profession and his associates all that Oxford would have given, and escaped whatever harm it could have done.

He saved, meanwhile, nearly ten years of life, and spent these on churches, chiefly old. He has not the marks of the University man, but for that he is none the worse. No more in truth has Morris. Instead of culture he has energy, instead of urbanity he has self-control, instead of classical he has professional reading behind him. It is only in a very special sense, after all, that he did without what we call culture and what we call urbanity; in the sense of Newman's rather malicious definition of a gentleman as a University man who is too indifferent for enthusiasms and too sceptical for prejudices. If young Street never went to school after he was fifteen, and no record remains of his reading regularly or under direction, yet he read irregularly all his life; by middle age he had read everything that a man must have read. Beyond this, in the subjects that he had at heart he had gone wide and deep. He must have mastered and spoken, besides French and German, both Italian and Spanish, and he carried on his research into Latin documents, it seems, with ease and speed. After meals and on journeys the busy man found his opportunity; he took up and took in a vast deal of contemporary thinking; finished the newspaper quickly, and reviews and the graver sort of periodical literature almost as fast. In his case, as rarely happens, another art could give what most men seek in literature if they ever seek it, and the taste was refined and the spirit inspired not so much by fine poetry as by pure Gothic. The churches of England and the cathedrals of France taught him that perfect measure, that economy of force, that high seriousness, that austerity of beauty, for which others are sent to the *Iliad* and the *Divine Comedy*. Barring *belles-lettres* and biology, there is little indeed, whether in science or in mathematics, that the University can offer, which the arts do not exact. If architecture is on the one side an art, it is on the other a profession, and partakes as little of the tradesman's mean-mindedness as of the artist's irresponsibility. It is probable, moreover, that his passion for landscape had as much to do in forming the character as Wordsworth's. By the living rock and the ancient wall, by the perfect fabric of Notre Dame and S. Marco, by the worship in chanted psalm and antiphonal prayer, his spirit was forged and tempered.

At school he had sketched and scrawled, and when after his father's death in 1840 he was recalled to live with his mother and sister at Exeter, he studied painting for a while as painting was taught in the provinces, learning the management of oils and the science of perspective. No harm could come from this except that in landscape sketching later he was shy of strong colour, and set down Spain and Italy more pallid than he liked; but already the current of his life was running by church walls. In the year before, his brother, who was eight years his senior and was brim-full of mediaevalism, had taken him on a short walking trip for what they called ecclesiologizing. For a while he lived near Exeter cathedral, drawn to it at that time by every sentiment: grief for his father — since his domestic affections were stable — and anxiety for the future, strong religious feeling, aesthetic feeling as strong, the beauty of the service and the beauty of the building. Thence he made another trip with this same brother, Thomas, around about through the West of England to Barnstaple, Bideford,

Torrington and Clovelly. The diary of that tour, written shortly after his sixteenth birthday, is simply the first of the always happy notebooks which record his many journeys in the interest of landscape and art. It sets down the lay of the land and the aspect of the streets where they passed; it notes that he got up at six to sketch out of his bedroom window; and it preserves more fact than comment, and less of the trivial than of the significant. Within another year he was articled to an architect in Winchester, studying the cathedral from every point and at every hour. The two brothers tramped the country for twenty miles about, and as they could pushed further, for the most part on foot still. In the spring of 1843 they walked to Chichester; in the autumn into Lincolnshire; the next year into Sussex. In 1845 they reached Northampton, returning thither in 1846 and again in 1850. The same autumn he went to the Lake Country and thence across to Durham and home by the Yorkshire dales and abbeys. Jervaulx, however, he missed at this time, nor does it appear among the sketches of other abbeys in a notebook of 1875. In the spring of 1847 the two brothers were among the churches of the fen-land in Norfolk and Cambridgeshire. Meanwhile in 1844 Thomas, who was the eldest of the brothers, and had succeeded to his father's practice, took a house near London and fetched his mother and sister to live with him there.

George, who was lonely and heartily sick of Winchester, came up to share it, with a letter for G. G. Scott and drawings of his own to show. Taken on because work was pressing, he was kept on because his work was good, and stayed in the office of Scott and Moffatt until he was ready to set up for himself five years later. Thomas Street by 1849 was married; the requirements of his profession, if not more serious, were more exacting. He made fewer tours, but his taste for architecture, and apparently his taste in architecture, remained sound. "At this time, they were all living together at Lee, and afterwards at Peckham," says the *Memoir* written in 1888 by George Street's son. "My aunt relates how the two young men used to arrive with sketch-books full and rolls of rubbings of brasses, and would then sit up till the small hours, in all the excitement of archaeological discussions and arguments. My uncle [Thomas] was quite untaught. His love for and appreciation of good architecture were quite spontaneous, and the proficiency which he attained with his pencil and the knowledge he had of this subject, more than considerable."

As the first knowledge of architecture had come through a brother, so Street's first commission came through the sister. Miss Street worked at ecclesiastical embroidery. She heard through another lady embroiderer of a clergyman who intended building a church in Cornwall. The story turns prettily on the scrupulous girl's anxieties. Mr. Prynne, the clergyman, begins — "Has your brother got much work going on?" The sister, who wants to make him out as important as possible, yet cannot bring herself to a fib; and the sorry truth that he is quite at leisure from affairs of his own, unexpectedly satisfies the impatient projector. The commission for Biscovey church led to others in Cornwall. Between restorations and new churches and schools, commissions accumulated, and Street at this period was in those parts for several weeks together, three or four times a year, overseeing the work in progress and finding new work ready always at hand. In 1849 he had chambers in London and was "on his own": at the end of 1850 he went to Wantage to be within reach of Cuddesden, being appointed by the Bishop of Oxford, diocesan architect.

Two main interests mark this time. He was engaged to be married, and he was at the well-spring of the Oxford Movement. He spent his Sundays at Maidenhead with Marquita Proctor, on the river, seeing churches and sketching; he spent his working days at Wantage.

"Mr. Street, having no special ties to any locality, desired to live at Wantage where daily service and weekly celebration had been established at a time when such were rare. He took, therefore, in conjunction with Mr. Stillingfleet — one of the clergy of the parish — a little house in Wallingford Street. During the time he lived there I saw him almost daily." This is Dr. William Butler, later Dean of Lincoln. "When not called from Wantage on business, he regularly attended my service, and took his part in the choir. He had, I remember, a baritone voice, and took a tenor part. He was much interested in the improvement of services, and, although at this time far from wealthy, he offered a large annual subscription, I think it was £20, toward the payment of an organist. . . . Never was there a man of simpler or less luxurious habits. In those two years he dined with us and the clergy of the parish, he drank no wine, and had only the plainest food."

It was an energetic wholesome life, simple not so much

by limitation as by renunciation, full of interest and expression, keeping a right line, as always, by the force of the initial impulse. The energetic, wholesome figure stands firm in a clear sunlight that is hardly dimmed by the space of sixty-odd years intervening. With nothing of the prig, as little of the aesthete, he was alien to both types by virtue of his vitality, his mirth, his essential soundness. A daguerreotype taken about 1850 shows quiet strength with a sort of sweet gravity. The hands are strong and flexible, not large, with tapering fingers and fine modelling on the back. You would have turned in the street to look after the head, with a big square brow jutting over blue eyes, brown hair very soft and round chin very firm, a mouth poetic and self-controlled. If poetry were (as once was rashly said) merely an affair of genius, and genius the affair of energy, Street would have been infallibly a poet. Energy and beauty in him were mingled in unusual measure, and he found expression in active more than in abstract creation: in loving landscape and sketching it, in hearing music and singing it, in building Gothic churches and restoring them.

His invention was inexhaustible; he designed not only all the mouldings for his churches, and all delicately various, not only reredos and pulpit, baldachin and font, and once a whole book of organs, but equally as a matter of course the windows, the stalls, the ironwork, the very altar-cloths. About this time he painted the ceilings to some of his churches after Fra Angelico, and elsewhere from his own designs. His early work may have been a trifle severe at times, and at times a trifle daring, but it had always freshness, vitality, one might say vibration. His capitals ring clearer than

GEORGE EDMUND STREET AT ABOUT TWENTY-FIVE

glass when it is struck; his mouldings sound as true a note as a violin when it is tuned. His building expresses, beyond possibility of mistake, as specific a sentiment as any composition of Palestrina or Fra Angelico: — viz., religious emotion, a combination of reverence and action, a solemn joy. But with this power to express an emotion from within himself and furthermore to create it in others, went an indefatigable energy. He was tall and very ready of movement, thickset and thin-skinned, blue-eyed and brown-bearded, ruddy, compact of strength and gentleness.

The energy found outlet normal and adequate in three directions — his work, his affections and his religion. He worked apparently as a young dog runs, from accumulated motor impulses, from strength that brims over. You have never the pang of our brother the ass, over-ridden, over-laden, that agonizes under the goad. You have never the fever craving for work as anodyne, that drives on desperately at the straining task as the only escape from the hell-hounds that bay hard after the sickening soul. The work is never done for work's sake. It is a pleasure always, but only by the way. It is done to support some one he loves and to add to the glory of God.

The affections are close and sweet, those of the hearth. His mother was a good Christian but even more a Stoic, and Street held her the better for it. Theirs was a love undemonstrative but recognized, of the most exacting sort, neither of them accepting from the other anything short of the very best. After he went to Winchester, being then seventeen, she treated him like a man, and rarely praised him for doing what he should. If a pleasure was renounced, she said, "I knew that under the circumstances you would be Philosopher enough to give it up." Her grandson wrote: "It is enough to read the mother's letters to see the source of the son's strength and steadfastness of character. She was one of those women who, in some indefinable way, have a powerful influence for good on all those into whose company they are thrown; who, themselves rather sparing in outward signs of affection, create in others a warm love and a perfect confidence. Her pride in her son was unbounded, but was left to be inferred rather than expressed; while her love was shown more in the demand for sacrifices, in the confidence with which she appealed to her son's sense of duty and obedience, however severe the test."

Besides a wide and wakeful kindness and untiring interest in others of his own profession, he had full, warm friendships, but where he could he took his pleasure with his nearest of kin. The early journeys were made in his brother's company, the continental with his wife, and later with his son. The brothers, George and Thomas, were married to cousins, and up to the very last the longest and most frequent visits abroad were made to his son's grandfather. After his wife's death he took for a second wife her close friend, an intimate of the household and frequent companion.

The relations not of choice, the intimacies sweetened and consecrated by tender use and wont and all the sanctities of the hearth, the blind impulses of the blood and yearnings of the flesh toward kindred flesh and blood, were for him alike inevitable and dear. Here also he expresses the genius of the English stock. The northern race stood out long for the righteousness of the married life even in the priesthood, and the English church has at all times tended toward the family life as distinguished from the cloistered, and elaborated and adorned those services and sacraments which celebrate marriage and the birth of children and their coming to maturity.

The Church of England may be in a position undignified, uncomfortable, or even ridiculous, coupled up with the State as it is; the doctrine of the great English churchmen may be honeycombed with Erastianism; but the English church has the virtue of providing for every one of her children, lay not less than clerical, a daily office in which they may take an intelligent, a personal, and a common share. The first characteristic of the primitive church was apparently the fact of worship done in common, action in some sort not merely simultaneous but mutual. There are some — the Society of Friends for instance — who define religion by that collectivity of feeling, and in expectation of the Holy Ghost assemble themselves together. They draw most profit from thirty minutes of silent meditation where a hundred people in presence make up that silence and meditate each one. The monastic life, with its multiplied choir offices, met in another way this same desire for the warmth of human contact, this same enhancement of the experience of the whole far beyond the several experiences. The Roman church, with its sodalities and confraternities meeting regularly for special services, its litanies and rosaries recited by tired, troubled women together after nightfall, has recognized this and is busy recovering hereby what has been lost out of the Sacrament of the Mass. I remember after three weeks' incessant travel finding myself in Siena cathedral, among women unquestionably devout, who held well-thumbed books, and, having lost count of the Sundays after Pentecost, as I opened my *Paroissien* I asked my neighbour on the right what Sunday it was. She shook her head and questioned her neighbour; I turned to the one on my left, but there was no one within decent whispering distance who knew what the priests and the choir were singing that day. Against such a chance, their church service assures Anglicans. The English Prayer Book may be a compromise, the office for morning and evening prayer may be patched up and anomalous, but it is an order of common prayer. The instinct of kind enhances the personal expression of psalm and antiphon, and daily service and saints'-day celebration have the sweetness and warmth of the family life, the dearness of the sacred ritual of the hearth.

Into his religion Street was born, as he was born into his family. In the dawn of consciousness he found it about him; with adolescence he felt it an influence and a motive. In the months at Exeter he was anxious often, but always there was the cathedral. In the last year at Winchester he was lonely and sick for home, but at hand there was the cathedral. While in Scott's office he used to go with his sister to mattins before walking into town; in the later years in London he never missed with his wife the early celebration on saints'-days. Church-going was as natural as eating, and as satisfactory. He loved God as consciously as he loved his mother and his wife; and said even less about it. After he gave up the hope of taking Holy Orders he made a plan for a sort of half-monastic fraternity of artists and architects, who should be in art what the Templars were, selected, set apart, and dedicated. It was patterned after his own life unawares.

Younger than any of the great men of the Oxford Movement, he was born in the Promised Land. What they had hardly won, he inherited untroubled. Among the many things the average Englishman would rather go without than talk about, even to himself, may be counted his religion, but the strain of enthusiasm in the temper of Street, the genius that leavens his English substance, would not let him rest without a reason for the faith that was in him. He read and thought much at this time. In later years, while the phrasing is reticent yet the architecture is eloquent. In carved stone and hewn timber, in chant and carol, in the colour and contour of his records of the visible world, he let loose the strong inward impulse that burned upward like a flame. His natural element was creation not conflict, and though he could strike a good blow at "pagan" architecture and services restricted to the clergy and the seventh day, he seems to have had small joy in fighting and it, perhaps, killed him at the last. On the ground, already won, of English Catholicity, he stood firm and built strong and fair. Webbe and Neale and Wilberforce, and I suppose Keble and Pusey, were friends and advisers, but his real contemporaries were the Pre-Raphaelite Brotherhood with their allies and admirers who launched the Aesthetic Movement.

How that was born at Oxford, and was baptized into the English church with the *Heir of Redclyffe* for godfather, is hard to keep in mind. But Morris and Burne-Jones knew each other there and knew Street, who had married in the June of 1852 and taken his wife to a house in Beaumont Street. To us in another century it seems that in those years, from 1852 when the two boys from Walthamstow and Birmingham met and matriculated together at Exeter College, even to 1857 when Rossetti brought them back to paint the walls of the Union, Oxford must have been a place of lightnings and splendours. It sheds the same radiance that a great city just beyond the horizon's bound throws up at night against low-hanging clouds. To them it seemed spiritually grey and dull enough. The Oxford Movement was in a sense ended; some men had broken away, some had got to cover, and in the rest religious emotion, having gone past the stage of smoke and flame, glowed clear but very still. Burne-Jones, according to his wife, "had thought to find the place still warm from the fervour of the learned and pious men who had shaken the whole land by their cry of danger within and without the Church. . . . But when he got there the whole life seemed to him languid and indifferent, with scarcely anything left to show the fiery times so lately past."

"Oxford is a glorious place," he wrote home, "Godlike. At night I have walked round the colleges under the full moon and thought it would be heaven to live and die here." He described it later: —

"It was a different Oxford in those days from anything that a visitor would now dream of. On all sides, except where it touched the railway, the city ended abruptly, as if a wall had been about it, and you came suddenly upon the meadows. There was little brick in the city, it was either grey with stone or yellow with the wash of the pebble-dash in the poorer streets. It was an endless delight with us to wander about the streets where were still many old houses with wood-carving and a little sculpture here and there. The chapel of Merton College had been lately renovated by Butterfield, and Pollin, a former fellow of Merton, had painted the roof of it. Indeed, I think the buildings of Merton and the cloisters of New College were our chief shrines in Oxford."

These two undergraduates, both alike so young and so typically English, lived at a high pitch in those years; each strong impetus pushing hard upon the foregoing. There was, to begin, an intention to take Orders, with a real and inward sense of dedication in both. Out of that flowered Burne-Jones's dream of a Brotherhood very like that which Street had earlier nursed. "A small conventual society of cleric and lay members working in the heart of London," his wife called it soberly, many years later, but he himself, at the time, "the Order of Sir Galahad." To a friend he wrote at the end of a letter — and the postcript is like one of his own exquisite pencil drawings, all archaic, and altogether lovely: "You have as yet taken no vows, therefore you are as yet perfectly at liberty to decide your own fate. If your decision involve the happiness of another you know your course, follow nature, and remember the soul is above the mind and the heart greater than the brain; for it is mind that makes man, but soul that makes man angel. Man as the seat of mind is isolated in the universe, for angels that are above him and hearts that are below him are mindless, but it is soul that links him with higher beings and distinguishes him from the lower also, therefore develops it to the full, and if you have one who may serve for a personification of all humanity, expand your love there, and it will orb from its centre wider and wider, like circles in water when a stone is thrown therein. But self-denial and self-disappointment, though I do not urge it, is even better to the soul than that. If we lose you from the cause of celibacy, you are no traitor; only do not be hasty. *Pax vobiscum in æternum*— Edouard."

That summer they went to France and saw Amiens. Their companion said: "Morris surveyed it with calm joy and Jones was speechless with admiration. It did not awe me until it got quite dark, for we stayed till after seven, but it was so solemn, so human and divine in its beauty that love cast out fear." They went to Beauvais, Paris and Chartres. "There we were for two days, spending all our time in the church, and thence made northward for Rouen, travelling gently and stopping at every church we could find. Rouen was still a beautiful mediaeval city, and we stayed awhile and had our hearts filled. From there we walked to Caudebec, then by diligence to Havre, on our way to the churches of the Calvados; and it was while walking on the quay at Havre at night that we resolved definitely that we would begin a life of art and put off our decision no longer — he should be an architect and I a painter. It was a resolve only needing final conclusion; we were bent on that road for the whole past year and after that night's talk we never hesitated more— that was the most memorable night of my life."

They were to start *The Oxford and Cambridge Magazine*, and Burne-Jones was to meet Rossetti and very heartily worship him but never to be drawn, even by that blazing, fiery star, out of his own orbit of art deliberate and devout. Morris meanwhile, as soon as he had taken his degree, addressed himself to work under Street. Afterwards, as we know, he tried painting, before he found his happiest outlet in decorative designing, in dyeing and printing, and surely his finest and most enduring expression in the writing that came so easily we can only wish that he had taken it harder. A note of Burne-Jones's in the year 1856 is so charming and so characteristic that it may well serve as the note of the whole set when they had really found themselves. "There was a year in which I think it never rained nor clouded, but was blue summer from Christmas to Christmas, and London streets glimmered, and it was always morning, and the air sweet and full of bells."

Their lives were, however, what could not be called less than intense. Their emotions were all fervid and their sentiments all impassioned, their enthusiasms fairly militant, their convictions even intransigent. Lady Burne-Jones communicates an exquisite sense of their way of being something better than human nature's daily food:

"I wish it were possible to explain the impression made upon me as a young girl. . . The only approach I can make to describing it is by saying that I felt in the presence of a new religion. Their love of beauty did not seem to me unbalanced, but as if it included the whole world and raised the point from which they regarded everything." Again she quotes from a letter of her husband's, written long afterwards, an impression of that first journey into France. "Do you know Beauvais, which is the most beautiful church in the world? I must see it again some day — one day I must. It is thirty-seven years since I saw it and I remember it all

— and the processions — and the trombones — and the ancient singing — more beautiful than anything I had ever heard and I think I have never heard the like since. And the great organ that made the air tremble — and the greater organ that pealed out suddenly and I thought the Day of Judgement had come — and the roof, and the long lights that are the most graceful thing man has ever made. What a day it was, and how alive I was, and young — and a blue dragon-fly stood still in the air so long that I could have painted him. Yes, if I took account of my life and the days in it that went to make me, the Sunday at Beauvais would be the first day of creation."

Emotion exquisite and almost as frail as the dragon-fly, almost as quick to pass as the Sunday sunlight! It is the impression of a boy, an aesthete and a poet, who kept to the end of his days the same sensibility and the same delight in beauty tangible. What he expresses, however, he felt with his generation; his associates had a like organization and a like attitude. In that very year Street, who had gone first to France, at a like age, not so long before, wrote from recollection, in a paper that was read at Oxford and published at Cambridge:

"One of the first elements is height. I know of no one thing in which one is so much astonished, in all one's visits to foreign churches, as by the luxury of that art which could afford to be so daringly grand. From the small chapel, not forty feet long, to the glorious minster of some four hundred, one feels more and more impressed with the sense which the old men evidently entertained of its value; and exaggerated as it often is, even to the most curious extent, it is never contemptible. It is indeed a glorious element of grandeur, and not the less to be admired by Englishmen because we seem always to have preferred length to it; whilst they, so they could have height, cared little as to the length to which they could draw out a long arcade, and prolong the infinite perspective of a roof. And there is perhaps this advantage of height over length, that whilst the one seems entirely done for the glory of God, the other is always more apparently for use. So in a church, height in excess seems to typify the excess of their adoration who so built; whilst the greater length makes one think of possible calculations as to how many thousands of men and women might pass through, or how long a procession. . . . And as I have said so much about foreign examples I will but observe that the wonderful beauty of the apsidal east ends abroad ought to be gladly seized upon. . . . No one who has stood as I have at the west end of such a cathedral as that at Chartres, and watched the last rays die out from all other windows and at last gradually fade away from the eastern crown of light in its five windows; or who has seen the mounting sun come through all those openings one after the other, with matchless and continued brilliancy, would deny that such glorious beauties are catholic of necessity, and not to be confined by custom or etiquette to one age or one nation."

There is the expression of the man, mustering his facts, enforcing his conclusions, weighing his estimates, recording of his pleasure the least possible part. The comparison is hardly fair to painter or builder either, but it is none the less significant. His power of expression, to be sure, is less, and his determination toward self-control is greater, but all the while the source of delight, though stiller, is no less deep. Street's private notebooks are as reticent as his public papers. Like everything else that he did, they illustrate the characteristic maxim which opens *The Christian Year*, that, next to a sound rule of faith, there is nothing of so much consequence as a sober standard of feeling — strong feeling, but sober. A better notion of his response to beauty could be formed from some personal letters that he wrote in 1845, being then twenty-one years of age.

"I got out at Milton station and trudged off for Lanercost Abbey, an enthusiastic ecclesiologist, with everything upon earth to make my enthusiasm higher than usual — a glorious autumn day, a beautiful walk and an abbey in prospect, in ruins it is true, but so lovely and admirable in its ruin that in my admiration of it, the day, and the scenery, I had almost forgotten to be enraged with its iconoclastic destroyers; but it was not in mortal temper, after having seen and sketched it and studied it carefully and lovingly as I did, to ascend the hill away from it, to look at the river still rushing along as beautiful and as swift as when holy men planned its bridge of yore, to look at the sunny fields first cultivated by them, and not to feel sorrow and indignation at the thought that avarice and sin could so far have transported men as to lead them to the destruction of so fair a scene." "O that the abusers of the monastic system would trouble themselves to examine this once happy valley, and watch the soothing influence of the lovely building and landscape, and would ask themselves whether they did not, in looking, feel more of reverence, more of awe and of love for the religions and for the men than they have heretofore felt."

Street was twenty-six before he crossed the Channel. A foreigner may be pardoned for feeling it a piece of his good luck that he should have learned and loved the English Gothic before seeing the larger beauties and the grander styles of France, lest otherwise his own should have seemed to him fair but pallid, pure but cold, bearing much the same relation to the continental that the English service bears to the Roman use. It was not in him, however, to withdraw the affection once given for due cause, nor yet to withhold that just devotion the larger excellence could command. For him the greater glory would not dim the less. Both shared henceforth in his life.

The foreign journey was omitted only twice, in the year 1855, when his son was born in October, and in 1870, when the Germans had invaded France. In the latter year Street went to Scotland; in the former he stayed at home on the Thames with Mrs. Street's people, bringing out his Italian book and working on the buildings for the Bishop of Oxford at Cuddesden. Towards the end of the year he moved to London and took a house in Montague Place. The plans which he submitted in competition for a new cathedral at Lille won a second prize, and the Frenchman to whom the actual building was given in the end had been rated originally below him. He had by this time at least three assistants working under him regularly, Edmund Sedding, Philip Webbe, and William Morris. He was perpetually occupied with parishes and private persons — on schools, chapels, restorations, residences even, country churches fitted to a village community, town churches designed for the artisan populace and their employers. He had finished Cuddesden College and carried work far already on the whole important cluster of diocesan buildings; he had begun building for the Anglican sisterhood at East Grinstead; he had been praised not a little in the competition at Lille; he was to take a second place, the next year, with his design for the Crimean Memorial and in the end to build the church; and shortly thereafter he sent in plans for new Government Offices. About this last he reasoned, with the spendthrift logic of youth, that while he could hardly expect to win the commission with a Gothic design, the premium offered to him among others of the best was a hundred pounds and would give him another trip to Italy, while he would gain, furthermore, from the public exhibition of the drawings.

The undertaking cost, to be sure, time and strength, but of these he was never stingy. He seems to have known how to be at once thrifty and generous of himself — generous perhaps because thrifty. All his life he seems to have done three men's work in a day and all work in a third of the time that other men would take. He mentions once, being on a journey, that "it rained, so we read, wrote, and occupied the many hours in the rumbling diligence as best we might." The notes were written often in diligence or train, as the firm clear writing betrays, while it remains characteristic and legible. He worked habitually till half-past twelve at night, yet with all the incessant occupation of the most exacting sort, in large measure creative labour, you never think of him, as he never can have thought of himself, as overworked. The essential soundness, the vital force made his way of life spontaneous and inevitable. The strong, even, white teeth, the strong, curling, brown beard, were the visible token of bodily sanity and power, a sort of physical validity of which the cause was not merely physical.

As the mediaeval builders reared and poised their great churches by a calculated balance of thrust and strain, and hung aloft in stone a proposition in proportion, so, you feel, with Street, it must have been some extraordinarily just measure, some perfect balance of temper, some secret of self-control, only comparable to the engineer's control of his crane or hammer or locomotive, that gave him life so abounding and yet so temperate, so huge in accomplishment and yet so undistressed. If we know that at times the pulse and the invention flagged, yet it is only because we know by testimony that tasks designed in hours of gloom were not, indeed, fulfilled in hours of insight, but instead they were destroyed, to be replaced later by designs better because of more vitality and more *élan*.

Doubtless in this a fine natural constitution played a large part, but even a larger part, one is tempted to think, belongs to faith. *Nisi Dominum*, says the Psalmist, but here the Lord did keep the house and their labour was not lost that built it. One thinks of Huxley coming home exhausted from his lectures to lie on a sofa at one side of the hearth, that on the other side being permanently occupied by his wife. There can be little question which of the two men did more for his generation, but also there can be no question which found more substantial and untroubled happiness. "It is *not* lost labour that ye rise up so early, and so late take rest, and eat the bread of carefulness, for so He giveth His beloved sleep." By every reasonable standard of happiness we must admit that Street's work, untiring, joyous, faithful, done in direct loyalty to God Almighty, bore the fruit of a constant blessing.

The domestic affections and the service of religion filled up a life singularly pleasant to contemplate. Boating, cricket matches and riding, plain-song meetings and the Philharmonic Society, opera, exhibitions and sales of pictures, all found place without crowding. If he did not ride he wrote letters for an hour and a half or two hours before breakfast. He had his office in the house and kept long hours in it without interruption except from clients, but his little son was admitted as something less than a trouble, and watched him designing. An assistant said, later: "We worked hard, or thought we did. We had to be at the office at nine o'clock and our hour of leaving was six o'clock, long hours — but he never encroached on our time and as a matter of fact I am sure I never stayed a minute past six o'clock."

After dinner there might be music, at home or abroad, cards or reading, or a cigar and talk on the balcony over the square — a London balcony, dingy and flower-beset, above a London square in summer, dim with twilight and coal-smoke, smelling of soot and dewfall on green leaves. At half-past nine came tea and thereafter three hours more of good work alone. He travelled, of course, more than a little, and on the journey put in the normal day's work. The same friend goes on: "I well remember a little *tour de force* that fairly took our breath away. He told us one morning that he was just off to measure an old church, I think in Buckinghamshire, and he left by the ten o'clock train. About half-past four he came back and into the office for some drawing paper; he then retired to his own room, reappearing in about an hour's time with the whole church carefully drawn to scale, with his proposed additions to it, margin lines and title as usual, all ready to ink in and finish. Surely this was a sufficiently good day's work. Two journeys, a whole church measured, plotted to scale, and new parts designed, in about seven hours and a half. He was the *beau-ideal* of a perfect enthusiast. He believed in his own work, and in what he was doing at the time, absolutely; and the charm of his work is that when looking at it you may be certain that it is entirely his own, and this applies to the smallest detail as to the general conception. . . . No wonder we were enthusiastic with such performances going on under our eyes daily."

Yes, it is good to know that such lives can be, filled with pleasure in the exercise of conscious strength, sufficient unto the day, with enough for all needs and to spare. It is like watching a blooded dog or a thoroughbred horse. As a rule we compare men to pleasant animals only when they are unpleasant men, and say they are engaging only when we cannot say they are trustworthy. Here was one singularly engaging. Every one in remembering him recalls his wit, fireside mirth, good temper, ready answer. When a dull gentleman, having dissected at great length the old mare's nest about mediaeval irregularities in design, wound up after a pompous question about the secrets of freemasonry: "Now Mr. Street, what do *you* think?" Street flashed back: "What do I think? I think the beggars could not build straight." When a young architect consulted him about going to law to recover his designs from a client — would it be wise? Street answered, "That depends on what sort of man your client is and whether you have any expectation of further commissions from him." "His experience and natural shrewdness," wrote an acquaintance at the time of his death, "made him a valuable adviser on points of professional practice, and he had a humour very often caustic, which one could not help sympathizing with."

He was a good son and brother, a good husband and father, without loss of manliness. No man was less a prig. No man, indeed, was ever more respectable, but the touch of genius makes respectability itself engaging. He was not subtle, but his directness can make subtlety look devious and insincere. He was not complex, but his straightness can make complexity look morbid and mean-minded. In 1863 Crabbe Robinson wrote in his diary:

"*October 17.* Dined with the Streets. Our amusement was three-handed whist. Both Mr. and Mrs. Street very kind. On every point of public interest he and I differ, but it does not affect our apparent esteem for one another. I hold him in very great respect, indeed admiration. He has first-rate talent in his profession as an architect. He will be a great man in act — he is so in character already."

He lived afterwards in Russell Square and then in Cavendish Square; always in the dear, unspoiled, substantial, smoke-stained professional quarter, the London of those that live there all the year, where autumn lights vistas of tawny splendour down every street, and spring offers nosegays of early wall-flower and narcissus from the Scilly Isles at every corner; where the air perpetually tastes of soft coal, damp mud, and warm malt; where in December the moist pavement glistens with a permanent slime, and in May the porch roofs burgeon into azaleas pied and trailing pink geraniums.

His life thenceforth falls into such periods as Ezekiel counted, — a time and a time and half a time. Ten years, from 1855 to 1865, were given to church-building, to travel for the sake of study, to writing, beginning with the *Brick and Marble in Italy* and culminating in the *Gothic Architecture in Spain*. Mainly within the next ten fall the great commissions — for the Law Courts, for building the nave of Bristol cathedral, for rebuilding the cathedral at Dublin, for restoring that of York. If this period is closed with the death of his second wife, in 1876, there will remain just five years for bringing all to a conclusion, finishing wholly or very nearly the great works, lending a strong hand to such public undertakings as saving London Bridge, adorning S. Paul's, rescuing S. Marco at Venice, and serving on the council of the Royal Academy. Finally, he was President of the Royal Institute of British Architects. He delivered, as Professor of Architecture to the Royal Academy, six lectures on Gothic Architecture in the spring of 1881. Those were widely read at the time, printed in the weekly journal, the *Builder*, as they were delivered, and in the *Architect;* and reprinted by his son as an appendix to the *Memoir*. In that same year he died and on the twenty-ninth of December was buried in Westminster Abbey. He was only fifty-seven and he had been ill only a month.

With Street's actual building I have little here to do. Immense in quantity, admirable in kind, it stands and long will stand, not only amid the dense green of English hedgerows and in the bitter grime of English towns, but beside the graves of Alpine valleys and in the Stranger's Quarter of continental cities. Of its technical excellence, the way it meets and happily resolves the builder's problems, I am not competent to speak. Architects have praised him well. The distinguished American who has devoted his own rich and exquisite talent to the quest of Gothic, tells me that Street, of them all, had the most genius. To the mere ecclesiologist, who comes to the American church at Paris, or the church and schools of S. James the Less, in Westminster, or the village spire of Holmbury S. Mary, it seems that if new churches must be at all, they should be thus. Where Scott's work seems colder than death and Butterfield's trivial or thin, Street's alone has a kind of present life, a pulse, an inner glow. It is again the abounding life of the man which communicates of itself. Many have put their heart into their work, but only a great heart lives and burns in it.

Of architecture, apart from technical questions, structural or archaeological, there is little profitable to be said. Like the other arts which deal directly with bodily experience, it suffers from the necessity of translating into an alien speech. You may talk about Shelley forever, since poetry is made of words, or about Plato, since philosophy is made of ideas, but the truest praise of the *Passion according to St. Matthew* is reserved for the organ, and the real right comment on any Perugino is the Granducal Madonna. Criticism may take a

IN LEON CATHEDRAL

lawful pleasure in explaining, first, how a given work of art came to be what it is — which is matter of history; and, second, why we enjoy it as much as we do, — which is matter of psychology; but the enjoyment itself criticism cannot express except by a laborious process of transmutation and translation. Of all the arts architecture is least apt for this sort of evocation. Even Pater hardly knows that song to which the memory of Chartres would, like a mist, rise into towers, though he could reweave by his magic the very spell of Botticelli, and recall with his subtle harmonies the very presence that rose so strangely by the waters of Leonardo. Those who have lingered at nightfall in the nave of Chartres until through mounting darkness the blue windows burned as by their own proper light, may know, some of them, that a great church, like the deep sea, like the ancient woods, like the starry heavens, can liberate for an instant the soul from the limitations of the conscious intelligence. But even if a man would tell of that, and no man would, there are no words for the telling. To put the matter another way: — the experience of music is a matter of the auditory sensations and their recall in memory; the experience of painting a matter of the visual, for the most part; that of architecture is a very curious combination of the tactual and muscular with certain respiratory and vaso-motor functions. Words, in each of the cases, are at the second and third remove from the actual appreciation; and moreover architecture shares with music, except where figure-sculpture enters in, the supreme condition that representation merges in presentation, that form and content coincide.

The love of thirteenth century France flowered in the beauty of Street's designing; the knowledge of Catalan city churches bore fruit in the frequent use of the lofty nave arcade, which barely marks the aisle off, and opens all the church to sight and hearing of the preacher; the long acquaintance with Italian brick construction led to his perpetual endeavour by bands of colour to lighten the monotony of English stone. But marbles under a southern sun will fade and stain and modulate together, where other material and other skies will not effect the combination, and while I feel that some of Street's essays in colour have been less happy than his other audacities, I feel stronglier yet that the fault lies more with the material at hand than with the shaping spirit of imagination.

He is supposed to have been at his best in designing middle-sized churches for general use, like All Saints' at Clifton, and S. Margaret's, Liverpool. I know he felt that he never worked more to his own mind than when he built his own church at Holmbury. The American churches in Paris and Rome, the English churches in Rome and Genoa, the Anglican churches at Lausanne, Vevey and Mürren are all his. The list of his buildings published in his son's *Memoir* stretches from Constantinople to Trinidad. I notice that at the time of his death some called the new nave of Bristol cathedral his most entirely successful work. That may in a way be reckoned as restoration, if one likes, and remain equally characteristic, for Street did much work of restoring, and the list of original work is followed in the *Memoir* by a longer list of ancient work to which he lent a reverent hand. Against any restoration but the most reverent he protested, both generally and in such particular cases as that of the Lincoln doorways. He was a member of Morris's "Anti-scrape" society, though once at least that body fell foul of him. The mere ecclesiologist in this case is again disposed to admit that if, to keep a church above ground, some restoration must be done, it had better be in such hands as his.

In truth all the best work of Street was done in the spirit and in the terms of mediaeval work, as the best poetry of Morris was written. Each by a rare chance found himself of blood kin, born to the same language, gesture and emotion, with those long dead. I do not know that Street's church building was ever blamed for not being of its own age: certainly such a criticism would be peculiarly unjust, for it is the translation into brick and stone of *The Christian Year*. The Tractarians and Street gave their lives to the same task, and they patched up their churches so well that these will stand for generations yet.

His knowledge, in truth, of the Middle Ages was often enough made a reproach. He was accused by competitors, by church-wardens and committees, by journalists and critics, of allowing an undue influence over his work to foreign styles. No one would be likely now to hold that for a ground of grievance, but the charge is the less plausible considering how early mature were both the man and his workmanship. It was in 1850 that he went to the Continent for the first time, already knowing his England well. Rarely, thereafter, he let a year go by without crossing the Channel, and often he added, especially in later life, an autumn or a winter holiday. There would be interest in drawing up a table of his journeys, if one could be made complete, year by year, and in supplying from letters and diaries his fresh impressions, if these were available. With the help of old notebooks, even without other material, may be made out a list tentative and imperfect, indeed, but still suggestive, — by the change in recurrence, for instance, by the perpetual discovery of fresh interest on ground no matter how familiar. From what he saw he took refreshment and suggestion, never precisely a model. There would be no use in setting off, against the table of his travels, a table of his buildings. These were the growth of English soil, and from his masters, the cathedral builders of France and Spain, the masons of Germany and Lombardy, he asked not what they did but how. More often, the direct outcome of travel, the transformation of observation into activity, was not the high-reared vault but the written word — figuring in the *Ecclesiologist*, in the *Transactions* of Diocesan Societies and Architectural Associations, in the Italian and the Spanish volumes, and in at least two more that he projected but did not live to finish.

Street never went to Greece or Russia, nor, I think, to Dalmatia. The Gothic lands he loved, there his genius renewed its mighty youth. For him as for the young Pre-Raphaelites in 1845 and then for the young Aesthetes in 1855, the first sight of a great French church, say of Amiens, marked as much the close of one stage and the commencement of another, as if they all had not known Westminster and York Minster, Iffley and Fountains Abbey; as if they were, in effect, young Americans fed on nothing more ancient than those white wood pillars of a front porch, that rough-dressed stone or bluish brick of a central square with flanking wings, which appear in our earliest and only, our "Colonial," style.

If one is tempted to press the American parallel in the matter of enthusiasm, as the only one adequate to express the degree of it and the surprise, fresh as a May morning, irrevocable as falling in love for the first time, one is even more tempted to push the same parallel in the matter of method — of "doing" churches and "doing" towns at an incredible rate. Burne-Jones and Morris on their memorable trip arrived at Abbeville late Thursday night after a Channel crossing, and on Friday had an hour in Amiens cathedral before dinner and stayed there afterwards till nine, reached Beauvais on Saturday and went to Sunday Mass and vespers, thence on to Paris the same night, spent sixteen hours Monday in sightseeing, and had only three days there in all with which to see the Beaux-Arts exhibition, the Cluny, Notre Dame, the Louvre, and hear *Le Prophète*. Thursday and Friday they gave to Chartres — a longer time, one likes to remember, than they spared for any other cathedral. So, of Street, his son writes: "In September, 1850, . . . in ten days he saw Paris, Chartres, Alençon, Caen, Rouen and Amiens, sketching all the time with might and main." That would be a fair record now for any but the shameless, even if you substituted kodak and motor-car for sketch-book and infrequent trains. "In the summer of 1851 three weeks sufficed to make him acquainted with Mayence, Frankfort, Wurtzburg, Hamburg, Nuremberg, Ratisbon, Munich, Ulm, [Constance], Freiburg, Strasburg, Heidelberg, [Cologne], and three or four of the best of the Belgian towns." The next trip was his wedding tour and reached the great churches of what might be called in architecture, conveniently, the Burgundian March — Dijon, Auxerre, Sens, Troyes; and the year after that, late in August, the pair came to Italy. The things done and seen, and, even more the things thought, in something like five weeks, crammed the notebooks and bore fruit in a volume that Murray published in 1855, *Brick and Marble in the Middle Ages.*

The first thing, and, even on reflexion, the most surprising, in all this travel, is of course the quality and the quantity of what Street did in his vacations, the incredibly rapid and inconceivably hard work, no less than the enthusiasm and endurance of the man. The labour, in the very doing, passes into creation. Besides the great sketch-block he carried a leather-bound luxurious notebook or two, of heavy and beautiful paper, some five or six inches by eight, and thick as would go into a coat pocket, in which he put down alternately sketches and notes, plans and measurements, names of local building-stone or extracts from a parish register, and occasionally a memorandum of railway trains or addresses and dates for forwarding letters. These worn little volumes are evocative, are potent. He begins sketching, always, the moment he reaches the Continent and keeps it up till he touches the Channel again, but he rarely repeats a subject or an observation. The text records facts and inferences, judgements and estimates, more often than impressions; and emotions, I think, never. The drawings preserve more often a plan, a detail, a profile, than a façade or an interior — in short, a picture. In a sense everything is a picture, in its vitality of line and unerring selection. For the rest, the great views of ambulatory and transept, west front and apse, were done on a larger sheet, and such of them as were not later used up or given away still preserve in books the itinerary of the successive years. Whoever has known churches hitherto by photographs only will turn the leaves of these with strong delight. It is hard ever to say fully why all drawings of architecture should satisfy more than any photographs, and these overpass comparison. The camera, after all cannot see around a corner and an artist can.

The solar print is a dead thing, and here is the living line. Street can afford, with great economy of line, immense vitality; his son says that he never carried an india rubber and never put in a line that he was not sure of, and on the pages of the dusty note-books the line lives and vibrates. One of 1874 may open at a chapel of the abbey at Vézelay or a capital from the choir arcade of Auxerre, or another of 1860, at the church of Ainay or the gateway of Nevers; but all the work of all the years is interchangeable in respect of firmness and life, certainty and authority; and what you see on the page is not merely knowledge, accuracy, dexterity, it is genius. The quick notes, as surely as the large studies and the great original designs, show never lack of it. Architecture is a craft, a thing a man by application can learn, like journalism, and architectural drawings may be merely exact, neat and compact, and give pleasure. But genius is like the grace of God in a man's work, it is all in all and all in every part. The vitality of the line in sketching, the vitality of the design in building, are the outcome of it. The very handwriting, rapid but neither negligent nor meticulous, is as much a part of him as a man's hair.

The original notes, written from day to day, are never slight, or stupid, or cock-sure. The *Brick and Marble* volume has kept their fresh, quick finality. Thanks in part most likely to *Modern Painters*, landscape in the early journeys counted nearly as much as cities. Street had seen the Alps in 1851 from the Lake of Constance, and looked at them and stuck to his work. The next year, apparently, he visited Switzerland with his wife and walked up as many as possible. On the Italian journey two years later he literally made the most of the mountains, going and coming — through the Rhineland and the Vosges, by the lakes of Zurich and Wallenstadt, down the canton of the Grisons and over the Splügen to the lake of Como, one way, and the other by Lake Maggiore and the S. Gothard, climbing the Furka and including the lake of Lucerne. As, on another visit, he comes down through the Tyrol by Grauenfels and the Pustertal, the bare hints are electrical, the reader's imagination catches fire. In this first book, the landscape gets more attention than ever again in print, but all his life he loved a mountain about as well as a cathedral, he saw the Alps as often as Amiens. His pencil was almost as often and as happily set to landscape sketching as to any other; it caught the profile of a bluff and traced the swelling and subsidence of a mountain's flank. Now that in the pursuit of colour and light most painters have abandoned form, and second-rate Impressionists are content to let a landscape welter in blues and mauves like a basket of dying fish, his forcible contours and cool washes awake a tingling of reality.

In 1854 he went to Münster and Soest, and wrote for the *Ecclesiologist* during the following year three pieces on the architecture of northern Germany, besides another for the Oxford Architectural Society. Summary as are these brief and practical papers, they remain still so entirely and beyond dispute the fullest and most suggestive account of German brick work, they are so good to steal from and so indispensable as adjuncts to Baedeker, and finally, so characteristically foreshadow and supplement the Spanish volume, that they are reprinted bodily in the appendix here. It is precisely sixty years since they were written, and they are not only not superseded, they are still unapproached. Back of the energy which enabled him to cover a vast deal of ground and never miss a detail, beyond the personal acquaintance, and not mere book-knowledge, of the twelfth, thirteenth, fourteenth and fifteenth centuries in England, France, Germany, Switzerland, Italy (to which later he was to add Spain) — beneath all this learning lay the happiest instinct for what was either first-rate or important or both. He rarely went out of his way to look at a church that was not worth his while, he rarely failed to look at every church in a town that would repay him. The *Memoir* quotes a letter from this journey, with the characteristic prelude, "he worked hard, as he always did, up early and in late": — "I have got a great budget of sketches; indeed, I have done pretty well, for in a fortnight I have mustered about fifty-five large sketches besides filling a goodly memorandum book. We enjoyed Lübeck immensely, and amongst other feats astonished the natives by making rubbings of some magnificent brasses, of which Marique did her share, to the delight of the sacristan."

His interest in German building was more practical than aesthetic; he found suggestive parallels to his own problems in those of the rich merchant cities, set down, often, in a country without accessible stone. He recurs a dozen times, in his writings, to the similar solutions found in S. Mary's at Barcelona and S. Elizabeth's at Marburg, and the same type of building in brick developed about Lübeck and Saragossa, Toulouse and Cremona — in the great plains of the north of Germany, the north of Spain, and the north of Italy.

Though in 1855 he took no summer holiday, he went over in the fall to see the designs at Lille with William Morris, and pushed on to S. Omer. The notebook of that journey is particularly rich in detail, both personal and architectural. The trip supplied material for papers in the *Ecclesiologist*, supplemented by another two years later, through Normandy, the Soissonnais and the German border. Even to-day when that country has been written to death, ploughed up by pedants and harrowed by illiterate motorists and photographers, the papers are almost too good to leave in the dust of old libraries, with their tang of a spring morning early enough to taste of frost. The notebook still is more than half a journal, coloured with detail not so irrelevant as the writer fancied, and I have snatched out a bit about Laon to reprint.[1]

[1] Since these words were written that country has seen another harvest time; the fields have been ploughed with the trenches of armies and harrowed by the bomb and bullet: Street's record of what men saw fifty years ago has grown precious for us who shall never see it more.

Far more brief are the notebooks, however, of 1860, when he went to the Bernese Oberland and took in the country that lies westward from Lyons — Le Puy, Brioude, Clermont-Ferrand, Nevers, — and many of the smaller churches of that curious Auvergnat type which was to help him so well in the interpretation of Spanish Gothic during the following years. There are sketches and plans aplenty, with the scantiest jottings of fact, and then a few fragments of bibliography; lastly terse notes of reading done, I fancy, in Paris on the way home. These served for an essay on *The Churches of Velay*, which has been printed twice in the *Transactions* of the Royal Institute of British Architects, once at the time, and again, long after his death, in 1889. It is still inaccessible to most, and I reprint it once more, partly for the bearing on his interpretation of Spanish building, and partly because I know nothing better on Auvergne.

Nothing missed him, not the paintings on the wall at Brioude nor the Liberal Arts on the pavement at Ainay. A scrawled road-map on one page would be still the ecclesiologist's best guide for the region. The village of Monistrol which harbours, thereabouts, a characteristic church, and to which he refers again for comparison in the Spanish volume, is not, I take pleasure in noting, the scene of the first meeting with Modestine. If it had been, you should not know from Stevenson that a church stood thereby, for the good creature had no great taste in churches, and though the *Inland Voyage* lay through a cathedral country, small good was that to him.

The volume shows how Street's published books were made, and it shows furthermore, what any other of these little leather books could equally illustrate, how his instinct drove straight at the truth and needed from documents only confirmation. He wrote once:

"For that period of just five hundred years so regular was the development that it is not too much to say that a well-informed architect or antiquary ought always to be able to give, within ten or at most twenty years, the date of any, however small a portion, of Mediaeval architecture with almost absolute certainty of being correct when his judgement can be tested by documentary evidence."

That was his practice, the *élan* of his own judgement, as certain as the stroke of his pencil, which other architects, of other nations, have delighted to honour.

Señor Lampérez, in his great book on Spanish architecture, bears generous and graceful witness to the justness and certitude of Street's conjectures. He even gives him the credit of finding the date of S. Maria at Benavente, now known to be 1220, though in point of fact Street had set down as opinion and not knowledge that the church must have been built between 1200 and 1220. The only case in which I know his instinct at fault is that of the belated churches of Galicia, where Romanesque forms persisted sometimes even into the fifteenth century. There, knowing few dates of buildings and fewer of builders, he hardly estimated them enough of laggards, and guesses wrong sometimes by a century, or nearly.

Precisely in a case like this, where an unknown condition vitiates the experiment, one sees how just is his method and how right in all but the actual year of our Lord, even here, is the outcome. The steady judgement, the wide knowledge, the happy divination, which we call genius, cannot play false. While the saint, by ancient dogma, cannot sin, the foredamned cannot do right; and the provincial-minded, even though all the data lie before him, is foredoomed by his *campanilismo* to come out wrong. It is, moreover, a trifle ungrateful in a few young Spaniards and a few fretful Hispanophils to scold at Street, for he was the best friend and the most practical, outside the Peninsula, that Spain had ever had — not forgetting either the Duke of Wellington or Murray's Ford. Let me quote again Señor Lampérez, what he has to say at the opening of his admirable *Historia de la Arquitectura Española Cristiana:*

"Two foreigners deserve especial place and mention in this survey, the English Street and the French Enlart. Street was an architect, profoundly versed in Christian art, Gothic in chief; he had studied the monuments of it all over Europe; he visited Spain and before her churches he sketched and took notes with so sure a vision that his book on Gothic Art [*sic*] in Spain has come to be, if I may say so, classic. It is the greater pity that Street saw of Spain only one very small part. On any count, his work is of exceptional importance. His text is too widely known for me to need to analyze it here; suffice it to say that his method is based on a technical study of each building, without any divagation into poetic descriptions or literary lucubrations."

Some account of Gothic Architecture in Spain, published in 1865, was the outcome of the journeys in 1861, '62 and '63 and (I suppose) of two more summers spent at home in research and actual composition and publication. At any rate I find no record of autumn travel in '64 and '65.

It is hardly fair, in truth, for Señor Lampérez to say that he saw only a small part of Spain. His journeys covered, geographically speaking, much more than two-fifths of the Peninsula, and archaeologically speaking, all the best of the Romanesque and Gothic, both Gallegan, Castilian, and Catalan. What he missed was the pre-Romanesque, as it is found in the Asturias, and the true Moorish, *i.e.* the Asiatic and non-Christian. If he neglected the Mudejar work and the Renaissance period, it was deliberately, because when he looked at them he misliked them. The real difference between his field of labour and that of Señor Lampérez consists not so much in the latter's possession of Estremadura and la Mancha, Seville and the south-east coast, as in his fuller knowledge and more minute experience of the northern provinces. The Castiles and Leon, Galicia and Navarre, and the ancient domain of the kings of Aragon, have been examined league by league and published both fully and frequently, since 1865. The peculiar styles which give their importance to the regions of the Biscay shore and the Sierra Morena, the Latin-Byzantine of Asturias and the Mohammedan of Andalusia, are special phenomena and must always be treated apart; they may therefore at need be omitted, without grave loss, from the general consideration of mediaeval building in Spain; and if these are struck out, for instance from the lists of Señor Lampérez, there will remain, as the significant monuments and the important regions, precisely those which Street had already treated. Cuenca and Soria, Poblet and Ripoll, Tuy and Orense, Toro, Jaca, the

Seo de Urgel, were all unvisited and other churches yet; but the list is not long nor are the places vastly important.

Some of them, if it must be known, are still but little studied; and with all the fine enthusiasm of Spanish architects, and societies learned and popular, treasures of the great age still remain unexplored. Only last summer the present writer rode over the flank of a hill to salute, all unprepared, a superb transitional church of the thirteenth century. It was not cathedral nor even collegiate, but mere *parroquia*, and perhaps the finest parish church in Spain: — and it is even to this hour, so far as may be ascertained, completely *inédite*. When Street went to Santiago he was much in the same case. "I had been able to learn nothing whatever about the cathedral before going there," he records, with ironic amusement; "in all my Spanish journeys there had been somewhat of this pleasant element of uncertainty as to what I was to find; but here my ignorance was complete, and as the journey was a long one to make on speculation, it was not a little fortunate that my faith was rewarded by the discovery of a church of extreme magnificence and interest."

The three journeys were so planned as not only to find out much that was new each time but to repeat and verify earlier impressions. With his usual sobriety he sets down the itinerary in the opening pages:

"In my first Spanish tour I entered the country from Bayonne, travelled thence by Vitoria to Burgos, Palencia, Valladolid, Madrid, Alcalá, Toledo, Valencia, Barcelona, Lérida, and by Gerona to Perpiñan. In the second I went again to Gerona, thence to Barcelona,

Tarragona, Manresa, Lérida, Huesca, Zaragoza, Tudela, Pamplona, and so to Bayonne; and in the third and last I went by Bayonne to Pamplona, Tudela, Tarazona, Sigüenza, Guadalajara, Madrid, Toledo, Segovia, Avila, Salamanca, Zamora, Benavente, Leon, Astorga, Lugo, Santiago, la Coruña, and thence back by Valladolid and Burgos to San Sebastian and Bayonne. Tours such as these have, I think, given me a fair chance of forming a right judgement as to most of the features of Spanish architecture; but it would be worse than foolish to suppose that they have been in the slightest degree exhaustive, for there are large tracts of country which I have not visited at all, others in which I have seen one or two only out of many towns which are undoubtedly full of interesting subjects to the architect, and others again in which I have been too much pressed for time."

Street is too modest here: his acquaintance with Spain if not indeed exhaustive, like that with France and England, is entirely representative; and however pressed for time, he never scamps his work. The present writer may testify, having followed his tracks with an exact piety all the way, that he exhausted every town. He passed through Miranda at dawn, but he described, classified and dated the church; he went up the coast, from Barcelona to Port Vendres, by train, but he saw more churches and towers than the careful observer after him. He continues:

"Yet I hardly know that I need apologize for my neglect to see more, when I consider that, up to the present time, so far as I know, no architect has ever described the buildings which I have visited and indeed no accurate or reliable information is to be obtained as to their exact character, age, or history."

In that sentence is written down the debt Spain owes to Street.

He took his wife on the first journey but not afterwards. She was both patient and spirited, but it was a little too rough for a lady. His own endurance and good temper are unfailing, and infallible his sense of due proportion. He never tells you what was for dinner, or how the bed ailed, or when he quarrelled with the landlord. It is much if he mentions, in a sort of postscript, that the journey to Compostela in diligence took sixty-six hours, and, elsewhere, that in autumn a man can live largely on bread and grapes. He is not, like Mr. Hewlitt or Mr. Hutton when they go on the road, writing a picaresque romance, but an account of Gothic architecture in Spain. The structural analysis of Santiago, the discussion of the date of Avila, the appreciation of the Catalan type of church-building — everyone knows that famous parallel with "our own Norfolk middle-pointed" — such passages provoke comparison and command praise, for substantiality and lucidity, with the very best of writing on a technical subject. The dexterity with which he singles out the English or Angevine elements at Las Huelgas, and those of the Isle-of-France at Toledo, and signals there the gradual interpenetration of local influences, has the happiest certainty and the most admired ease. It is hard to say where he is at his best, — whether in dealing with a style like the Romanesque of Cluny or the Gothic of Paris, where he has a vast store of experience long accumulated, and makes comparisons and illustrates distinctions from England or

Italy indifferently, or whether coming upon fresh matter like the domed churches about Zamora or the brick building around Saragossa, or even something so much out of his line as the Mudejar work scattered about in the Castiles, he applies reason and method to the unknown, and, arriving at conviction, he enforces it. Nothing could be more succinct and more satisfying than his dealing with the dates of Don Patricio de la Escosura, in *España Artistica y Monumental*. "I see no reason," he writes easily, "for believing that the plaster decorations are earlier than 1350 or thereabouts."

Only once in a very long while, a slight twist or tang of perversity relieves the even good sense and good taste. Of the lovely sepulchre in Avila of that young brother of Joanna the Mad, too early dead, he remarks that the great tomb "is one of the most tender, fine, and graceful works I have ever seen, and worthy of any school of architecture. The recumbent effigy, in particular, is as dignified, graceful and religious as it well could be, and in no respect unworthy of a good Gothic artist." The quaint anti-climax has the very, sweet, *gaucherie* of a woodcut by Rossetti or a bit out of Scripture by the young, unspoiled Holman Hunt. We have come, since that could be said, a very long way.

It would seem that he finished a great piece of work only to be free for another. When he had published *Brick and Marble* he moved to London and went in for the Lille and the Government House competitions; when he had published *Gothic Architecture in Spain* he was to go in for the National Gallery and the Law Courts. It is a great piece of work. The reading it implies, that would have been for a mere student no trifle,

THE OLD CATHEDRAL OF SALAMANCA

was done by a professional man already more occupied than most. The drawings for it were made on the wood by a working architect, already designing for his own churches every several moulding, every piece of ironwork, every free-flowing tracery. Though the task took all he had to spare out of five years of his life, that was, after all, a life filled with other and more important interests; yet the proudest nation in Europe has gone to school to him. Every Spanish ecclesiologist knows this book, not by repute only but by heart. Even those who disclaim all working knowledge of English have the volume on their shelves and the substance of it in their heads. The part which deals with Cataluña has been translated into Catalan and published separately. A Castilian version of the half-chapter on Valladolid, with rich and appreciative annotation and comment, appeared in the *Boletin de la Sociedad Castellana de Excursiones* in 1898. He is still cited as a final authority. The effect of it was to teach the rest of Europe that the glory of mediaeval Spain endured; that one could actually see something south of the Pyrenees, neither Saracenic nor Jesuit, a great religious art surviving, not decadent, not moribund nor morbid nor corrupted by the gold of the Indies, strong, virile, spontaneous, the expression of personal independence and manly piety. No one ever packed up fewer prejudices in his baggage, no one ever brought out more truth. On his accounts we still may confidently rely. The most important truth was, of course, the debt to France, which Spanish pride still at times shrinks from acknowledging. But what some amiable enthusiasts are loth to admit for love of Spain, and others less amiable are fain to deny for a grudge against France, the stones of the towns cry out to testify, and they have Señor Lampérez and Don Rafael Altamira, let them hear them! The glory of Street is that by the light of his intimate knowledge and love of France, he saw it fifty years ago. To-day, as then, his is the one book that cannot be spared. The great lover of Spain, who set himself, on the first journey thither, to follow in the steps of the Cid, reckoned also on planting his foot in the track of Street. The casual traveller writes back to London for a copy and sits down by the way for it to overtake him. It is the best companion in the world, never irrelevant, or peevish, or stodgy. It never fails in sensibility to exalted beauty; it is never betrayed into unction and the professional whine, or what Swinburne once called rancid piety. The English sobriety and good breeding just sufficiently are leavened with enthusiasm — yet that temperate admiration was really, I suppose, the betrayal of an inner passion: the sound rule of faith and the sober standard of feeling being again in play.

With the National Gallery in mind, Street had gone abroad in 1866 to study great halls, and swept a wide round through Munich, Vienna, Prague, Dresden, Berlin, Hanover, Hildesheim, and the Belgian towns. The next three years he was in Italy, and after the war oftener there than elsewhere, coming or going by way of the Val d'Aosta or the Engadine, the Bernese Oberland or the Austrian Tyrol. The sad summer of 1871 he spent in Switzerland. Street could not, indeed, have been born and lived and died in England in the Victorian age, without feeling that same passion for high mountains which makes so touching the letters of Meredith, in whom it was thwarted perpetually, and so inspires the letters of Leslie Stephen, for whom it seems to have supplied a source of spiritual regeneration. The two Stephens, Tyndall, Clifford, Arnold and the rest of that strong mid-century race that broke, most of them, with the church, and repudiated, all of them, religion as by law established, found literally in the Alps a substitute for God. Street was able to keep God and the Alps too — since "all these things shall be added unto you."

In 1874 he published a second edition of *Brick and Marble*, augumented by notes gathered in journeys as far back as 1857. Both editions have long been out of print. It would be a good work if the ancient house of Murray would republish it, for the author's most fantastical reactions against Palladio cannot affect — shall I say, its solid worth? Accurate observation, close and careful description, knowledge that can read into every detail its implications, would make the dullest book indispensable for reference, and this runs lightly as a traveller's tale. You are surprised when you find how few of the books, with pictures and without, that every year unloads on the subject of Italy, give any substantial information beyond the hotel door-step. Upon my faith, every author, from the venerable Mr. Howells to the diligent Mr. Hutton, will run on and on discoursing most excellent music — but if you would know what a church really looks like, without or within, he is not your man. Forms shift and dyes mingle in their descriptions as in sunset clouds. Mr. Pennell will turn you off a wonderful portfolio of pictures, each worthy to be framed and glazed and hung on the wall, but if the church be Gothic or Romanesque, if the square be classic or baroque, who can say? If you need to know, down comes the shabby Street from the shelf, and after you have consulted the page and the drawing you may have, belike, more than the author had when he set down what he saw. His son notes somewhere that on referring to an old landscape sketch they found accurate record of details they had not known till later: so truly does truth stand by her lovers.

Meanwhile he had planned the companion volume on central and southern Italy, to which he refers in the preface. It is a sad pity he could not have found the time nor the heart to write this, for with it in mind he pushed as far in 1873 as Ancona, Lucera and Benevento. The MS. notebook, I fear, has perished which should have gone with a square thick book of sketches more than usually stimulating and lovely. The choir of the S. Chapelle at Chambéry shows the way he went; then plans of S. Ciriaco, at Ancona, the crossing and dome seen from the nave, the south porch, the eastern and western apses, with a tenderly faithful drawing of the innumerably-arcaded front of S. Maria, imply the kind of close study that culminates in a book. Had he but followed up his observations there and elsewhere, at Lucera for instance, where he recorded not only the cathedral and the castles, but a whole group of churches and a cluster of castles that front the Adriatic coast thence southward; or at Foggia, where, with a sketch of the façade of the cathedral and a separate study of the most characteristic Pisan and Pistojan traits he fairly underlined the relation and suggested Troja to a surprising degree; — had he merely knotted up the syllogisms that he laid out ready on the page, and written his Q. E. D., then, beyond a question, from his intimate knowledge of the Royal Domain he would have made out and declared, here as in Spain, the determining influence of northern France, and anticipated the thesis of M. Bertaux. That would have been such another triumph as the Spanish volume, for English intelligence and English taste. But in these Christmas holidays of 1873 he snatched, as the train passed, a castle at Recanati and a portal at Giulianuova, then from Foggia made a great leap to Salerno, and ended for the nonce with careful detailed drawings of the ambons and towers throughout the wonderful Salernitan group, at Amalfi and Ravello and Scala.

Year after year he went back to the south-west coast in winter; in 1874, after his wife's death, spending Christmas with her father as usual, going down by the Riviera and coming back by Florence and the Brenner. It is this year, I fancy, that we may thank for a record of Spoleto cathedral before the restorers had it, for a series of notes in the Umbrian towns, and for another series of the churches of Asti.

This was all familiar ground, of course, to him. The MS. notes on central Italy belong mostly to a journey to Florence made in 1857, reinforced by another, in 1872, that carried him the rest of the way to Rome. Of these notes I am reprinting not a little: in part because such analysis as that of Assisi is profounder than any that has been written since: in part because such comment as that on Siena and Orvieto if not palatable is yet salutary even to those who have learned to love the Tuscan Gothic. Of Florence, others have written more eloquently though not with more sincerity. To the MS. of the Florence episode the privileged reader will turn with keen curiosity indeed, but without apprehension, to learn how Street felt about Donatello and the primitives, having the assurance beforehand that he will not like the wrong thing. If one has to forgive Shelley the tinkling guitar of Jane, and to forgive Browning the thick legs of Guercino's Guardian Angel, and both an occasional lapse upon Guido Reni, Street wants no allowance made. His taste is hardly out of date, even yet. His friends at home had always been the young painters, his house in London held not only some good pieces of theirs but some early Italian panels and tondi.

Inevitably he transposed his taste in architecture bodily into painting: Giotto and Fra Angelico are sure of his liking, so usually are their pupils; but Donatello's S. George is "a poor knock-kneed figure, and no one of the statues [at Or San Michele] comes near the early French figures in any way." Well, recalling the S. George on the south porch of Chartres, on what ground shall one dispute that?

Not merely the dates that Street will like may be foreseen, but the intellectual attitude and spiritual style: as he cared little for the architecture of the Renaissance, he will care no more for the masters of chiaroscuro, and the baroque style he will feel equally distasteful in the two arts. Lastly, his abiding love for Perugino and Francia is utterly in keeping with his Anglican faith; it recalls the very tone of the boyish letter about Lanercost.

"It is particularly characteristic of Lanercost that all is in harmony, every portion seems designed upon the same principle and with the same amount of reverential feeling, and all is so simple as to indicate truth and solidity and the absence of gaudy and hypocritical religion. I dare say you have smiled at the way I come at architecture and religion, it may perhaps be the bias of a profession which makes me do so, but I cannot but think that architecture as well as, not more than, the other fine arts, is a great and most important assistant to religion. Again in the matter of abbeys, I know there will be an outcry when you read my journal [*if we could but read that journal!*] against my admiration of them and their system; but when I lament their destruction I lament it because I venerate the men who founded them."

Rome he never cared for so much as Tuscany and Umbria, that, too, being temperamental. In the early weeks of 1876, after his second marriage, upon making the usual visit to Naples he came back by Rome again, taking the time from his business to see Subiaco, Albano, Palestrina, and Frascati. The brief wedding journey, when almond trees must have been in flower all the way, though it was to end so cruelly in a Roman fever, had begun in a strong fresh flow of happiness that found outlet in a set of MS. notes on Amalfi. That is the last bit of writing which I can trace that is not strictly exacted by the circumstances of his profession.

Occasionally always, when something called for it, he had written an open letter or a brief pamphlet of protest or vindication. Like all men of strong creative imagination, Street cared more for doing than for undoing. He was not a man of war, but he was a good fighter when the issue was clear and the charge laid upon him. Having taken part in the stormy competition over Edinburgh cathedral in 1872, he said forcibly during the proceedings, in the name of the English architects engaged, that the award did not comply with the conditions. As finally made it complied less than ever, and thereafter he said nothing. It was a hurt and he held his peace. Some other great controversies in which he was engaged, fell later and lasted longer. One's own opinion to-day is apt to sustain Street. In the matter of the younger Scott's restoration at S. Albans the work was generally challenged and came out unsatisfactory; in that of his own dealing with the Fratry at Carlisle, he felt himself at liberty, in the face of late and ugly alterations, to replace and piece out such fragments of the original work as he found embedded in the building; in that of re-adapting to general and cathedral use the Minster at Southwell, his proposal respected the visible indications of the architecture. The present writer, being at Southwell not long ago, had contrived to make out by mother wit, from the signs of vault and arcade, of structure and carved decoration, just such intentions as Street, it appears, presumed. His superb scheme for rearranging S. Paul's, with the altar under a great baldachin at the crossing, stood no chance of liking because it ignored the average English habit of mind, it made religion splendid and brought it near. Now the English like their religion chilly and infrequent and a long way off. His stubborn adherence to Gothic for all uses may have cost him the award for the National Gallery, and cost England a new and intelligible building in place of that which still survives. Street's plan would have brought forth, in a way, something not so unlike in effect, while quite different in style, to the Boston Public Library, stately and gracious, a pleasure to the passer-by, adapted not only to its use but to its dignity. The question of Gothic with him was not only a matter of conscience, it was more, a matter of temperament: all his life, all his religion, the very fibres of his body, were strung to that interplay of thrust and strain, were tuned to that upward reaching of the mountain's heart toward God. He could not otherwise. The battle of the Law Courts echoes still, though faintly, in Englishmen's depreciation and guidebooks' disapproval. The great pile, notwithstanding, in every aspect is noble, and the question must turn merely on the style. Modern Gothic granted at all, little can be said against it, and if the sixties and seventies of the last century had not used modern Gothic, what else could they have used? It seems unlikely that the new Law Courts in New York will be better, built on the plan of the Colosseum.

That work was to outlast his life. Meanwhile private commissions did not fall off and ecclesiastical appointments multiplied. At Oxford he had long been diocesan architect; and he held somewhat the same relation to the cathedrals of York, Ripon, Winchester, Gloucester, Salisbury and Carlisle. With all this he had building of his own in which to take delight. In 1872 he bought land at Holmbury, near Dorking, and made himself a garden there and in time a house, lastly a church.

The country is there of very ancient occupation, essential England. The buxom contour of the hills, the generous leafage of the woods, are richer than elsewhere. The lawns are springy with delicate turf of grass fine like hair, the close hedges taller than a man, the stocks and gillyflowers heavy-scented, the dahlias and snapdragons dark-hued and gold-dusted. From the ridge the eye can range — but the English landscape needs an English pen.

"The house he decided to place on a brow, with a terrace running all along its front, the whole, or nearly the whole of the garden being disposed in the hollow below. A certain formal effect had been obtained by sunk rectangular lawns and banks. As the views to the south-east and the south were almost equally good, he planned the house in two wings, forming an obtuse angle one with the other;[1] one facing southeast and the other full south over the sunken garden . . . Below the hill the ground swept down in an amphitheatre open at one end to give a glimpse of the blue distance seen over a bit of park-like foreground, whilst above it rose one spur behind another of the near hills, clothed with junipers and grand bushes of holly, and over them again the farther edge of the hill crowned with masses of dark firs."

He had, as he maintained the architect should always in truth have, a right judgement in all things, interior decoration as well as structure, secular and domestic detail as well as ecclesiastic. When he had thought of giving up the house in Cavendish Square a friend "told me he never saw so charming a room as this drawing-room and he was rejoicing that I could not leave it just now — nearly every one seems to be of the same mind. . . . All my happiest associations are with these rooms

[1] Your man of genius has run ahead of fashion by forty years. This description reads like the account of a house finished last week somewhere up the River or on the Main Line.

GEORGE EDMUND STREET IN 1877

and I begin to think I should be less happy anywhere else."

He was to need the happiness of associations. The work begun and carried out by the nest-building instinct, that faculty which shapes after one's own desire a shelter for one's own kind and kin, was to prove a solace for grief at the last. His wife had died in 1874; two years later Street married "a lady who had been of all my mother's friends the most highly prized, and had been so intimate with us as to have been her companion on many of our foreign tours" — her step-son writes. It is typical of the homing breed, of the instinct that holds in the old paths, to rebuild with the least possible of novelty, and recommence without snapping one of the old threads. The blind impulse of solidarity finds its wants in the ancient walks, the ancient intimacies, the ancient affections.

Mrs. Street lived only eight weeks after her marriage. Thereafter Street kept men's company mostly. He had for friends all that was most living in London, the Rossettis and Holman Hunt, George Boyce and J. W. Inchbold, William Bell Scott, Madox Brown, Morris and Burne-Jones. That *enfant terrible* of the last generation, Mr. Ford Madox Hueffer, has probably reminiscences of him. He had, before all, his son, who on quitting Oxford came up to work under him; he had his associates in his own profession and in the Royal Academy. In that last year he made a tour with Arthur Street among the German cities, but the drawings that could date it are few, and one of the latest notebooks passes within a few leaves from pulpits in southern Italy to the landscape around S. Gervais. Thither he had gone in the autumn to take the waters: "he was troubled more or less by headache the whole time, but he did a good deal of walking and sketching in spite of very bad weather." That was in September. The stroke fell on him the middle of November; then he was better, was planning a long journey in Egypt. On December 18 he was dead. The tireless energy never knew a real abatement. He lies in the nave of the Abbey as Pierre de Montéreau lies in S. Germain-des-Prés, and in Rheims Robert de Coucy.

It is not a long life as you count it over: five years with Scott and Moffatt; five in and near Oxford; twenty years in London of triumphant work; then five of honours like the pause at flood-tide, and never the ebb. Like such a great river as that he knew so well and frequented all his days, his life flowed steadily and strongly, the brimming stream augmenting always, deepening and widening, the heavier current moving, at the end, more slowly but not through slackening of power, until, at the last turn, the majestic estuary opens and broadens, as, with no hurry of fretting waves, no straining through silted sandbanks, undiminished, the mighty mass of waters mingles with the sea.

NOTES OF A TOUR IN CENTRAL ITALY TO
WHICH ARE APPENDED A FEW NOTES
FROM A LATER TOUR

II

NOTES OF A TOUR IN CENTRAL ITALY

(*From a notebook of 1857*)

August 20, 1857.

LEFT town at 8.30 P.M. by South-Eastern Railway for Folkstone. A close push for it, as I was an unwilling auditor of Lord Riverdale in the House of Lords till 7 P.M. I then had a conference with the Bishop of Oxford.

I left them to settle if possible the Divorce question and rushed home just in time to pack and be off. A very quiet passage over to Boulogne was seconded by a weary hour's waiting at the station before the train started.

We reached Paris at 9.10 and drove to the *Hôtel de l'Europe* and then wandered about for the day seeing sights. Tried for but could see no good MSS. Drove to the *Bois de Boulogne* and went to the *Pré Catalan*, for which I cannot say much. By dint of watering the grass vigorously they get it to look very green, but it is coarse stuff, more like a water meadow in texture than an English lawn. The *Pré Catalan* without a soul in it except the show men, etc. eating *al fresco* dinners, is rather slow, so we came back soon. In the afternoon went to the Hippodrome. The best thing probably was the racing between three men each riding a four-in-hand and going at a great pace. Dined at Véfour's and then off to the station, and in a rash moment, and in submission to the peremptory order of a grand railway clerk, booked ourselves through from Paris to Turin. The train was very full but I rested tolerably well and awoke in the morning just in time to get a glimpse of the cathedral at Tournus.[1] At Mâcon we changed to another train and crossing the Saône turned off toward Geneva; the country invisible in a thick fog till we reached Ambérieu, the junction with the line from Lyons, where it rose sufficiently to disclose an exceedingly picturesque situation. From this point up to Culoz, where we left the line, the country is very wild and beautiful. The railway runs up a very narrow winding valley hemmed in with grand hills, showing here and there fine bold bluffs of rock. The stream, a mountain torrent, was nowhere — but wide banks of well-worn stones show that it is powerful enough after rain or in the winter and spring. At Culoz we embarked on a long and very shaky steamboat, the "Coquette," and going stern foremost a half mile down the rapid Rhone (here a dirty white colour) we finally turned out of it into a sort of canal which connects the Lac du Bourget with the Rhone. Our steamer was so long that in getting along we invariably just touched land at one end and occasionally at

[1] Note from the sketch-book: Tournus has a fine Romanesque church with one complete and one unfinished steeple at the west end and another complete steeple on the north side in about the position (I think) of a transept. These two steeples have two arcaded stages of about equal height above the roof and are finished with square tiled spires in a very characteristic manner. (These square spires seem to be of very frequent occurrence in this district.) Just in front of the church are two round towers which seem to form a gateway and the space between the western steeples of the church is finished horizontally with a crenelated parapet on a machicoulis — the battlements pierced with openings of this kind ✠ — the whole looks as though done with a view to defence.

both, but by dint of great energy in the steering and by aid of men who ran along the bank to push us off, we were safely discharged into the lake. The water here is of the blue green which one remembers at Geneva. The banks are precipitous and the lake, though not very large, very pretty. The Dent du Chat on the south-west is a fine hill, and the high bold hill above Culoz stands out to great advantage over the immense, perfectly flat, meadow which occupies the space between the Rhone and the lake, and which to-day is full of haymakers, — I should say some two or three hundred — all hard at work. We embarked at a temporary kind of port called S. Innocent and went thence by railway to Chambéry. Here we stopped for five hours to see the cathedral, wash and eat. The cathedral is of small interest. Its flamboyant west front is fairly good of its kind. On the whole the church wants dignity, and gives the impression of a parish church more than of a cathedral. The castle which rises above the west side of the town has not much old remaining. The chapel is poor flamboyant with some good stained glass in the apse. The king has a fine papered and cushioned gallery at the west end. I looked into one or two other churches but found no old features.

The situation of Chambéry is exquisite. It is hemmed in on all sides by mountains, and their outlines are generally unusually sharp and bold, finishing as many of them do with great bluffs of rock. A figure resting on the fore-quarters of four elephants who spout water from their trunks is the most remarkable modern feature in the city. It is to the memory of General———[1], a great

[1] General de Boigne, d. 1830. — G. G. K.

benefactor. The streets contain few old houses: I saw one of the sixteenth century nearly all windows. The fronts of the shops have the old arrangement of a stone arch the whole width of the front and a bold stone counter.

We left Chambéry at 5.30 P.M. for S. Jean de Maurienne. The scenery as long as we could see it was beautiful, but the clouds were low and at the point where Mont Blanc ought to have been seen they effectually prevented our seeing anything. At S. Jean we took possession of the diligence for Turin and saw nothing till we were well up on the mountain from Lons-le-Bourg. It took us two hours to scale this height, pulled at a slow pace by nine mules and two horses. The ascent was uninteresting but we gradually came upon more and more snow and the pass increased in interest. There is a small lake at the top and a dreary drive across a crest led us to the fine part of the descent. This is, for the last hour and a half before reaching Susa, singularly fine, finer indeed, I am inclined to think, than any descent I have yet seen. The mountains are fine in their outlines, and the road winds backward and forward between chestnut and walnut trees. Susa is mainly remarkable for its beautiful situation among mountains with snowy peaks always in sight, and a burning sun just now. The cathedral has a good campanile of brick and a west front built on by the side of an old Roman gateway, whose scale makes that of the church seem very small. The spire of the cathedral is covered with small pieces of copper (I think) cut like slates. The interior is painted all over in the worst possible taste. Indeed throughout the Sardinian dominions there seems to be a passion for painting shaded imitations of tracery upon walls and groining. Chambéry cathedral is a notable specimen of this and Susa not much better. We left Susa at 8.30 P.M. and reached Turin at 10.30. I expected nothing here and was agreeably disappointed. A city cannot fail to be charming which has at the end of every street such a view, of mountains and snow at one end and hills at the other, as Turin can show. And then, though quite modern, its streets have that narrow picturesque character so universal in Italy, and in every way leave a pleasanter impression than one would expect from maps and descriptions. . . .

The women in Turin wear handkerchiefs on their heads. The streets are some of them arcaded, by arcades filled with stalls of all kinds of wares — but fruit is the staple commodity now. The effect is to make the place look rather shabby and rubbishy. There is not one church of any interest. The view of the city from the opposite bank of the Po is charming, owing to the immense chain of Alps spreading from right to left all behind the city, and the hills above the Po are very respectable, rising as they do about 2000 feet above the city to where they are crowned by the church called the Superga.

We left Turin at 5.30 and reached Genoa at 9.30. The views of the Alps by sunset very charming. At Asti we had a bottle of the effervescing *vin d' Asti* brought to our carriage, and could not resist indulging in the pleasant draught. . . .

The notes on Genoa appear in the second edition of Brick and Marble.

August 29, PISA.

My expectations were very high here and were a little disappointed. The Gothic work in the grand group is mainly confined to the Campo Santo and the baptistery, and in the former the traceries are, as Pisano's always are, very unscientific and more like a confectioner's work than an architect's, whilst the latter has undergone such an amount of "restoration" that not one old crocket is left and barely one old piece of tracery. There is abundant evidence however in the Spina chapel and in the few portions of the original marble still left in the Baptistery that Pisano could do his work in a way very different from what we do, and I therefore prefer to think only of what his work once was and not of what it is. The external design is very striking and if the cone above the dome were properly finished with a circle of canopied traceries and figures I have no doubt its effect would be perfect. The traceries, carvings, etc., when looked into are very bad, and it should be seen therefore from a distance. The interior looks much older than the exterior and there can be no doubt that this must be the case, notwithstanding the inscription which says it was "ædificata de novo" in 1728. Unquestionably this must refer to the destruction of the exterior which left the interior all but untouched. The dome is in part covered with red tiles and in part with metal.

The Campo Santo is architecturally not pleasing. Its large traceries, unskilful and long, never at all fit on to the capitals of the shafts that support them — but its great length and size are very effective and the court with its greensward and some tall cypress trees at the centre, the mountains blazing in the sun and the deep blue sky above, combine to make a very charming picture. The great treasure here is the frescoes with which its walls are covered. Orcagna's great fresco of the Last Judgement quite and more than came up to my hopes. It is a wonderful work and full of exquisitely natural treatment of figures in most delicate colours. The aureole round the figure of our Lord is too green, I think, otherwise the dignity of the figure is unmatched if not unapproachable.

The cathedral is not to my mind a pleasing structure. Like most of the great churches in this part of the world, it is raised on a basement of several steps extending in front of it on every side. It is Romanesque in character throughout, its nave of great height and the crossing covered with a low and ugly tiled dome. The columns between the nave and aisles (there are two aisles on each side) are either antique or closely copied from the antique and have nowhere any trace either in their proportions or sculpture of any really Romanesque character. The columns everywhere have the entasis distinctly developed. All the walls are arcaded externally and striped with black marble. All the Pisan and Luccan buildings are similarly striped and (unlike the architecture at Genoa) the black forms but a very small proportion of the whole wall. It is generally spaced regularly, and introduced at springings and sills of windows and under cornices, and there is no approach even to irregularity in its arrangement. The roof is one of a class of heavy panelled wooden roofs which were common here in the Renaissance period, similar in idea to the roof of the Banqueting House at Whitehall. The aisles are pleasing, vaulted without ribs. In the old glass, of which some quantity remains, the colours are very rich, there is scarcely any white (if any) and the designs are almost entirely made of lead lines and not by painting. The pulpit has two figures and some lions under the columns which were preserved from an older pulpit said to be the work of Giovanni Pisano. The detail of all the ornamental mouldings is completely Roman, the egg and tongue being everywhere finely introduced. . . .

Of domestic buildings Pisa retains very extensive remains, inasmuch as almost every house bears evidence of being mediaeval, but they have been so much cut about that there is little to be seen now at all perfect. There is an elaborate brick and terra cotta front to a house on the Lungarno but it is of very late date — almost Renaissance in much of its detail and very flat, regular, and ineffective.

On the opposite side of the Arno is another old house now used as the Custom House; this is of stone but its traceries and details are poor, very much like those of the Ptolomei palace at Siena. The windows are shafted, but the capitals of the shafts are generally too large for the arch mouldings which they have to support, and the mouldings, if they may be called so, do not unite properly and are singularly ineffective. Most of the old houses seem to have had a row of plain pointed arches rising some twenty feet from the ground line, but I could not make out whether they had been filled in with windows, or whether they belonged to the stage of stables and coach houses so universal in these Italian towns. The work is either brick or stone, but in no case did I see the two materials countercharged.

On the Sunday evening there was a grand procession of a figure of the B. V. M., with a vast number of attendants all with lighted candles, a military band, and a few cavalry to bring up the rear. The view from the lowest bridge looking up the Arno, with the picturesque outlines of the bold hills above Pisa behind the towers, is one of the most charming I remember.

A railway journey from Pisa of an hour brought us to Lucca. The railway cuts some fine hills, and passes by the ruins of a large castle close to the station before Lucca.

Lucca is entirely enclosed within elaborate brick fortifications, there being, I think, no vestige of suburbs on any side. The ramparts are well planted with trees, and the view of them from below, giving an impression of the tall walls covered with trees and these surmounted by the tall towers of the town, is fine. The view of the surrounding mountains is, too, very exquisite.

Of course our first object was the cathedral. Its west front need hardly be described. Its detail is very rich and beautiful and there is a great deal of very good inlaid work. In the upper part subjects from field sports are introduced, whilst lower down they are mainly geometrical patterns. Some of the shafts are inlaid. The three great arches which stretch across this front give a dignity to it in which S. Michele, Lucca, Pisa cathedral, and the other imitations, are quite wanting. They are remarkable for the way in which their arches are treated; these are semicircular and the width of the voussures is two or three times as great at the crown as at the springing — the effect is good. An image is cut in the right-hand upper end of this front.

All the walls and arches are partially striped with black, the black courses being very thin with a considerable space between them. The north and south walls of the nave and transepts are cased in much later work than the west front and are good specimens of Italian pointed of the thirteenth century. The carving of foliage in this work is very bad and what little moulding there is hardly looks like the work of Gothic men. There is a good inlaid string course under the windows. A fine campanile stands a little in advance of the south-west angle of the cathedral. It is of Romanesque date and built of brownish rough stone below and of white stone (or marble) above; it is of very considerable height and effect. The interior is certainly grand but disappointing — almost all the arches are semicircular but (as the groining bays are not square) the wall ribs of the groining bays are pointed, and this gives in some way a general effect of pointed to the whole work. The main arches are round, but they were so covered with red hangings that it was impossible to see much of them. The triforium is of great height and consists in each bay of two round-head windows, filled in with slight tracery — the whole is of poor character and badly proportioned. Above these two windows is a small circular window which serves for clerestory. The groining of the nave is painted richly. It has broad borders next the ribs and the wall is painted blue, and figures in the centre of each painted in a circle. The borders have a good many white lines, but there is no gold in any part of the work.

The planning of the transepts is very singular. They are divided by an arcade down the centre, and as the nave arcades and triforia are continued across them some singular combinations are produced. The pavements have small compartments of Italian fifteenth century geometrical patterns in mosaic, surrounded by square arrangements of plain black and white.

Close to the cathedral is S. Giovanni, which, though not otherwise remarkable, has an immense baptistery built on against its north transept; it is a square of about fifty-seven feet internally and covered with a square vault of a domical form. The old font has been removed.

Near the south end of the cathedral is the little chapel of S. Maria della Rosa. It is a small low building of about the proportions of the Spina chapel, and mainly remarkable for the window tracery in its side wall. This is, like all other tracery hereabouts, unpalatable to me. The windows are shafted and I suppose therefore that they must have had their glass put in frames inside. This seemed to have been the case in the Spina chapel. There are dates of 1309 and 1333 on the building, the latter on part of a door which in England I should venture to call Renaissance. We could not get inside but saw through a window that the interior had been completely modernized. . . .

When we reached Siena we found the station elaborately decorated with wreaths and flowers in pots, banners, and every possible kind of railway utensil (even portions of engines), and all in honor of the Pope who had left that morning for Città della Pieve on his way home after a tour through various parts of Italy. He seemed to have been greatly fêted at Siena.

Siena is situated on the irregular summit of a considerable hill. All streets are up and down and in some places very precipitous. A sort of natural amphitheatre in the centre of the city — the Piazza del Campo — is the chief point round which the rest is built, containing the Palazzo Pubblico, a grand Gothic building, out of the end of which soars the finest campanile, after that at Verona, that I have seen. On the circle of the Campo opposite the Palazzo Pubblico are some old houses but not any of special interest. The Palazzo Pubblico is of the usual type of brick buildings here and very regular. . . . The campanile is brick without break or ornament of any kind for a great height, and then is boldly corbelled forward on all sides; the whole of the work is in stone. The arches of the machicoulis, the bands round them, and some older parts, are rendered much more distinct by the introduction of lines of black marble. Seen by a bright moonlight this campanile possesses such an exquisite contour that nothing can be much more beautiful. The contrasts of colours too are most admirably arranged, and the exceeding simplicity of the lower part cannot be too much praised.

A considerable ascent leads from the Campo to the east end of the cathedral. This has a central door and on entering you find a small chapel under the altar of the cathedral gained out of the slope of the ground. The detail of this chapel and of the east end of the cathedral above it is by far the best example of Gothic work in the city. There are all kinds of things which, to an eye used to the exceptional skill and care in fitting one part to another usual among northern architects, are very unscientific-looking, but nevertheless this work is original in its character and certainly beautiful in its effect. It is of white marble striped sparingly with black. A flight of steps leads up from the east end to a north doorway in the east wall of the immense unfinished work which, though in the position of a south transept, would really have been rather larger than the existing nave of the cathedral.

This south transept is quite unfinished though very considerably advanced. Its south wall shows that the vaulting was to have been semicircular in section like that of the nave. The proportions of the whole are very bold and fine. . . . The rest of the exterior has been much modernized. The west front is much like that of Orvieto but I don't know how much is original. There is very little in it which I should accept as really pointed architecture. The foliage and the feeling of the whole is very Renaissance and the steep gables are all sham and are very unpleasantly conspicuous in a distant general view of the church. The campanile, coursed in black and white in nearly even proportions (two courses of white material for one course of colours), is Romanesque, of very great height, and follows the usual rule of increasing its number of openings in each stage. It is capped with square spirelets at the angles, and a low octagon spire, I think of stone — this I thought had crockets, but I found they were only some arrangements for illumination in honour of the Pope's visit. . . . Internally the church has been painfully modernized; a row of Popes' heads — about as artistic as a row of barber's blocks — is ranged all round above the nave arcade, and the whole of the church has been plastered and painted in the most abominable manner. The walls are striped in exactly equal courses (about eight and a half inches in height) of black and white. The effect is certainly too bizarre. There are no good specimens of carving, and the detail of groining ribs, arches, etc., is hopelessly bad. All of the pavements are covered with subjects formed by inlaying and incising the marbles which compose them. There is a certain grandeur in the completeness of the idea but the effect is not good. . . .

We spent some hours to great advantage in the *Accademia*. The collection of pictures of the early Sienese school is wonderfully rich and gave me a very high idea of the power of some of the men whose names one does not often hear.

There are three or four tondos similar to that at San Domenico and a considerable number of reredoses of various sizes. A favorite subject is the B. V. M., surrounded by saints in the outer compartments. Nothing can exceed the beauty of some of the angels. In all, the wood seems to have had canvas laid on it which was prepared with a thick layer of size, and on this gold was laid all over preparatory to painting. In some the colour has peeled off and left the gold with lines for the outline of the figures scratched on it. Generally speaking the preservation of the colours in these pictures is something quite marvellous, not a crack being visible anywhere; may this be attributed to the gold ground?

The later pictures are not so interesting nor is the collection of them so complete as it is of the others. Room III is that in which the work is most beautiful. There were several students at work drawing from the life, and in one of the rooms all the designs submitted in competition for prizes were exhibited. The architectural designs were generally very commonplace but one or two for a holy-water stoup showed power of drawing and some fancy. Renaissance is the only style thought of. . . .

September 2.

The view from Cortona is very fine, over the broad Val de Chiana with the end of Lake Thrasimene full in view, and the irregular mountain outlines of Monte Cortona and other heights filling up the whole of the background.

We left after only two hours' pause and soon reached the head of the lake. We were busy making out all the sites of the battle (which may be done with great vividness), when we reached the Papal dogana. There were two difficulties — first, my passport was improperly viséd but this I got over; and second, our driver had no visé at all, and it was half an hour before he was allowed to take us on as far as the next village under strict promise to come back again at once. It rained heavily as we started and we lost some of the beauty of this the best part of our drive. Thrasimene is a grand sheet of water but wants some striking feature on its banks, some jutting out rocks or mighty hills plunging perpendicularly into its depths, to make it thoroughly attractive. Now it has a deserted look: its banks are not grand and yet no houses or villages show there and one gets a rather gloomy impression. The place at which we changed our horse, Pasignano, is a miserable Italian village, — and how miserable that is I can hardly say — with its fair proportion of beggars, *i.e.*, every one whose eye you catch holds out a hand immediately for a *mezzo baiocco*. It is prettily situated, and, as one of the places at which *vetturini* stop on the road to Rome, ought to be rather better favoured as to an inn. The only one did not look promising and we preferred fasting to trying it. A few miles more and we left the lake, and aided by two bullocks climbed a steep hill above its banks, reached the cathedral and village of Magione, and drove the rest of the way by moonlight to Perugia where we were heartily glad to find ourselves at 10.30 P.M. very ready for something to eat.

September 4.

Lucca in its flat, surrounded by mountains, Pisa grand with water and hills, Genoa with the blue Mediterranean at its feet, Siena on its lofty though arid hills, and Arezzo with its fine prospect of cultivated valley girt with hills, must all, lovely as they are, give way to Perugia, seated on the irregular summit of a mountain, looking one way toward Thrasimene and Monte Cortona, another toward the irregular peaks of the Appenines, a third down the rich flat valley of the Tiber, and last of all toward the noble mountain against whose streaked side stands whitely shining in the distance the object of many an artistic as well as many a religious aspiration, the shrine of the great saint of Assisi. Add to this beauty of situation a beauty of atmosphere which we never dream of in England, and the picture is complete.

Certainly since we have been here this has been no land of cloudless blue skies. We have had glorious weather, and yet without any doubt the most glorious cloud scenery we have ever known anywhere. Sometimes a violent storm in the distance and another close at hand, sunsets short in duration but brilliant to excess while they last, and in midday a purple, blue or violet tint over every portion of the wonderful landscape. . . .

September 6.

We started at 5.30 A.M. for Assisi. . . . The sacristan took us up through the sacristy by a staircase which opens into the north transept of the upper church. From the gloom of the lower church to the flood of coloured light in the upper the contrast is very great. The latter is in all respects one of the most joyous buildings I have ever seen, bold, nervous and simple in its design, exquisitely harmonious in all its colouring, and in most respects unharmed by the hand of the restorer. Obviously however the frescoes on the roof are losing their colour and being gradually washed out. This is not difficult to account for when one sees the state of the outer roof of the church, which, I have no doubt, admits an ample supply of wet at the top of the groining. The upper church is used only on some few great days during the year and is I suppose even less cared for. It gave me a pang to be shown into such a building by a door in a corner, to see the principal door permanently closed, grass growing thick upon the dreary piazza in front of it: it was even more mournful, I think, than is the sad solitude of the great group at Pisa.

I am much puzzled by the interior of this upper church. I cannot get out of my head the impression that they [the two "churches"] were designed and *in part executed* by Frenchmen. The detail of the groining piers and their capitals and bases are so peculiarly and characteristically French that (seeing how very different Italian work of the same date was) I cannot believe that they were ever wrought by Italian hands from French designs, because sculpture of foliage was just one of these things in which the character of different schools was so marked that it was impossible to get any but Frenchmen to do such work as this. Above this point I do not feel the same thing because I see that the window traceries, though very fair, have a feature peculiar to Italian Gothic — in the way in which the circles, etc., in the tracery are put under the main arch, just touching but not uniting with it. The string under the windows has for a considerable portion of its length a complete English dog-tooth. The whole of the walls are painted. Below the string course, which is very high from the floor, is, first a painted imitation of hangings (much like our thirteenth century patterns) in which the diaper is continued regularly without reference to folds in the draperies; then a row of noble frescoes by Giotto; and above the string on each side of the windows other frescoes by Cimabue. The roof is by the latter, and the groining bays are alternately blue studded with stars, and frescoed in subjects. The latter have a predominance in the ground of a rich chrome — reddish yellow — and the ribs throughout are bordered with wide patterned borders. The contrast of colours is admirable and finer than anything I have seen. The borders round the work done by Giotto are very inferior to those in Cimabue's work. The latter [1] are all severely flat and geometrical,

[1] These must be those now given to Cavallini and his school; and Street's taste comes out right where knowledge was a-wanting. —G. G. K.

indulging, after a few feet of plain pattern, in a quatrefoil ⟦⟧ or one inscribed on a square, painted with a head on a blue ground. Giotto's, on the other hand, though in some respects very beautiful, indulge too much in perspective, *e.g.* each division between the groining piers is divided into the subjects by painted and shaded imitations of twisted columns bearing cornices. There are some features of interest in the work beyond the exquisite beauty. To me it was new to find Cimabue painting with so little rudeness and so much magnificent simplicity and breadth of purpose. I note another of Giotto's frescoes is interesting as showing the original use of the painted roods of which we have seen so many. I think there can be little doubt they were to be placed on the rood-screen, as he distinctly shows them, and, curiously, I find in this upper church the two ends of the ancient rood-beam sawn off a foot from the wall. This was a few feet west of the crossing. The transepts, altar and stalls are all modern in their arrangements.

Externally there is nothing to notice save the fine west door and circular window over it, of a type peculiar so far as I have seen to the churches of Assisi. The glass in the nave windows is certainly old and good, very little white introduced.

After seeing this most interesting building well, we betook ourselves to the not very easy work of climbing about the city to see the other churches. The whole place is as decayed, forlorn and dirty as the smallest and rudest of fishing villages in the worst out-of-the-way parts of Cornwall, spread out to ten times the extent. Old walls remain nearly all round, with gateways, and at the highest point the picturesque ruin of a castle.

The west end of the cathedral is fine and the campanile by its side is also of noble size and good character though built with very rough stone. . . .

September 7.

We left Perugia this morning at 6 A.M. in the banquette of the diligence for Arezzo. The day was charming so that we enjoyed the ride throughly, though we had done it all so lately on our way to Perugia.

Here I shall note down a few of the things we have discovered on the road: —

Hay and corn stacks are all made round a tall pole fixed in the ground. Another piece of wood nailed across often converts this into a cross over the corn.

In Arezzo cathedral during tierce a black cat was howling about the cathedral in a most ludicrous manner. It belongs to the church and is always howling about, sitting on altars, and so forth. Foreigners never care about taking animals into church with them. Dogs are special church-goers in Italy!

About Perugia the women's costume is good: white sleeves, blue skirt, pink bodice and bright handkerchief over the head. The women usually wear immense straw hats about two feet six inches in diameter, generally pinned on to the back of the head and flapping back to shade none of the face. Between Arezzo and Florence the women often wear round beaver hats with broad flat brims — and very ugly they are. Women carry a fan instead of a parasol. Women in Genoa wear white veils.

The staple production of much of Tuscany, Siena, and the Papal States seems to be olives. The trunks of the trees are always very old, crushed down in the centre and sometimes two or three feet in diameter. The branches are young wood and always trained out so as to leave a hollow circle in the centre. The colour is a very blue green and as they are planted everywhere in lines and at regular intervals, they do not improve either the near or the distant view of the landscape. Maple trees are trained in the same way for the purpose of growing vines. The vines are festooned sometimes from tree to tree and at others festooned round the tree itself.

The ploughs here are very clumsy, they have a very heavy wooden frame with an iron shoe put on in front. It does not turn the dirt over but only digs a rough furrow in the ground. Oxen are always used for all agricultural work. They are ringed through the nose and a cord, fastened to this ring and passing under a rope between the horns, serves as a rein. The carts are so made that they are loaded far out on the pole to the shoulder of the men.

All houses here have a pigeon house raised above the roof. On it are painted some flying pigeons on a white ground. It is generally a large construction and looks like a look-out room at first.

It is curious that we never see a bird flying about, yet we eat at dinner every day portions of two or three. Where do they all come from?

All the houses are built over stables.

Wayside churches seem almost always to have a small window on each side of their western door protected by a grating and with a shutter inside. Often there is an arcaded porch above.

September 8.

We left Arezzo at 6 A.M. in the diligence for Florence. With such a bourne the pace of an Italian diligence is very aggravating — five and a quarter miles an hour is the average speed, and the poor wretches of horses have to go stages of twenty miles without stopping. The road is very interesting. It passes nearly all the way through hilly country rich in olives and vines and with the grand outlines of the Appenines in the immediate neighborhood. I saw not one architectural feature in the entire journey. We passed through two or three small towns busy with festivities in honour of the Nativity of the B. V. M. but their churches seemed to be all modern.

After passing ——[1] we recommenced a long ascent and aided by four mules and ponies achieved the highest point after about two hours of the hardest work under the hottest of suns. Here I caught a glimpse of Florence in the distance; but about three miles further the whole city suddenly opened to the view, filling up the valley of the Arno with its campanile and dome thrown out grandly by a passing shadow upon the delicate blue and violet tints of the Pistojese mountains in the background. Fiesole was on our right and the whole country between it and Florence seemed to be dotted over with villas, looking gay and lovely in the brilliant sunshine. Behind Fiesole a long hill of rich reddish brown stood out from the rest and afforded by its contrast with the other colours of the landscape as complete a whole as can be imagined. It is in vain to describe such a view: it is the most exquisite of the kind that I have ever seen, and words cannot carry the impression of an effect not produced solely by facts but in part undoubtedly by sentiment.

[1] If Street did not know the name, how should the editor? — G. G. K.

A long drive through suburbs brought us to an old gate (shorn of its old Florentine machicoulis, however) where we were detained nearly half an hour about our passports and luggage, and this done we soon arrived at our inn, crossing the Arno by the Ponte alle Grazie and passing in our way the Palazzo Vecchio, Or San Michele and Giotto's tower. The latter was looked for eagerly and rewarded my anxious eyes. It is certainly the most lovely piece of building I have ever seen. I shall say no more but go on to journalize on the buildings as I am able. . . .

Street's appreciation of Florence was intelligent, ardent, and characteristic, but is, more than any other of his notes, a journal intime. *I have respected his sincerities.*

September 13.

We spent the whole of the afternoon very profitably at Pistoia. The cathedral has not much architectural character. The west front has a good simple Romanesque door and an open arcade all across in front. At the northwest stands a very lofty and massive campanile, plain below but arcaded richly above with arcades that have the appearance of being put on in front of the real tower instead of helping to support it. They have semicircular arches and then have their tympana filled in with chequer patterns in white and black marble. The whole of this arcaded part of the steeple is coursed in alternate white and dark green: the lower part is of stone. Internally the cathedral has little to show. There is a moderately good monument near the west end to a professor who is represented lecturing; no mark of his religious faith (I think) is introduced.[1] . . .

[1] This will be Messer Cino—of Dante and Mr. Hewlett.—G. G. K.

Opposite the cathedral's west front stands the fine baptistery. This is octangular in plan and built in equal courses of white and dark marble. Its external effect is very good indeed. It has a western door[1] and north and south doors and a small chancel projected on the west side. The design recalls in some respects the baptistery at Pisa and must have been built about the time that was altered. The interior unfortunately is as plain and bare as whitewash can make it. The great octangular font in the centre is of the same kind of work as the screens at S. Miniato, Byzantine in the character of its sculpture, but delicate and elaborate in its detail and altogether a good specimen: it is executed mainly in white marble. . . .

In another church, S. Bartolomeo, I found a pulpit (also dated, etc.) made by Guido da Como in 1250. This is square in plan, supported partly in the wall and partly on three shafts, two of which rest on lions' backs and the third on a sitting figure of a woman. The sculpture is rude but vigorous. The whole of the sides is covered with subjects, and at the angles are three figures, or rather one figure with two others looking out from behind him. The subjects are described by inscriptions under each in Latin.

Going from here to the church of S. Giovanni Evangelista, we saw a similar pulpit of later date and superior workmanship but evidently very closely copied from the work in S. Bartolomeo. The two angle columns remain, both resting on lions' backs. The lions have been turned round so as both to face the west wall, — a most ridiculous position. It is clear indeed that

[1] Eastern? queries Street in pencil.

all of these pulpits have been taken down and reconstructed. In this work the central column at S. Giovanni has been taken away. It seems to me that this pulpit at S. Bartolomeo is the prototype of all those for which the Pisani have so much credit. Giovanni Pisano is said to have sculptured the pulpit in S. Giovanni and if so (and I think it seems probable) he simply copied the older work. I do not know what the pulpit of S. Andrea is like, but I have little doubt that it was really from this pulpit that they obtained their idea for all their very similar works.

The south front of S. Giovanni is arcaded in the Pisan fashion (with lozenge panels in the arches) and above arcaded with two rows of elaborate arcading. The whole elevation is remarkable in its effect. The roof is of the usual type, with long tie beams, and quite flat in pitch. . . .

We were followed about everywhere here by two very dirty and very ragged urchins who took us to see everything. They knew about the pulpits, talked about Luca della Robbia, etc., and when I gave them an indivisible coin, about which they quarrelled, they settled the matter by putting it into the poor box. How unlike any English boys altogether! We were immensely amused by their sharp impudence.

The inn at Pistoia looked out on green shrubs and gardens, very pleasant: the consequence was not so pleasant — the being kept awake half the night and bitten in all directions by our troublesome enemies the mosquitoes. We had to turn out early to join the diligence whch arrived by railway from Florence at 7.30 A.M. We made a brilliant start but very soon altered our pace, the road beginning to ascend almost immediately, and then for about four hours we toiled slowly up the slopes of the Appenines, at first with six and afterwards with eight horses. The day was fine but misty so that we lost very much of the distant view. The scenery is fine but not alpine. It reminded me more of the Jura, save that the hills seem here more to be shaken confusedly about and not to range themselves into regular lines or masses. The olive tree was seen for the last time as we went up and then we came through great numbers of Spanish chestnuts, and lastly for half an hour at most through a bleak, open and treeless country.

The descent was very different, down a narrow valley, following the windings of the mountain stream, with fine combinations of scenery and views. Stopped at La Porretta for dinner, and then on through a fine country but along a miserable road constantly crossing the (now dry) beds of mountains torrents. The soil is exceedingly liable to land slips and seems to be sliding about in all directions — of course road-making is difficult. At Vergato, a small village or town on this part of the road, the old Palazzo Pubblico was passed, covered with coats of arms in the usual way and distinguished by its Ringhiera still perfect and jutting out into the narrow street. We reached Bologna at 8 P.M. A wall and gate was passed about a mile from the town; I could not understand what wall it was.

September 15.

S. Petronio is the grandest church in Bologna. Its west front is of immense size and width but left nearly all in rough brick, the door and basement alone being finished. This part of the work is of poor character and the sculpture[1] (except in a stela on the south-west door which I thought very vigorous) not particularly good. The interior is magnificent. . . .

S. Francesco is one of the finest churches in the town but shabby and decayed outside and "painted and decorated" to such an extent inside as to have destroyed nearly all its good effect. I never saw anything more vile. The whole church is of brick and it has an apsidal east end with an aisle all round the apse and chapels beyond. The buttresses are "flying" but very heavy. The west door is good and indeed the whole west front is striking. The windows are new but appeared to me to be probably copies of the original windows. The campanili are curious. There are two — one much smaller than the other and both on the south side of the choir. They form a curious combination in the views from the east. . . .

September 16.

The ride to Ferrara was very uninteresting — about four and a half hours; we had left the hills altogether and saw nothing at all of any distant country. The land was rich with vines, mulberry trees and rice plantations, but certainly not picturesque. The grapes were being picked, and we met everywhere here and in Bologna waggons bearing magnificent casks for the reception of the grapes. These carts have a great beam from back to front elaborately carved and ornamented with colour, and wheels also carved and ornamented. They are really very handsome and put one in mind of the frame-

[1] Attributed to Jacopo della Quercia; it is not hard to divine why, when Donatello had failed to satisfy, Jacopo should offend. — G. G. K.

work for guns of Queen Elizabeth's time. They are always drawn by white oxen.

Here the Brick and Marble *volume takes up the tale. To 1872 belongs a notebook particularly spirited in text and drawings. It opens:*

1872 — With M. S. and Jessie Holland (afterwards J. M. A. Street)

February 24.

Left London at 8.35, and reached Paris at 7 A.M. . . .

Towns generally built on hills. Curious number of churches in which the tower and spire at one end and a very high choir at the other have a low nave between them. The scenery has the large French character, owing to absence of hedgerows and the very long lines of trees — generally lanky poplars closely set. Just before Dijon, at Plombières, I saw a very pretty tiled spire, tiles of golden yellow, green, etc., very rich and charming in colour; — green not at all blue-green.

Reached Mâcon at 8.30 and after coffee walked out to try to see something. Moon rose beautifully over the opposite side of the Saône, here a very fine looking river. Walked about nearly in vain but came at last on remains of a church of some interest.[1] It has two octagonal towers, the lower part of which seems to be Romanesque, and a nave of some forty feet long with an enormous central doorway of the fifteenth century, and aisle arches on each side of it (now glazed) of the twelfth century, — choir entirely destroyed, and a small cloister arcade built up in front. The whole has been all but destroyed and then I suppose just patched up by

[1] Qy.: S. Vincent? — G. G. K.

some good-intentioned antiquary. It is (at least in the dark) an architectural puzzle.

February 25.

Called at 4.30 and off by train for Genoa via Turin at 6 A.M. As we left and crossed the Saône saw that the church I had discovered last night was the only old looking church, and that the cathedral is an entirely new stone building. It was a fine frosty morning and we could do no more than keep ourselves warm by shutting up windows, and so seeing but little through the hoar frost on the glass.

At Culoz we had a second breakfast and found the hills all about us suddenly looking like mountains owing to the snow on all their higher points. When we came back from Geneva last year, fresh from the Alps, we hardly deigned to look at them, and to-day they seem to all of us about as lovely and grand as they could be. At Culoz we changed carriages and then, keeping by the pretty Lac du Bourget, were soon at Chambéry, and then all the way to Modane we entertained ourselves by the discovery, first on one side then on the other, of snow mountains of the first magnitude! At Modane carriages are changed again for Italy, passports are examined, and then we start for the tunnel. The railway runs round Lons-le-Bourg, where we used to take sledges for the Mont Cenis, and then ascends winding round until the mountain above Modane is reached. Here the tunnel begins and we were just twenty-six minutes passing through it. I promised every one spring, oranges in fruit, and trees in full foliage when we really reached Italy; but it was just the opposite, for there was more snow, by very much, when we reached Bardonnecchia than when we left Modane. We caught one or two views of churches and I just managed to secure a note of Susa seen in the most picturesque way far below us. We reached Turin at 6.42, got some dinner at the railway station and had some much too sweet *vin d'Asti*, and started again at 7.35 for Genoa, where we arrived at midnight.

February 29, GENOA.

A glorious morning welcomed us to this most delightful town. It was really like summer and the views in all directions were most exquisite. Even before I got up I saw through my window the beautiful outline of the mountains of the Riviera all covered with snow, and just a line of the blue Mediterranean above and beyond the crowd of vessels below us in the port. We had rooms at Feder's hotel — now Trombetta's — and our bedroom had an oratory in it with a very elaborately carved altar, etc., which has been not very reverently turned now into a sleeping room.

I spent most of my day at the new English church directing the workmen, etc. Lunched with the Shelbells, but did not see Brown the consul, who had gone off to a castle he had bought near Sestri. The church looks fairly well, but it is difficult to make anything lofty enough to compete with the enormous houses which it is the fashion to build now in Genoa and with which it is surrounded.

Walked a little about the city: into the Via Nuova which is straight for the greater part of its length (instead of curved as I fancied) — up and down the goldsmith's street which seems always to lead to everything — into the cathedral and some of my other old friends among the churches. Noticed particularly the sumptuous effect which the painted palaces produce. The palace now used by the British consul is covered outside with painting, a good deal of which remains in fair condition whilst the two arcades round the courtyard are in a very fairly perfect state. The doors to the houses in Genoa had commonly an oblong panel of sculpture over them. These were cut in slate at or near Savona. The Gothic houses here have arcades below, and corbel tables under the second floor, and the windows divided into lights by very delicate shafts. The best samples are the Doria houses close to S. Matteo.

We left Genoa at 9.00 by steamer for Livorno. The boat was small and full of passengers, but I slept well on the floor of the cabin till we reached our port soon after 5 A.M.

March 1.

Started by the 9.12 train for Empoli. Murray describes Empoli in such terms as made us feel no regret at having to stop there those three hours. Unfortunately his description turned out to be all wrong, and we found but little to see or sketch. The best thing there is the steeple of the collegiata. The front of this church is a work of about 1600 in white marble and serpentine. And the Pallei building opposite to it is entirely seventeenth century, but has some wall painting outside which somewhat redeems its otherwise uninteresting walls.

Our train left Empoli at 2.25 and did not reach Orvieto till nearly 10. During the first part of the journey I was well employed making sketches from the windows of the carriage of Certaldo, S. Gemignano, etc. We caught some beautiful glimpses of Siena as we dashed by, and then as we passed through the wretched country just to the south of it, we gradually lost the daylight, and slept away the hours till Orvieto was reached. Here the station by daylight looks just under the town, but it took us forty minutes to drive up.

March 2, ORVIETO.

I was out before breakfast and spent a long, busy, and happy day here. The town is perched on the top of a rock which is on most sides a precipice at first and then a long slope carrries the eye on to the river and valleys at the bottom. Beyond on all sides are distant hills to be seen, one of them very picturesque in outline. In summer it must be a perfect view, but now the olives are the only trees in leaf, and their colour is so sad that it does not do much for the landscape.

The old walls exist round much of the town. They are generally set back a few feet from the edge of the rock so as to leave a passage outside, which in its turn is defended by battlements built on the cliff. The lay of the ground reminds one of Toledo, but the country is more open, and the river is not a Tagus and does not produce much effect on the landscape. The views which may be had from various points of the rocks and walls are, however, superb, and I have seldom seen anything more striking. On the other hand there is no building of sufficient importance in the town to give the best effect to the views. The cathedral, not having any tower, produces but little general effect, and the only towers are some of the plain square family fortress towers like these sketched at S. Gemignano.

The cathedral more than fulfilled my expectations. The west front is in its way very beautiful, delicate and

MASTER MATTHEW'S PORCH AT SANTIAGO

refined — perhaps over-refined everywhere, and beautiful in the symmetry of its arrangement. But it is still not a great success. My great interest here is in the sculpture of the piers between and at the sides of the doors. First of all, I must say that they strike me as too small and delicate for their place. This is their one fault. If they were to be there they ought to be, as they are, small and in low relief so as not to interfere with the flatness and look of strength in the walls. The sculpture in the northern pier — the days of creation — is perhaps the most beautiful of the four. Nothing can be much more refined in feeling or treatment. The heads are a little exaggerated. The next pier which contains the succession of the seed of Abraham seems to me to be altogether inferior to the others. The third and fourth (from the north) are equal, or nearly, to the first, though a little more crowded. In the last the figure of our Lord surrounded by an aureole of angels, in the Last Judgement, is beautifully designed. The foliage decorations of all this work are very natural in their treatment and extraordinarily skilful. The play of relief in leaves, whose extreme projection from the face of the marble is often not more than an eighth of an inch, is of the most delicate, subtle and artistic description. Contrast the skill with which it is treated with the workmanship in the south door, and the difference of power will be seen.

The interior is very large and simple — the architectural detail generally very poor. Columns (large cylinders with exaggerated capitals of queer semi-classic detail) carrying alternated arches, show the characteristic faults of the Pisan school of architects. The clerestory has long, simple, traceried windows, and the best detail is in the east window, which has good geometrical tracery, is of very long proportion, and is filled with stained glass of beautiful design — subjects in square panels. The effect of its colour is perfect. All round it are paintings by Agnolino of Orvieto, not very fresh now, but giving a colour of the most tender kind to the interior, to which the simple black and white striped construction of the columns and walls leads the eye up gradually and well. In the east window the glass is divided into small panels. There are four lights but in spite of the irregularity caused by this even number the grounds of the subjects are all countercharged, alternately ruby and blue. . . .

What Street said, and what he thought, of Siena and Orvieto, is nearly unique. At Viterbo and Toscanella, he could only see and feel the first what others have since made familiar. Corneto is less known.

March 4.

Looking back to Viterbo I saw it lighted up with beautiful effect by a sudden burst of sunshine. Its towered walls were in deep shade whilst a cloud of light, wind-started from the town behind, caught the bright sunshine and seemed to set the steeples of the town in a sort of halo. Behind rose the high mountain and to the left of this, in the far distance, a line of snow-capped mountains which added immensely to the beauty of the view. This open country is very charming — clouds casting their shadows here and there and a horizon always lovely in the pure colour of the mountains or hills which fringe it. All the way we had Montefiascone in full view.

Corneto stands on a steep hill above the marshy flat which borders the Mediterranean. Its old walls and towers standing generally on a rocky base give it a very imposing appearance, but its interest seems to be mainly Etruscan. The inn at which we stopped made amends for any lack in the churches by its extremely good character. It is of late fourteenth century work, but the internal courtyard with its open arcades on two sides is most beautiful. The front towards the street shows in some of its detail and especially in the construction of the masonry in its upper portion, the influence of the Renaissance. The building formed originally three sides of a quadrangle with a passage-way corbelled out on the wall which forms the fourth side. The lower storeys have fine open arcades, and the third a series of delicate shafts with very effective capitals oblong in plan, carrying a white marble lintel under the wall plate. The whole scheme is one of extreme beauty and has much of the effect of being earlier in date than it really is. . . .
With a few notes on Rome, and the exquisite drawing of a living acanthus leaf at Paestum, the book dies away into a sort of Journal, that records talks with the Bishop of Gibraltar and Père Hyacinth, — "I found him very pleasant and intelligent."

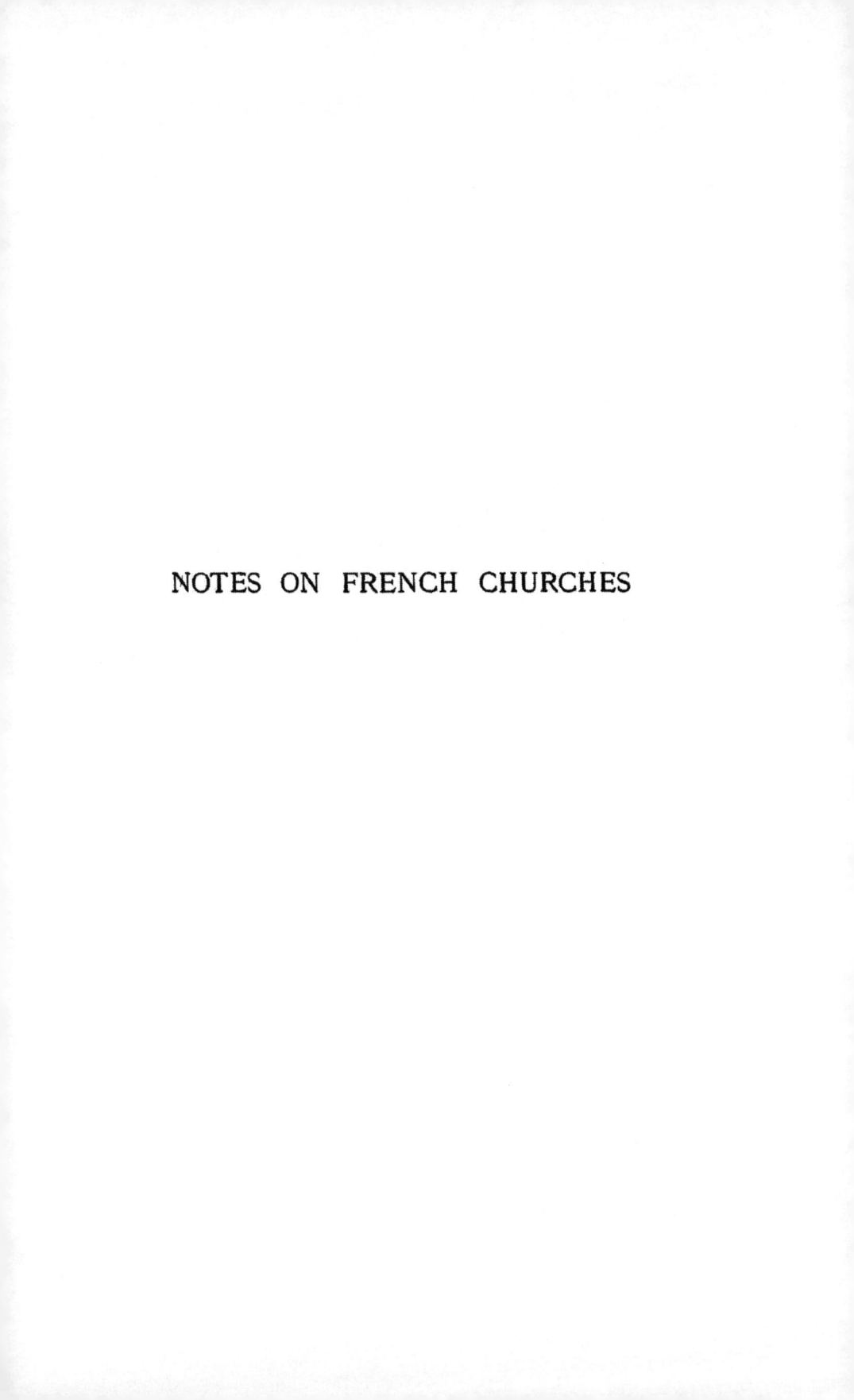

NOTES ON FRENCH CHURCHES

III

SOME FRENCH CHURCHES CHIEFLY IN THE ROYAL DOMAIN

(From a notebook of 1855)

June 13.

SOMER has lost much of its original interest by the destruction wantonly in 1830 of nearly the whole of the abbey of S. Bertin. It is wicked, but I did not lament this so much as I should have done, had the church been of rather earlier date. From what now remains it appears to have been entirely in one style, and that an early phase of flamboyant — much more like some of our English late middle-pointed than flamboyant, and really very effective in its mouldings and sculpture, the two great tests of all architecture. The west front and the north wall of the nave are all that now remains of the once magnificent church, and the latter has lost all its window tracery and is in a sad state of decay.

The west doorway of the tower (which is central at the west end) is fine, and has cut in the lintel stone of its door an inscription: — "*Castissimum Divi Bertini templum caste memento ingredi.*" The tympanum had a painted subject and much of the rest of the stone work still retains traces of decorative colour. The west window of the south aisle is an unhappy example of the worst kind of flamboyant, the tower is covered all over with vertical lines of panelling but is nevertheless, from its great size, imposing, and indeed gives S. Omer all the character it has when seen from the railway. A sentinel keeping watch warned me off as I was measuring the aisle: I suppose having lost so much they were nervously alive to the chance of architects' hacking off what remains!

A long winding street leads from S. Bertin at one end of it to the cathedral of Notre Dame at the other. This is a church well worthy of a visit for several peculiarities and not less for its generally fine effect, especially in the interior.

The original fabric — of which the choir with its aisle and two apsidal chapels thrown out from the aisle, and the south transept and one and a half bays of the north, are all now remaining — is of the earliest pointed, with occasional round arches to windows, etc. The character is very simple and mainly remarkable for the great beauty of the profusion of sculptured capitals to all the shafts. The section of the piers is singular and gives great lightness of effect; they are in fact thin slices of wall, and not piers formed in the usual way, and as the weight of them is not a crushing weight, I look upon them as excessively scientific in their arrangement. The triforium is very lofty as compared with the rest of the design, and consists of a very simple arcade of pointed arches, supported only by long and slender shafts set near together.

The groining is good, and in the chapels a small shaft rises from the capitals for some feet and carries the wall rib: this gets over a difficulty in mitring the mouldings. The Lady-chapel appears to have been remodelled at a later day but upon the foundation of one coeval with the choir. A very grand effect is produced by the great size of the transepts — which have aisles on both sides — and by the placing of a chapel in the re-entering angles between them and the choir aisle. In this way an internal effect of lightness and space, of very fine character, is obtained.

One of the most remarkable features about this cathedral is, however, the extent to which, in later days, the old design was persisted in: *e.g.* the remarkable triforium is carried round the entire church, varied a little in its details and quite different in its sculpture, but still evidently a copy and from its great size giving an air of great unity to the whole design. In the clerestory windows generally there is a good deal of poor flamboyant tracery with a little glass of the same date, but in the choir the original windows all happily remain. These are, in the apse, rather wide lancets, and in the rest of the clerestory simple triplets. In the aisle there were windows of two lights with a simple quatrefoil above. Many of the windows have the dog-tooth ornament round the external labels. The choir still retains on the outside a very fine and original corbel table.

In a chapel south of the choir are extensive remains of some most singular work for pavements — they are squares of stone slightly sunk in regular patterns and then filled in with some very hard black or red substance. The same work is carried up against the walls of this chapel, and in other parts of the cathedral are several small fragments of similar pavements. The stone is of a yellow colour and the system seems to admit of being turned to most useful account.

Of the exterior, the south transept door is about the most remarkable feature. It is very simple, almost plain, but nevertheless its great size and the deep shadow cast by its outer arch combine to make it a very magnificent work. The sculpture of the capitals is very good and the delicate arcade, containing figures on either side below the base of the columns, is thoroughly French in its beauty of detail and exquisite finish. Unhappily it has decayed much. There is a stoup inside against the pier dividing the doors; this is not used now. The western tower is like that of S. Bertin, engaged, and has but little to recommend it to notice.

In the interior there is a very fine high tomb of a bishop — I think S. Omer — early in the thirteenth century, about of the same date as the south transept door. The altar now stands on the east side of the crossing; either side of it, a range of music-stools affords fitting accommodation for the clergy, whilst behind, stalls are arranged in the choir around the apse, encircling an organ which stands about where the altar ought to stand. In front of this organ is a group of music stands etc., for the accommodation of the orchestra. The choir is enclosed with high stone screens toward the aisles — old but quite unornamental. . . .

At S. Leu we had a very *maigre* meal at a small *café biliard* close to the station and left at 7.45 for Senlis. The road was rather pretty and took us in sight of Chantilly, a prettily situated town on the Oise with a château which belonged to the Duc d'Aumale. In little more than an hour we rumbled through the old narrow street of Senlis and took up our quarters at the *Grand Cerf*. Before dark we saw the church of S. Pierre, desecrated and used as a cavalry stable. A soldier who spoke some English insisted on our seeing the thirty "Hawks," as he called them, who occupied the church. This we agreed to in order to see the building, which has, however, little to remark on save its elaborate west front and flamboyant architecture. Near this church is the cathedral and near this a desecrated church, but I must reserve them until to-morrow.

June 16.

My first visit in the morning was of course to the cathedral, of which the west front with its magnificent south-west tower and spire is the most delightful portion. The rest of the church, though retaining many of its old features and arrangements intact, has been overlaid on the exterior with flamboyant work to an unpleasant extent. The two transept fronts are very elaborate and entirely in this late style. At the east end some of the chapels which surround the apse are of Romanesque date, semicircular in their plan outside and roofed with lean-to roofs of stone. The west front was intended to have two similar towers and spires: the towers are both built but only one spire. The detail of the lower portion is very simple, that of the upper part of tower and spire very elaborate and covered with ornament of varied description. The whole surface of spire and turrets is covered with patterns which contribute very much to the general richness of effect. The most remarkable features are however the open pinnacles at the point where the tower becomes octangular, and the delicate spire-lights which are set on every side of the spire and rise nearly half its height. The spire-lights are remarkable in their arrangement at the top;

instead of going back horizontally at the ridge they slope down rapidly to the spire so as to produce a very piquant effect. The detail of all the sculpture and mouldings is most carefully executed throughout, and though the scale of the steeple is not large it produces a very great effect of height. The crockets and finials on the spire are very vigorously carved.

The construction of the spire is very ingenious and allows of passage-ways in the wall to the base of the spire-lights. At this point it is constructed in two thicknesses, one of which slopes and forms the outer line of the spire; the other is perpendicular from the inside face until it meets the external sloping portion and dies into it; the two are occasionally bonded together with large blocks of stone, and a passage-way is formed between them. The view from the steeple is fine.

Close to the cathedral on the south is the desecrated church of S. Frambourg, a simple parallelogram in plan and finished with an apse, rather broad and low in its proportions, but nevertheless very effective. The groining is all sexpartite. The original windows remain only in the apse, and there is but little to be said of the building farther than that its west front is remarkable for the outer line of moulding of a prodigious rose window, (now blocked up), and for a west doorway which though mutilated has much beauty. There seems to have been a tower at the north-west of the nave. This church is now used as a store by a builder. . . .

We left the city of Senlis with some difficulty. *Imprimis* we had an extortionate charge for a bad kind of accommodation at the *Hôtel du Grand Cerf,* and next had great difficulty in getting places in the omnibus to

Pont S. Maxence. But all is well that ends well, and we succeeded, happily, in getting away. The view of the cathedral as the town is left behind becomes very fine, but it is soon lost as the road plunges into the woods through which for the best part of the way it runs. One village, Fleurines, was passed, with a poor late church; some large stone granaries are passed and then the long street of Pont S. Maxence. The Oise is crossed at its end and a few hundred yards bring us to the station; from hence we booked to Noyon, passing on the way Compiègne, which has an old town hall and two churches, one of which, as seen from the distance, seems likely to repay examination. Noyon was reached at four o'clock and we walked off to the cathedral which towers up most conspicuously above the town.

The general character of the church is, internally, much the same as that of S. Leu, etc., but it is very much loftier and has a singular arrangement into four stages in height. There are in the nave: — 1. the arcades, 2. the triforium, very large, with windows and groined, 3. a small arcade more like an ordinary triforium, and 4. a clerestory. In the transepts there is no groined triforium and the two upper stages, being of similar height and both of them glazed, give the impression of a double clerestory. I do not at all like this quadruple arrangement of the interior. The columns of the nave are alternately of clustered and single shafts. The groining is divided into compartments of two bays by reason of the transverse ribs from the clustered piers being much larger than any of the others. Both the transepts terminate with apses and there are many very noble points in the internal effect. Here as at S.

Leu the aisles are very narrow compared to the width of the nave, and the spaces between the columns of the arcades are also very small indeed. Of the exterior, the west end is perhaps the more striking part. It has two immense and very simple towers with a grand triple porch in front of its three great doorways. This porch was constructed weakly and has been boldly buttressed up. North of the north-west tower is a long building connected with the church, of exquisite beauty, and other old buildings enclose a considerable space on the north side of the cathedral. These buildings are remarkable, *inter alia*, for the bold foliage which is introduced beneath the parapets in a fashion very popular in this part of France.

There is a small porch of fine early pointed character on the east side of the north transept and above it a very fine rose window. The ground at the east end is planted out in a garden and the whole effect of the choir with the restored steep roofs above the apsidal chapels is very noble. There is what appears to be a distinct church (now desecrated) attached to the east side of the south transept. It is of simple early pointed and has in each bay two lancets and a round window above. It has several bays of length, and an apse, and is parallel with the choir. Careful works of restoration are going on here. I saw no trace of any other old building, saving a portion of very late domestic work.

We left Noyon at 8.40 and reached S. Quentin at 10 P.M. . . .

June 17.

I turned out early and got a sketch of the great church before breakfast. Its height is very imposing but in its general character it disappointed my rather high expectations. It appears to me to be a kind of late imitation of early work. For instance the triforium and clerestory have almost geometrical tracery differing only in slight points from the best kind of geometrical work. The proportions too are good and the groining very simple. Many of the shafts in the choir are single columns, but the carving of their capitals is very inferior to that I have seen elsewhere. The choir has, too, a triforium which seems to be much earlier than that of the nave, probably early in the thirteenth century. One of the best features is the management of the chapels and aisles round the apse. There are two transepts; the eastern one does not show however in the ground plan. The tower was central at the west end, but has been all modernized and does not now rise above the immense pointed roof of the nave, so that in the distance the church wants distinctness of character and outline, badly. The flying buttresses are very elaborate and are steadied by arches thrown across from pinnacle to pinnacle, so as to keep them from falling laterally; notwithstanding these precautions the church has fallen out so much in some parts as to look very unsafe.

In the market place there is a quaint old town hall standing on open arches and rather elaborate in its details but very late in its date. There was less to interest in S. Quentin than in most places I have visited as yet, so I was very well able to get away at 11 to Tergnier by railway; here we waited for an hour and then started in a slow diligence for Laon through La Fère and Crépy. I could not see any church in the former place, but in the latter — a good sized village — are two, both of first-pointed date and one with a remarkably good chancel having an east window and side windows of two lights with a distinct circular window above, and all adorned with dog-tooth ornaments. The other was remarkable for a very striking western porch. The road was pretty and soon after passing Crépy brought us in sight of the cathedral of Laon crowning its noble hill in right royal style. A drenching storm of rain prevented our seeing much of the beauty of the view as we climbed the steep road that winds round the hill into the town, but in the evening when we walked round the ramparts we found that it was one of most uncommon magnificence — a vast expanse of flat country generally green in its colour, dotted here and there with woods or villages, and bounded in some parts of the horizon with distant hills. . . .

Our first object in the morning was the cathedral. The original idea of the church (which is said to have been built in the extraordinarily short space of two years) was a great nave, choir and transepts, the west front and both the transept fronts being flanked with two towers of nearly equal height and even fairly similar design. Four of these were completed, those on the east side of the transepts having been only carried up to the height of the roof gables. There is a combination of intense simplicity with an intricate and delicate transparent effect in the open pinnacles at the angles which is wonderfully fine. The scale is larger and the whole treatment though similar is finer than that of Senlis, and though it was imitated it was not, I think, rivalled, even in the magnificent steeples at Rheims.

There is a lantern at the intersection of the nave and

transepts which, had it been carried up some vast height above the other towers, might possibly have helped to reduce them all to order; but there is no sign of any such intention, and the only reason for it that can be seen is the desire to elevate the groining at the intersection to a great height above the rest of the roof. I have sketched and measured these towers so carefully that I shall say no more about them, save that they are groined just below the summit and that they were evidently intended for some further finish than they now have, probably for spires like those at Senlis.

The interior of Laon is singularly like that of Noyon, having the same double triforium, but being finished at the east with a square end instead of an apse. Going from one church to another differing only in this respect seemed to give the best possible means of ascertaining with some degree of certainty their relative merits; and certainly it seemed to me that, of the two, Noyon was incomparably the superior, and entirely on this account. The east end of Laon is nevertheless fine for a square east end, and has the windows filled with very magnificent old glass of deep colour. The altar is now brought forward one bay so as to leave a passage beneath the east window.

The capitals generally of this church are very finely treated and would afford endless examples of good work in this early style. In studying the church one of the features most to be noticed is the frequent recurrence of carved courses of foliage which everywhere take the place of moulded string courses.

The south transept has double doorways, and above them a very beautiful rose window. This has now become curious because by its side there is the jamb of a middle-pointed window, evidently inserted by some ambitious man who was going on to put in an entirely new window but who was happily stopped here; I say "here" because he was unhappily not stopped in the south transept and so we have to regret the loss of a grand window suitable to the building and the insertion of one which in no way improves it. On the north side of the choir a great alteration was made in the thirteenth century by throwing out the outer walls to the face of the buttresses in order to gain a considerable number of chapels. This was done in very good style indeed and much improves this part of the exterior.

The only apsidal terminations in the whole church are those of two chapels thrown out on the east side of the transepts. They are carried up three stages in height, one of which opens into the transept aisle and the two others form another chapel out of the magnificent triforium.

Round the east end of the cathedral are large remains of old buildings of early date, connected probably with the church (which, by the by, is said to have been built in A.D. 1113 and 1114, dates which seem to me to be at least fifty years too early for such a structure). The main portion of these buildings consists of a long pile opening to a sort of garth or cloister, north-east of the cathedral, with simple pointed arches supported on low circular columns, and showing on the other side the elevation which I have sketched roughly, and which, standing just at the edge of the cliff, looks on a vast expanse of country until the far distance is lost in mist. These buildings are now converted into some Courts of Law, store houses and lumber rooms.

The Bishop of Laon lives elsewhere I fancy, as our landlord made much of his having come expressly to join in a procession through the city which we witnessed on Sunday afternoon. This procession was new to me and may as well be recorded: it visited a number of altars got up in a temporary manner, elevated on high flights of steps, and decorated profusely with flowers, garlands and drapery. These were erected in every available space, and I suppose by the zeal of the neighbors in each locality. As the time for the procession came, all the good people of the city hung up white sheets over the fronts of their shops so that the whole street bore a most singular appearance, though the universal white was here and there relieved by the old pieces of tapestry with some sacred story on it hung out by some more well-to-do person.

Presently through the dense crowd came the procession — first, girls bearing banners and draped in white, then other banners, clergy, acolytes, censer-bearers and lastly the bishop under a square velvet baldachin carried by priests, walking between two priests, bearing a monstrance with the Host.

At intervals the censer-bearers turned and censed and then went on again, till they reached an altar, which the bishop always ascended and gave the benediction from it, displaying the Host to the people all kneeling below. The procession was followed and kept in some order by soldiers whose band, alternately with the choristers, accompanied the march. In half an hour after the return of the bishop from his rather long procession the town had resumed its old look, the white sheets were gone, and the altars pulled down or denuded of all their ornaments. All the towns we had been in had been preparing for the same fête, which was to be greatest at Lille, where "*Notre Dame de la Treille*" — whose day it was — is looked on as the patron of the city.

From the cathedral we went to the church of S. Martin at the other end of the main street. The general effect of the exterior is very good, and very superior to the interior, — which is very simple, rather bad in its design, and much modernized. The south transept front is very fine and remarkable for the boldness of the mouldings on its buttresses and strings. The west front is, after this, the finest portion of the building, being a very ornate addition in middle-pointed to the old Romanesque church. It is very picturesque and I liked it much.

From the church we turned down into a walk which follows the line of the old ramparts and nearly surrounds the city. The view, from this part of it, of the cathedral standing on a sort of promontory, with the cluster of houses around it, the vine-covered hill sloping down rapidly to the valley on the right, and then the flat vale, lined all over with rows of poplars, and finished against the horizon with fine hills, was most charming. Indeed I have never seen any town of which the views were so invariably magnificent as they are always round old Laon. We saw no other old church here, save one below the hill with a central tower and low spire, which looked at all as though it might be worth visiting. In the street close to the south transept of the cathedral is a gable end of a good middle-pointed house.

We left Laon in the coupé of a small diligence at 6 P.M. for Rheims, grateful in the extreme for the one fine day which we had as yet had — nowhere so grateful as here, where every turn disclosed some view or some subject of which a bright sun was the most indispensable adjunct.

Our going to Rheims afforded no incidents. When we crossed the hills from Laon and descended towards the broad valley of Champagne we had a most glorious view, simple in all its detail, but full of beautiful colour, and rich and verdant in the extreme. One small village we passed on the way had a church of which I managed to get a sketch while we changed horses. I went inside and found the whole church fitted with open seats on a raised wooden floor. The central tower is groined and has only a small apse to the east, and the effect of this inside is exceedingly good. The south aisle consists of a series of compartments running north and south, the roofs boarded on the under side and coved or canted, and descending not on arches across the aisle but on beams. The steeple was, I think, the only part groined. From this village to Rheims our journey was made in the dark and it was nearly eleven as we drove along under the shadow of the great walls of the cathedral and into the gate of the inn which faces its west front, where happily we found rest for our weary limbs. . . .

June 19.

It rained fast when I turned out early this morning and continued to do so perseveringly all the day. This was miserable and perhaps has made my recollection of Rheims less pleasant than it ought to be.

The west front with its three great doorways is very magnificent. The two steeples, which are developments from the Laon idea, and like Laon unfinished, are at present not large enough for the porch and look too much like turrets, and yet they are of immense size. The substitution of second-pointed mouldings in these steeples for the first-pointed shafts of those at Laon, is unfortunately not an improvement. The whole porch is covered in the most lavish manner with elaborate sculpture of the very finest character and detail, but it is generally spread over the whole surface and gives perhaps an effect of littleness and fritter to the whole front. The detail of the pinnacles and flying buttresses at the sides is unusually fine, and all of the same fine early middle-pointed date — that of the apse and the chapels surrounding it is equally fine. The northern transept is also a fine composition, but the parapets were intended to have flanking towers and these are carried up in the same way as those both at Rouen and Chartres, hardly on a sufficient scale to be looked on as towers. Their great open belfry windows produce a fine effect. The three doors of the north transept are all very fine, though the sculpture on some of them is of earlier date than that of the west front, and of very ingenious execution.

On entering, the impression produced is one of exquisite proportions, colour, and decoration, but perhaps a little too much of all this and not so much of that indescribable feeling which some noble churches so eminently produce. It is in fact a work of faultless art rather than religious feeling, though so noble a work of art cannot help inspiring great religious feeling. The whole design is extremely simple and as free from superfluous decoration as the west front is crowded with it. Its triforium appeared to be poor and insignificant in the extreme, after the magnificent triforia of Noyon and the other early churches with their ampler open spaces and fine groinings. The treatment of the west wall on the inside is very curious. It is divided into a great number of trefoiled niches with very little in the way of moulding, each niche having a figure; and the background being coloured white throws out these figures remarkably. Borders, spandrels, etc., are filled in profusely with much delicately carved and very flat foliage, all most accurately copied from natural forms. In the north transept is a curious wooden clockcase of the fourteenth century. . . . We left Rheims at 6 o'clock in the evening by railway for Meaux where we arrived to sleep at 11.

June 20.

As is my wont, I was very early at the cathedral this morning. The scale is not large, and in particular the nave is singularly short, only three bays east of the towers. One tower only is completed, and that in a flamboyant style. The church is very open inside, having two aisles, and chapels on each side of the nave and a good arrangement of chapels, etc., around the choir. The great beauty of the interior is its generally fine style — very early third-pointed — the beauty of the triforia, and the particularly fine interior of the transepts. I managed to get some sketches to show its general character before we left, which was at 11 A.M. for Paris, and there seemed to be no old buildings of any interest in Meaux, though I saw one old pile with corner turrets near the cathedral.

We reached Paris at 12.30 having noticed a fine-looking church on our way, at the station of Lagny, which well deserves a visit. . . .

June 22.

Wrote letters and then to Notre Dame. . . . A fee gave me admittance to the new sacristy and small cloister. The detail of this is all very good, save the doorways; and the glass, which is a *grisaille* with subjects boldly drawn on glass of very pale tincture but thick in texture, was very good indeed. The encaustic tiles used here are very inferior to ours. . . . On our way we just looked at the S. Chapelle, the new turret on which appears to me to be most unsatisfactory.

At 12.20 we left Paris for Evreux, going by railway to Vernon station. I expected much here and was much disappointed. The cathedral is a building whose substratum is good first-pointed, but this has been overlaid by an accumulation of late flamboyant work, so as to be almost invisible. The west front has been rebuilt in bad classic. The north transept is a rich and picturesque piece of flamboyant work of the most ornate kind, and has across its angles internally some immense squinches to carry a passage from the aisle to the end walls. A great deal of very good grisaille glass of the thirteenth century has been retained in the flamboyant windows, and in the others there is a good deal of late stained glass which seems to be of fair quality. The church internally is very narrow in proportion to'its height and looks consequently more lofty than it really is. The other church at Evreux, S. Taurin, is a Romanesque church altered in flamboyant and adorned with a west front of pseudo-classic. It is a fine church, and its main ornament is the magnificent shrine of S. Taurin, of which I managed to get some slight sketches. It is of silver or other metal, gilt, with some very good ornamentation in enamel and niello. In the south transept wall is an arcade filled in with coloured tiles, but it hardly looks as if it would be original; nevertheless, it is said to be so and I see no reason for supposing it likely that such an enrichment would have been subsequently added in such a place.

June 23.

We left Evreux at 7 A.M. for S. Pierre station and passed through Lóuviers on the way. I had only time to run in for two minutes to look at the cathedral. It is like Evreux, an early pointed church with flamboyant alterations, but its scale is small. The triforium and clerestory in first-pointed are very good, with relieving arches inside. . . .

We reached Rouen at 11 and though I had seen all its curiosities before, I was glad to have another opportunity of looking at them. The cathedral gains rather than loses in my estimation. Its general proportions are fine and all its detail admirably good. Unfortunately it is whitewashed and not much cared for, and so people fancy it a poor church. It is on the contrary very fine, and much finer in all ways than its rival S. Ouen. . . .

After the cathedral almost everything in Rouen is very late in style and unsatisfactory therefore; it is an interesting town in many ways but in no way to be compared with such a town as Cologne for real architectural interest.

In the evening I made a sketch of the north-west tower, which with its quaint slated roof is a most picturesque composition. Indeed the whole west front is very grand and broad in its effect, whenever it can be seen without the detestable new cast-iron spire of the central steeple. . . .

June 24.

We left Rouen by diligence for Lisieux at 7 A.M. The ride is for much of the way very pretty, notably so between Rouen and Elboeuf, and again about Brienne, a small town with two churches, one of them undergoing some restoration of not good character. At Bourgtheroulde I went into the church and found all the roofs of wood, arched and boarded, with tie-beams and ring-posts. . . .

We reached Lisieux at 3 P.M. It was a fair day, and the *place* in front of the cathedral was crowded with people, shows and booths. The church was very full, and in the choir, suspended on a beam, were three great new bells just made, and I suppose in process of being blessed before being hung in the tower.

The whole church is very fine and of nearly uniform date, the choir rather more advanced first-pointed than the nave and with a late Lady-chapel added. The triforium of the choir is very charming; and here and in the side windows of the choir aisle — also very beautiful — there is a great fondness displayed for cusped circles sunk slightly in plain walling-spaces, as also in the spandrels of arches, etc. This is the case notably in the west front and again in the fine north-west steeple, where bands of circles are used as strings. This was seen also in the steeple of Senlis. In the west front, which has been elaborately restored, the side doorways are small but very beautiful, finishing with trefoil heads and remarkable for the great masses of regular foliage round their arches in place of mouldings. These are used with the happiest effect.[1] The exterior of the

[1] The same ornamentation appears in the doorways opening out of the Great Cloister at Las Huelgas (province of Burgos, Spain). — G. G. K.

south transept is also a fine simple composition and the interior of this and of the north transept are specially good. The church is apsidal with two chapels besides the Lady-chapel.

The music used here was strictly Gregorian; so also at S. James's, where the congregation joined most heartily. . . . The two western towers are very different, that on the south-west early and for a number of stages of Romanesque work; the other very beautiful, and in its belfry stage giving a type for others — as especially S. Pierre and others in Caen — to copy. The northwest steeple has no spire and that of the other has been much modernized. There is a low central tower which forms a fine lofty lantern internally.

The only other mediaeval church in Lisieux is on a large scale but entirely of poor flamboyant work. We were there whilst a collection was being made; a Gregorian psalm was sung and the collection was made by a priest first and then by a little girl dressed up very smartly in white. There was a crowded congregation composed mostly of women.

A good many old wooden houses remain in the streets of Lisieux; few however are of very rare character and all seemed of the latest date. Our inn was dirty, disagreeable, but cheap, — two dinners, two beds and servants coming to 8 francs only! But its merits were so questionable that we were very glad to find ourselves on our way to Caen. We left at 6 A.M. and arrived there at 10. There were one or two fine views on the road, but otherwise it had no interest until the many towers and spires of Caen rose before us. . . . I had seen Caen before, but five years had left me so far forgetful of the detail of its beauties as to be heartily glad to discover them again.

The church of S. Pierre was close to our inn and its spire was first of all looked at. It is certainly very glorious but not original. The spire is copied from S. Étienne and the tower is a repetition of what seems to have been the one idea of a tower in this part of France. Lisieux has an early example, and so too have Bretteville, Norrey and others; but giving up the point of his originality, the architect of S. Pierre must nevertheless have great credit for his mode of working up old ideas. S. Jean and Notre Dame in Caen have steeples copied from S. Pierre, so that we have here an instance of the same design being reproduced for three hundred years again and again, dressed only in different detail. This is a most curious fact and one not often paralleled, I think. . . .

The discussion in detail of the many churches in Caen seems hardly to call for printing as mere record, for the ground has been well covered by later travellers and not, this time, reached by the German army.

June 26.

To-day we changed our diligence travelling for a more agreeable mode, by hiring a phaeton to take us to Bayeux in order that we might be able to stop on our way at one or two churches.

At 8 A.M., we started; the view of Caen on leaving is fine, its towers and spires standing up well against the sky. A village is passed very soon with an early church whose bell-tower on the chancel end is of good character. One or two steeples with saddleback roofs are seen near the road, and at the end of about seven or eight miles the tall spire of Bretteville l'Orgueilleuse rises on the road. The design is most curiously like S. Pierre, Caen, but it is earlier and has been much mutilated. All the piercings in the spire are filled in, and one only of the spire lights remains in its place, though there are evident traces of others having existed. The tower rises above the chancel and east of it is a sacrarium of the same date, square-ended and with two lancets in the east wall, but groined in such a way as to make one think that its architect could not forget his apsidal terminations. The nave is modern, or perhaps I should rather say modernized. The windows of the tower and sacrarium and the doorway in the north wall of the former, are of very good detail — the transition from Romanesque. There is a piscina in the south wall. East of this chancel has been built within the last year or two a most frightful sacristy, intended I suppose to be pagan but at present not very definite, as all the stones which compose its wall are built up in block to be hewn out afterwards. This of course blocks up the curious east end, but the priest to whom I protested against this wanton piece of barbarism made very light of the matter. I cannot see that the clergy anywhere take the interest that one would expect in such matters, for I have seen nowhere any restorations of at all proper character, except such as are being carried out by government with public funds.

From Bretteville a drive of about a mile brought us to Norrey, whose church is so remarkable that I measured its plan and sketched many of its details.

It consists of a nave without aisles and a choir and transepts with aisles and two apsidal chapels to the choir aisle. The nave is similar in its detail of windows and doors to Bretteville, and in no way worth particular notice, but the rest of the church is most singular. Its decorations are extremely elaborate, the mouldings and ornamental carvings being carved out with a depth of elaborate elegance seldom rivalled. The mouldings are singularly deep and effective, and the carving all very good. The style is throughly good pure first-pointed, and looks more like English work than foreign. The dimensions are exceedingly small, the width in the clear of the choir being only about sixteen feet and of the aisle not seven feet, whilst some of the intercolumniations are not more than three feet and a half and three feet ten inches. The plan is nevertheless similar in all respects to that of a large church of the first order, save in the absence of a central chapel at the east end, and it is therefore much more properly called a "model cathedral" than churches so dignified generally are. The piscinae of the chapels are good and have one orifice and a large space of shelf. One of the altars is original and has a mass of masonry under it for, I suppose, relics. The whole church is in the most wretchedly damp, dirty and neglected state, and a disgrace to all who have any charge of it.

The main entrance is now by a beautiful porch to the north transept, which is, unfortunately, rapidly decaying — as much of the other work executed in Caen stone is doing everywhere. The small chapels of the apse are roofed with most extraordinary stone roofs, of very steep pitch, which at a little distance look like two great pinnacles, and when seen close at hand look like nothing else that ever was built or designed. There are very curious marks, in the exterior, of a change of plan in some respects as the work went on, some of the choir windows having been commenced with most elaborate mouldings outside as well as inside, but altered either in one jamb or at their heads into a plain double chamfer, in a most singular manner. There is some good arcading commenced outside, and a beautiful arcade runs all round the inside wall below the windows. The tower is just like Bretteville, but the spire must have differed considerably from it; unhappily it was struck by lightning some twelve years since, and there is now a poor slated roof in place of the spire. The angle pinnacles still remain and I think they prove that the transition from the tower to the spire must always have been very abrupt. I think from the character of all the detail and especially from the great love shown for the round trefoil, that this church must have been designed by the same man who built the eastern part of the cathedral at Bayeux. The mouldings are excessively similar and the abaci are constantly used octangular in plan in conjunction with square and circular.

An interesting road took us from Norrey to Bayeux, where we arrived at 3 P.M.

The general view of this cathedral is most magnificent, — owing to its two completed and similar western spires and to the great height of a central tower of flamboyant work capped with a pagan cupola which, though of bad details and inconsistent with all the rest of the work, certainly aids much in making the magnificence of the whole so great. This central steeple is on the point of being taken down, I believe, as the piers below are giving way; and the church is now filled with timber shores, etc. I do not like the steeple but cannot help regretting its loss. . . .

There is a curious old chimney near the west front of the cathedral, rising out of a modern house. Attached to a seminary near the Hôtel Dieu is a good simple chapel of first-pointed date. It is a parallelogram groined simply and lighted with windows of two lights in each bay. The whole is wretchedly whitewashed everywhere and contrasts strongly with the magnificent colour of the stonework throughout the interior of the cathedral.

June 27.

We left Bayeux at 11 A.M. in the diligence for S. Lô — I in the *coupé*, my unfortunate wife in the dusty *rotunde*. The country was very pretty indeed, quite like *good* parts of England, and very grateful to my eyes. The church of S. Loup, passed just after leaving Bayeux, has a good Romanesque steeple capped with a low square spire and remarkable for the great richness of its belfry stage and the eccentric narrowness of the windows with buttresses between them. Two miles before entering the town the cathedral of S. Lô comes in sight; and by the graceful proportions of its two western spires gives promise of pleasure to the ecclesiologist. . . .

June 29.

We left Coutances this morning at 7.30 for Hambye en route for Avranche. The road was all the way excessively pretty, and gave an admirable view of Coutances, with the cluster of towers and spires which crowns the hill on which it stands. . . . I walked off alone to the abbey. The situation is pretty; under a steep woody and rocky hill, with a clear stream near, and woods and *riant* hills and dales all around. The entrance is by a very simple gateway, double in front and single-arched behind. . . . A few paces from this gateway stands the church, of whose west front no traces now remain, and some old and rustic buildings to the south of it, which have only one old doorway remaining.

The church is remarkable in its plan, having a nave without aisles, a central tower, transepts with eastern chapels, aisles and chapels round the choir. The end of the north transept is divided off by two arches from the church, and was I think intended for a sacristy, corresponding somewhat in position to the beautiful sacristy at Coutances — of which cathedral this abbey church bears most marked evidence of being in great degree a reduced and simplified copy. Two small chapels are placed at the re-entering angles of the nave and transept, and, supposing the choir to have extended to the western side of the tower, these would have been most useful in allowing access to the choir aisles and transepts without passing through the choir itself. The same point of arrangement occurs at Rayham abbey — also an aisleless church — and would be necessary in all conventual churches of this type. The effect of the interior is striking, owing to the excessive lightness of the nave and to the great extension given by its aisles to the width of the choir. The design of the choir is much like that of Coutances — the same lofty proportions of columns, the same caps, the same kind of clerestory window, and the same double lean-to roof all round the choir, one side over the aisle and the other over the chapels of the apse. The whole work looks early, though there are here and there suspicious-looking mouldings and Murray says that the whole church is of late date. If he is

THE AMBULATORY, CATHEDRAL OF TOURS

ARCHITECTURAL NOTES IN FRANCE

(From the *Ecclesiologist*, 1858-59)

I

A SHORT holiday among French churches has left so many pleasant recollections of new ideas received, new thoughts suggested, ancient memories revived afresh, that it is as impossible as it would be churlish to refuse to communicate some notes of what I have seen; and as they are asked for I proceed to give them, though they must be more slight and generalizing than I could wish; for I have a very profound conviction of the great grandeur of ancient French art, and a corresponding sense of the danger of so treating it as to convey too small a sense of its value to those who have not studied it for themselves, or of offending those who are so happy as to have realized that value to the fullest extent and from actual inspection of its remains. It is needless to say that as the France of the present day is an agglomeration of ancient and distinct provinces, so also in its ancient buildings we can trace, without any difficulty, a variety of different national or provincial styles: it would be strange indeed were it not so. Even in England we have most striking varieties in style confined, generally, within the boundaries of particular dioceses; so that to understand ancient art aright, it is necessary to have an exact acquaintance with the third-pointed work of Devonshire and Cornwall as well as that of Norfolk and Suffolk, and to be able to perceive all the difference between the first-pointed work of the Yorkshire abbeys and that of Wells and Salisbury.

And if we have such marked differences in a country like this, we may well expect a much greater variety in a country which, like France in the Middle Ages, was not as now one great nation but divided into sections antagonistic to each other and exercising little if any reciprocal influence. It is easy, therefore, to map our France into certain divisions, each containing within its boundaries a special individual style of Gothic architecture, distinguished by notable peculiarities, and each affording a separate field for very careful study. Thus we have in the north of France distinct French styles, in, first, Normandy, and secondly, the old Île de France and the surrounding country, and thirdly, in the country bordering on Germany, a style which is rather German than French in all its leading features. Then going southward, we have, fourthly, a distinct Burgundian style, and another, marked by extreme peculiarities, in Poitou and Anjou, and (judging only by drawings, for I have never myself visited the extreme south of France), again other styles, whose centres are respectively at Clermont and at Arles. Of these various styles that of Normandy presents a very great affinity to our own. It is there, and almost only there, that we see the circular abacus, there only that we see much attempted in the way of deep and complicated architectural mouldings, whilst the general effect of many — especially among the larger churches — is extremely English. The likeness is one of which we may well be proud, for the architecture of this province is full of beauty and interest to a degree second only to that of the district of the old Île de France. Its very deficiencies, too, are English in their character, for in going from Paris into the heart of Normandy, the one thing which we notice more perhaps than anything else, is the general absence of the figure sculpture to which we have become accustomed; and this is the case also in England, where we have really hardly any at all extensive remains of sculpture, and certainly none which can be named with those whose pride it is to be the guardians of such churches as the cathedrals of Chartres, Paris, Amiens, Laon, or Rheims.[1] The study of the architecture of Normandy is therefore the proper and natural sequel of a complete and careful study of English architecture, and may be entered on with the less hesitation as I believe I may safely venture to say, that what is learned there will be in no sense foreign either to the precedents or the sympathies of England.

The churches of Anjou, Poitou, and Touraine, appear to me to be of much less value for architectural study: though from the connection which was maintained be-

[1] Our ancient sculpture is therefore of inexpressible value to us; and it is to be hoped that we shall hear less and less of that destructive and dangerous process called "restoration" in connection with it. The *Guardian* lately contained a paragraph stating that a London carver is employed on the restoration of the ancient figure-sculpture at Lincoln. I shudder to think of the havoc which (if I may judge of him by the former performances of his class) he must be making. If the Dean and Chapter of Lincoln possessed a picture by an old master, would they employ a painter to touch up the noses and put in new heads where the old painting was defective? Assuredly not. And can they not feel that any sculpture is just as much a work of art, owing all its interest to the genius of the artist, as any painting can be, and as far beyond restoration therefore?

tween our own country and those parts of France during a long period of the Middle Ages, it is impossible but they should present much that is of the greatest interest to the English student. I have looked, however, in vain for evidence, either in the general design or in the details of their architecture, of any influence exercised by the English upon their art. In fact, when we held the country, we held it as conquerors not as colonists, and we left no mark of ourselves, but let the people go on building for us and for themselves in their own way. And their way was full of peculiarity, perhaps more so than that of any other part of France. They had their own system of planning, their own system of groining: and this, it should be remarked, is sure, if it has any peculiarity, to exercise a most powerful and obvious effect upon the whole architecture. There is, however, a heaviness, a repetition of the same idea, and an absence of delicate skill, as well as of bold architectural inspiration, which to my mind marks all the buildings in these parts inferior, not only to the best French work, but also to that of Normandy and of England. And now I go on naturally to say that I believe the best work in France is that which I described shortly as that of the old Île de France and the surrounding country; it is that which I have studied the most carefully, and love the most of any architecture that I know; it is one which presents no features unsuitable for our country, or inconsistent with the demands of our climate; it is one from the study of which I believe we should all derive an immense benefit, for it were wellnigh impossible to spend much time among the works of art which it so bountifully affords without being strongly impressed with the stern grandeur and masculine character of the men who conceived it, and without being elevated in our whole tone of mind so far as we have been impressed. A district which affords examples such as Rouen cathedral, S. Quentin, Amiens, Noyon, Laon, Soissons, Meaux, Rheims, Troyes, Chartres, Notre Dame of Paris, Mantes, S. Leu, S. Germer, Senlis, Beauvais, and others, must be conceded to be, if not the best, certainly the richest field for the study of our art in all Europe; and it is mainly to this district that I will take you, with this expression of my extreme veneration for the art enshrined in its architectural remains.[1] . . .

At Beuzeville, where the Fécamp branch joins the main line of railway to Rouen, it is worth while to walk a mile and a half to the church, not because it is a fine building, but rather because it illustrates well enough the differences between French and English ideas about village churches. The unbroken nave, thirty-three feet wide and sixty-nine feet in length, with its arched boarded roof, — the central groined tower with a spire springing some four or five feet below the ridge of the nave roof, — and the hipped vestry roof, are all unlike English work, yet the whole effect is particularly good notwithstanding the poverty of style, which is late flamboyant. There are four rows of fixed seats all down the nave — modern, of course.

[1] I am, of course, aware that some of these churches are not locally situated within the Île de France, and one of them — Rouen Cathedral — might have been expected to be purely Norman in its character. To my mind, however, it represents a fusion between the Norman and the real French style, affected, moreover, at first to some extent by Italian influences. And Rouen, as well as most of these churches, was comprised within the *Domaine Royale* before the death of Philip Augustus.

From Beuzeville to Rouen the railway took me over ground well known to the majority of English travellers, and I would not say a word about Rouen, were it not that the strong popular delusion which has elevated the church of S. Ouen into its great attraction deserves to be protested against always. And, this, not because the church is not very fine and very pretty—it is both — but because S. Ouen-worship leads people to miss altogether, or only to half see and understand the extreme value and beauty of the cathedral. I have seen this often, and I find that, unlike some other churches, each time I see it I discern new beauties and new value in its art; and it lies so near to us, and teaches us so much not to be learnt in England, and yet of the utmost value to all of us, that I do not know how to express myself sufficiently strongly as to the advantage of a careful study of it to all workers in the revival. Indeed I think that the Architectural Museum could perhaps do more for art by helping young carvers to go for a time to Rouen for study, than by adding to their collection a multitude of casts which are often of necessity of doubtful excellence. The thing may be difficult to accomplish, but it ought to be done, for this one cathedral contains such an abundance and variety of sculpture as would almost put to the blush all our churches combined. The western doors of the north and south aisles are, to my taste, the most exquisite portions of the church. Their style is so early, and so immediate a deduction from Byzantine or Romanesque work that I can fancy a man, who had been taught to believe in the absolute perfection of our English fourteenth-century style, would be long before he appreciated to the full their perfection. They are moreover of a kind of work which is as rare as it is excellent. In England we have nothing, to the best of my belief, of similar style. I remember that Mr. Scott once suggested to me the probability that they were executed by the same man who executed the doorways in the west front of Genoa cathedral, and the suggestion evidenced fully his sense of the extreme rarity of the work. I believe, however, that they are examples of a style which was not that of an individual only. That it owed much to Italy I have little doubt: for even if there had been no trace of an Italian influence in the extreme delicacy of the whole of the sculpture, in the twining foliage of the door jambs, and the very singular and graceful foliage of the archivolts, yet it might, I think, have been detected indirectly. For in this same church, in the aisle round the apse, there still remains a monument of an Archbishop Maurice, the Italianizing character of which is most marked, and at the same time its details show that it is a work of precisely the same school as the western aisle-doorways. None who have been in Italy can forget the almost invariable type of the finer early monuments — a simple arch, surmounted immediately by a gable of very flat pitch, and supported on detached shafts. They will remember them at Verona often, in Venice, in Genoa, in Perugia, and indeed in all directions and of all dates; well, in this monument, we have the same thing, a round arch exquisitely adorned with angels (whereof two in the centre bear up the soul of the archbishop) and immediately above the arch a very flat pediment or gable. Perhaps, too, it is an Italian influence, which is evidenced in another respect in the decorations of the western doors. The alternate orders of the arch are simply chamfered, presenting in section three sides of an octagon, and these are covered with regular sunk patterns of the simplest kind, but marvellously effective. Go from Rouen to Genoa and you find the western doorways executed in marble, every plain surface in which is inlaid with geometrical patterns, — light patterns on dark ground, and dark on light. The effect is very similar in the two places: at Genoa the very best materials were to be had: and at Rouen where nothing but common stone was used, the artist struck out a system which produced an effect all but equal to that obtained at Genoa. And yet with all this similarity I am not disposed to class these two buildings together as the work of one man. The architect of Genoa loved mouldings much more than did the architect of these doorways; and I think I have met with a sufficient number of traces of similar work to convince me that it was the style of a class, not of a man, and one of those many and glorious phases through which our art in her rapid progress passed. The western doors at Mantes are very similar in their detail; those of Chartres — what a study they are! — partake largely of the same spirit; in the western façade of Notre Dame, Paris, there are traces of it; in Notre Dame, Châlons-sur-Marne, the south doorway was identical in character, and fragments of work of the same style have been discovered in the course of lowering the floor of that church to its ancient level; and in S. Germer, in the chapter-house of S. Georges de Boscherville, in the western doorway of Angers cathedral, and in parts of S. Remi at Rheims, I think we see the same style more or less developed. Undoubtedly the work at Rouen is the most excellent of all, just as it occupies the central position in point of date.

I am not afraid to confess that the whole of these examples are largely Byzantine in their character; in my eyes this is a virtue, not a fault; for I believe that it is here perhaps more than anywhere else that we may succeed in developing from our forefathers' work. There seems to be here a mine of untold wealth, the workings into which were no sooner commenced than they were abandoned: and the style seems to be one which affords special opportunity for meeting our great difficulty at the present day, as it indicates a mode of obtaining rich decorations without being dependent for effect entirely on a horde of slovenly carvers, who, without an idea in their heads, ruin all the rest of our work by their failure in its sculpture.

This is a digression, but the subject was tempting: I will only say further, as to these remains at Rouen, that they have the rare advantage of not having been restored, and that they are entirely covered in all parts with work of almost uniform excellence, though, to my taste, the north-west door (the tympanum of which contains the life of S. John the Baptist) is the finest. The effigy of Archbishop Maurice is singularly elaborated: the patterns on the vestments, the details of the censers, and indeed all parts, being finished with the elaboration of a genuine Pre-Raphaelite. Before modern sculptors sneer at these twelfth century works, I wish that they would themselves attempt to produce even one block of stone, a foot square, as well wrought, and I doubt not they would profit by the lesson, novel though it might be.

The western doors of the aisles are placed between large buttresses, and arches are thrown over them from buttress to buttress. Between the arches of the doors and these upper arches, a small space of plain wall remained, which has been treated in the most ingenious manner. Figures are marked in outline on the stone, which were, I think, painted, and the ground throughout is diapered with a very simple pattern sunk in the stone. Over the south-west doorway was the Last Judgement: and over the north-west, our Lord seated with angels and saints on either side. In the former our Lord is seated on a throne, between two candles: angels present souls to Him, other angels bear a soul in a sheet, and others again on the right drive the wicked into hell.

I must say little more about Rouen; but I ought not to forget to notice the fine and very varied treatment of the capitals throughout the nave, and the thoroughly Norman (and English) effect of the immense numbers of clustered shafts, of which all the piers are composed. The double division in height of the main arcade is not easily accounted for; but if it was owing to an alteration in the height of the building, while it was in progress, it is a happy instance to be added to many others, of the skill with which mediaeval architects seized upon difficulties as the best opportunities for achieving successes.

The ground-plan of this cathedral is, I think, altogether one of the best in France. In particular the *chevet* is of great beauty. The aisle round the apse, instead of being completely surrounded by chapels, has its alternate bays only so occupied, with great advantage in point of effect, both internally and externally. The arrangement is almost identical with that of the fine *chevet* of S. Omer cathedral, and appears to me to be a happy mean between the one chapel at the east end of Sens, and the cluster of chapels which crowd the apsidal ends of almost all the great churches in the north of France. Whilst in its plan it is more skilfully disposed than the somewhat similar *chevet* of Chartres, it is preferable to those of Mantes and Notre Dame, Paris, where there were no projecting apsidal chapels,[1] or Bourges, where they are so small as to produce no effect.

The north-west tower (that of S. Romain), should be ascended, if only to examine the framework of the roof and for the bells, and to note, among other things, the open wooden staircase in its upper stage. The view, too, of the city is finely seen; and I know few cities that reward more bountifully any trouble taken in the attempt to see them in this way. A city it is, indeed, of desecrated churches, but still a city whose situation on the noble river winding here under great chalk hills, and there along the edge of meadows green, flat and extensive, fringed with long perspective lines of poplars, is as beautiful and as happy as it can well be.

It is not a long walk from Rouen to S. Georges de Boscherville, and the view from the hill at Chanteleu is one of the best near Rouen. The church is but of

[1] The plan of an aisle or "procession-path" without chapels is, in execution, the only form of apse, the effect of which is decidedly inferior to our English square ends. It is on the exterior that its deformity is most conspicuous.

slight interest, though its flamboyant tower, with a grand open western arch, forms a fine sort of porch, and indicates a variety which might sometimes be introduced among ourselves with advantage. S. Georges de Boscherville is too well known to require description but if others have formed the same conception of it that I had, they will thank me for saying that the chapter-house is an exquisite example of the earliest pointed work, full of delicate and beautiful detail. The three western arches are circular, but not Romanesque in their character; some of their capitals have foliage, some sculpture of figures, and the thickness of the wall is supported by a miniature sexpartite vault. The vaulting of the chapter-house is also sexpartite, with additional cells at the east and west end to accommodate similar triplets. As I have before said, there is much in the detail of parts of this building, which indicates the same school as the early-pointed work at Rouen. The chapter-house is a parallelogram, fifty-four feet in length by twenty-four feet nine inches in width, and groined in three bays. Some of the western entrance shafts are elaborately carved. The vault inside is coloured buff, and diapered with red lines in a small regular pattern all over.

Between Rouen and Mantes, a pause of a few hours at Pont de l'Arche enabled me to see the interesting remains of the abbey of Bonport. The refectory is nearly perfect, and there is a great deal of simple quadripartite vaulting remaining throughout the modern-looking farm-house. But of the church, the bases of one or two columns, and one respond alone remain, and these of an excellence of design which make it very much to be regretted that it should have been destroyed. The groined refectory, of five bays in length, is well worthy of a visit. The side windows are of two lancet lights, with a circle above, and at the north end is a window of four equal lancets, with small cusped openings above. The south end and entrance from the cloister are modernized. The pulpit staircase is perfect, and very ingeniously contrived; but the pulpit itself is destroyed. Among the buildings, which are of considerable extent, are some admirable examples of domestic windows; and, to conclude, the whole is of the very best early thirteenth-century style.

The church at Pont de l'Arche is one of those ambitious but very picturesque buildings, of which we have no counterpart. It is flamboyant in style, very lofty, and intended for groining throughout. This, however, was never completed, and there is a coved wooden ceiling in its place. A good deal of late stained glass, of *very* poor detail, exists in the windows, the subject of one of them being the Tree of Jesse.

Of the ancient bridge over the Seine, at Pont de l'Arche, not a vestige, I think, now remains.

The cathedral at Mantes is in many ways of much interest. Your readers are, no doubt, well acquainted with Notre Dame, Paris, and with the singular changes which have been effected in it from time to time. In Mantes, I believe they may see almost the same kind of conception, left with such slight alterations as do not in any way conceal the original design. It is therefore of special value.

I have already referred to the western doors. They are much mutilated, and the south-west door was replaced in the fourteenth century by an immense and conceited composition of a doorway with pediment and flanking pinnacles which is very damaging to the general effect of the façade. The remainder of the front is uniform first-pointed, with two steeples connected by an open screen as at Paris. The north-west tower has been already nearly rebuilt, and the south-west tower is now suffering from the same process, "suffering" I say, because I believe firmly that the original design is being annihilated. In both the belfry stage, which rises above the screen between the towers, is now much smaller than the stage below; nothing can look much worse than such a sudden diminution in size, and I am convinced that the original intention must have been (as at Laon) to continue the shafts and arcading which surround the lower stage up to the top. I made as careful an examination of the work as was possible, and have hardly a shadow of doubt that this was the case; but whether the authorities did not know the glorious steeples of Laon, or whether they have a view of their own as to what looks best, they are certainly making the upper part of this unfortunate west front look as modern in its outline and meagre in its character as it is new and fresh-looking in its colour. It were better that old work perished altogether, than that it should be scraped, re-chiselled, cleaned and modernized in this heartless manner!

The most noticeable feature of the interior is the treatment of the triforium of the eastern portion of the church. This is groined with a succession of transverse barrel vaults, the effect of which is to give an immense addition of strength to the main walls. They spring from the capitals of a succession of detached shafts which are placed across the triforium, so that the perspective of its interior is singularly picturesque. It was not very long after the erection of the church that the western portion of the triforium was altered, a quadripartite vault being substituted for the barrel vaulting, and wherever this has been done, the thrust has been too great for the principal groining shafts, which have bulged considerably, and are now held in place by iron ties. In the apse, the bays being of necessity much wider on one side than on the other, the ridge of the barrel vault rises rapidly towards the external wall: and the triforium is lighted by a succession of immense simple circular windows. The internal elevation of one bay of this cathedral is nearly identical with the original design of that of Paris, though simple and (I fancy) rather earlier in date; but from the shortness of the church and the absence of transepts (in which one point it reminds me of the fine church of S. Leu d'Esserent) it has both inside and outside the effect rather of a choir only than of a complete cathedral. There are various additions to the church of later date, which add much to its picturesque character, especially a chapel on the south side, the chapels round the apse, and the sacristies on the north side. The stone roof above the groining of one of these is remarkable. The arrangement of coloured tiles on the roof is one of the best I have seen. The pattern is rather complicated, and is formed with dark tiles (green and black used indiscriminately) on a ground of yellowish tiles.

The church from the apse to the western towers consists of but three bays of sexpartite vaulting, each bay covering two bays of the main arcades. Between the towers is one bay of quadripartite vaulting.

Walking from Mantes across the river to the suburb of Limay, a fine view is obtained of the town and cathedral, which shows here the whole picturesque exaggeration of height as compared with length which distinguishes it. Limay church boasts of nothing save a tower and spire on the south side, of late Romanesque character throughout. The surface of the spire is covered with scalloping, and has spire-lights and fine pinnacles at its base. Some attached shafts against the face of the belfry stage, which seem to serve no purpose, are curious as being probably the type from which some similarly placed shafts in the steeples of the cathedral were derived. Here too, as in the cathedral, a most effective form of label is used, the section of which is a square cut out into diamonds like unpierced dogteeth. We see the same thing in England, and among other examples there is a good one at Lanercost. Its effect is singularly bold and piquant.

A mile on the other side of Mantes is the little village of Gassiecourt, whose cross church is of much interest. The glass in the three chancel windows is fine, and of late thirteenth-century date. The east window of four lights with twenty-five subjects has been restored, and two of the subjects — the thirteenth and eighteenth — have been quite wrongly placed. The window represents the whole Passion of our Lord. The side windows of two lights contain large figures under canopies of the early part of the thirteenth century, in a sad state, but of very considerable value. The east window of the south transept has subjects from the lives of S. Laurence and another. The internal arrangement is remarkable; the fifteenth century stalls, with subsellae and returns, being placed in the two eastern bays of the nave, leaving three bays to the west. The old altar remains in the east wall of the north transept. The walls and roof of the south transept are covered with painting; on the roof are four angels with the instruments of the Passion, one in each division of the groining; the west wall has a painting of the Last Judgement, and the east large figures on each side of the east window; on the soffit of the arch into the tower are angels playing on musical instruments. The whole appears to have been painted in the fifteenth century, and, though of no great artistic merit, is of value in France, where, as in England, such things are very rare. A grand Romanesque west doorway, and a simple gabled central tower with a good belfry stage are the principal external features of this interesting village church.

Before I conclude, I must say a few words as to the evidence of popular feeling in regard to pointed architecture in France. It is partly, doubtless, owing to the fact that all the great churches are national property, and entirely sustained by the State, that we miss so entirely any of that evidence of personal and widely spread interest in them, which so honourably distinguishes most people in our own country. But descending to the second and inferior classes of churches, we find unfortunately the same apathy, the same neglect: so that a tour among French village churches would leave an impression on the mind of any Englishman that the clergy and laity are alike careless of their fate and ignorant of their value. One of the very few village churches which I have seen in process of restoration was being done by order of the Emperor, and by a rate imposed upon the *commune*, aided by an imperial grant; but there, as elsewhere, the repair was entirely confined to the fabric; and pews, pavements, altars, — all remain still in their old state, ugly, dirty, and uncared for. I must make honourable exception in favour of one large parish church, Notre Dame, Châlons-sur-Marne, where, with the greatest care and love for the building committed to his charge, the excellent curé is carrying on a restoration which appears to me to be by very far the best and most faithful that I have seen on the Continent. I have seen, I grieve to say, but little evidence of any practical love on the part of the people or the clergy for their glorious churches, but I will let M. Viollet-le-Duc — than whom who can be a better judge? — say what can be said as to the real impression which they produce: —

"Dépouillés aujourd'hui, mutilées par le temps et la main des hommes, méconnues pendant plusieurs siècles par les successeurs de ceux qui les avaient élevées, nos cathédrales apparaissent au milieu de nos villes populeuses, comme de grands cercueils; cependant elles inspirent toujours aux populations un sentiment de respect inaltérable; à certains jours de solemnités publiques, elles reprennent leur voix, une nouvelle jeunesse, et ceux mêmes qui répétaient, la veille, sous leurs voûtes, que ce sont là des monuments d'un autre âge sans signification aujourd'hui, sans raison d'exister, les trouvent belles encore dans leur vieillesse et leur pauvreté."

II

Leaving Paris for Beauvais, the first station at which I stopped was l'Isle Adam, from whence a walk of two or three miles by the banks of the Oise brought me to the fine village church of Champagne. This is very unlike an English village church in its general scheme, but full of interest. In plan it consists of a groined nave and aisles, of six bays, a central tower with a square chancel of one bay, and transepts with apsidal projections from their eastern walls. The date of the whole church (with the exception of the tower arches, which must have been either rebuilt or very much altered in the fifteenth century) is about the end of the twelfth century. It is now undergoing repair at the joint expense of the Emperor and the commune, but this is being done in so careless a manner that it is to be hoped it will not proceed further than is absolutely necessary for the security of the fabric. The western façade has a very singular doorway, the tympanum of which is pierced with a window of six cusps, whilst the abacus of the capitals is carried across the tympanum, and a square-headed door pierced below. Above is a large wheel window of twelve lights. The aisles are lighted with lancets, whilst the clerestory has a succession of circular windows, which internally form part of the same composition as the triforium, the lower part being an unpierced arcade. The chancel is lighted at the east with a circular window enclosed within a pointed arch and on either side with early geometrical windows of two lights. The finest feature is the steeple, which rises in two stages above the roofs. The belfry stage is excessively lofty and elegant in its proportions, having two windows of two lights in each face divided by a cluster of shafts, whilst other clusters of shafts at the angles of the tower run up to a rich corbel-table and cornice, under the eaves of the roof. The finish is a hipped saddle-back roof of steep pitch and covered with slate.

Internally the most rare feature is a very light cusped stone arch of flamboyant character, with pierced spandrils, which spans the western arch of the tower, and no doubt originally carried the Rood. The capitals in the nave are boldly carved, and carry the groining shafts, which are clusters of three. At the west end of the north aisle, and projecting beyond the façade of the church, is the ruin of a small gabled chapel, the object of which I did not understand.

Altogether this church, owing to its fine character, and the retention of almost all its original features and proportions unaltered, deserves to be known and visited by all ecclesiologists, who travel along the north-of-France railway to Paris. A few miles farther on the left rises the fine church of S. Leu, which I have known for a long time, and which deserves, as I think, very much more notice and study than it appears to have received. The plan, situation, details, and style (early first-pointed) are all alike of the best, and I know few, even among French churches, which impress me more strongly with the thorough goodness and nobility of their style. The east end of the church rises from the precipitous edge of a rock, which elevates the whole building finely above the level of the *riant* valley of the Oise. It was attached, I believe, to a Benedictine abbey, the other buildings of which are all in a most advanced state of decay. The church fortunately, though much out of repair, and in some points altered into flamboyant, is nevertheless sufficiently perfect for all purposes of study. It consists in plan of two western towers (the north-west tower being only in part built) then six bays of nave and aisles, three bays of choir, and an apse (circular on plan) of seven bays; round the apse is the procession path, and four chapels, also circular on plan, lighted by two windows, so that one of the groining shafts is placed opposite the centre of the arch into each, and over the altars. In place of the fifth chapel on the north side, a circular recess is formed in the external wall of the procession path, so as to make space for an altar without forming a distinct chapel. I should be disposed to say that this was the original scheme of the church, afterwards altered and much improved by the substitution of larger and distinct chapels.[1] The central chapel of the apse has the unusual feature of another chapel above it, on a level with the triforium, adding much to the picturesque effect of the east end. In addition to the western steeples there are gabled towers which rise above the aisles on each side of the choir, and the church is remarkable, like the church at Mantes, for the absence of transepts. Perhaps, as the internal length is not quite two hundred feet, this is of some advantage to the general effect. A considerable change has at some time been effected in the external appearance of the east end, for on examination I found that each bay of the triforium was formerly lighted by two lancet windows between the clerestory and the roof over the aisles. My impression is, that this must have been altered when the chapels round the apse were erected and within a very short time of the original construction of the church; but whatever the

[1] The chapels round the apse of Senlis Cathedral form an intermediate link between the two plans at S. Leu. They form exactly half a circle on plan, and have only two bays, one of which is lighted with a window. Externally they have stone roofs, finishing under the triforium windows. These two churches should be studied and compared together.

reason, the church has lost much by the alteration. The six bays of the nave appear to have been built after the west end and the choir. The latter has a noble very early-pointed doorway, rich in chevron ornament, and this seems to have had a porch gabled north and south between the towers so as not to interfere with the window in the west wall of the nave. The southwest tower and spire, though small in proportion to the height of the nave, are of elaborate character. All the arches are round, and there are two nearly similar stages for the belfry. The spire has large rolls at the angles and in the centre of each face (an arrangement seen at Chartres and Vendôme) but in addition it has the peculiarity of detached shafts, standing clear of the rolls on the spire and held by occasional bands. They have a certain kind of quaint picturesqueness of effect, but were never, I think, imitated elsewhere. The whole face of the spire is notched over with lines of chevroned scalloping. On entering the church the first thing that is remarked is the excessive width of the nave (thirty-six feet between the columns) compared to that of the aisles (about twelve feet). The result is, that a grand unbroken area is obtained for worshippers, whilst the aisles appear to be simply passage-ways. The general proportion of the building is, however, rather too low in proportion for its great width. Almost all the arches throughout the church are, more or less, stilted, and with the best possible effect. When the eye is thoroughly accustomed to this it is curious to notice how unsatisfactory any other form of arch is. The fact is, that a curve which commences immediately from its marked point of support is never so fine as where it rises even a few inches perpendicularly before it springs. The capitals throughout the church are finely carved, and those round the apse are of immense size, and crown circular shafts of very delicate proportions, much as at Mantes, and (though on a heavier scale) at Notre Dame, Paris. The construction of this part is of the very boldest character, and exemplifies in a very striking manner the extreme skill in construction to which the architects of the day had arrived.

Great effect is produced by the profusion of chevron and nail-head ornament used on the exterior of the church; a double course of the former of the very simplest kind forms the cornice under all the eaves, and is also used down the edges of all the flying buttresses. On the north side of the nave there still remains a portion of the cloisters, of fine early character; two sides only remain, with a room of the same date with groining resting on detached shafts. Some remains of gateways in the old walls of the abbey are worth noticing, as also the old walls which surround the church, built for the most part against the rock on which it stands, with here and there very small openings, which make them look as though they were intended for defence. Whilst I was in the church some boys came to toll the passing-bell. They said that they always did so on Fridays, at three o'clock.[1]

I saw nothing between S. Leu and Beauvais, though in the part of France bordering on the Oise, I believe

[1] No one who visits S. Leu should omit to go also to Senlis. He will find a tower and spire of unusual — if not unique — beauty and elegance. There are two fine desecrated churches, and other remains which, with the charming cathedral, make a *tout ensemble* not easily forgotten. It is a walk of about six miles only from S. Leu — passing by Chantilly.

that every village would afford something worth seeing in its church. My time, however, was limited.

As you reach Beauvais, the country changes; there is a great deal of wood, a very scattered population, and but few churches. Of course the first object of every one at Beauvais is the cathedral; a building from the study of which I derived less satisfaction than might be expected. It is unpleasant to find an artist striving after more than he is really able to attain, and this was conspicuously the case with the architect of Beauvais. The church was consecrated in A.D. 1272 and fell in A.D. 1284. In order to repair its defects the arches of the choir were subdivided, and from the great size of the columns, and the narrow span of the arches, the present effect is that of a church in which the arches have but little to do, and in which everything has been sacrificed to keep the building from falling again. Then when the roofs and passages about the building are mounted it is seen that the great object of the architect has been simply to obtain one grand effect — that of height and airiness, and that to this everything has been sacrificed, the details throughout being poor, coarse, and slovenly in their mode of execution. The whole gave me the impression of being the work of an unsatisfactory architect, though at the same time it is impossible to deny the excessive grandeur of the vast dimensions of the interior so far as it is completed, or the beauty of arrangement which marked the original scheme of the ground-plan, unpractical and unstable as it was. It may be right, however, to attribute some of the failures, with M. Viollet-le-Duc, to the carelessness of workmen; though no good architect allows himself to be so excused.

It seems very like presumption to criticise such a building, yet I know not the use of architectural study if it is to be pursued with that blind faith which obliges one to admire indiscriminately everything that was built in the thirteenth or fourteenth century. The mere fact that the main intention of the people of Beauvais was to build something finer than their neighbours at Amiens is in itself suggestive; and I am not surprised that a building erected on such terms is unworthy of its age. It is one of the very few buildings of the kind which impresses me in this way; for usually the feeling derived from the study of mediaeval churches is one of respect for the absence of anything but the most thoroughly artistic feeling on the part of their builders. No doubt the architect of Amiens did his work in the best way he could, with little reference to what was being done by his neighbours; and it is curious that the grand success which he achieved should have led, both at Beauvais and (I think also) at Cologne, to unworthy and unsuccessful attempts at rivalry. I can quite see that a claim may be made for the architect of Beauvais, as a man of genius who was not quite so safe a constructor as his contemporaries, but who nevertheless conceived the grandest idea of his age, as far as size and height were concerned. I can only answer that this is not the character of a great architect, and would lead me to class him with the architect of the abbey of Fonthill, rather than with the architect of Amiens or Chartres. The first architect of Beauvais was, however, a better architect, in some respects, than his successor; for though his details (seen in the apse only) were not of the first order, those of the latter are about the worst

I have ever met with in a French church of such pretensions.

The glass in the clerestory windows has a band of figures and canopies crossing them at mid-height, with light glass above and below: this is an arrangement often met with, and generally productive of good effect, especially in windows of such great height. A museum attached to the west side of the north transept contains a few antiquities; but the feature of most interest is a late, but good cloister, noticeable for the extreme delicacy of the shafts and piers between the trefoiled openings. In the museum is a fair embroidered mitre, which belonged to F. de Rochefoucald, Bishop of Beauvais, in 1792.

The church of S. Étienne [1] is, after the cathedral, the great architectural attraction of Beauvais. Its west front has a grand arched doorway, with a sculptured tympanum, containing the Nativity, the Adoration of the Magi, and the Coronation of the Blessed Virgin, and four rows of figures of angels and others in the arch. The jambs and central pier are completely denuded of all their shafts and statues, and the whole work is much mutilated in all its parts; nevertheless, it is the best thing remaining in the city, as far as goodness of sculpture and detail can make a work good. The gable of this porch runs back into a triplet, and the main gable has a cusped circular window, now blocked

---

[1] I copied the following from the "Tariff" of the seats in S. Étienne:—

"Une stalle haute par année, 8 fr.
Une stalle basse   "   5 fr.
Les deux premiers bancs à chaque côté du chœur, 8 fr.
Les deux centres bancs derrière l'autel, 7 fr. 50 c."

up. The date of the whole front is early in the thirteenth century. On the north side of the nave there is a fine doorway, of very ornate Romanesque; it has been carefully repaired. An arcade of semicircular arches above the doorway is diapered with a pattern sunk in the stone and marked at regular intervals by red tiles inlaid, and about two inches square. The effect is good, and it is, I suppose, a restoration. The circular window on the north side of the church is remarkable for the figures sculptured outside its label; it is evidently a Wheel of Fortune window.[1] The buttresses of the aisles are valuable examples of late Romanesque work. They have a fair projection, but are weathered off some five or six feet below the eaves' corbel-table; and from their summit in some cases one, and in others two, shafts rise to support the corbel-table. The choir is lofty flamboyant work, but ugly. The nave, of early Transition character, internally has very heavy groining-shafts, and the far from admirable peculiarity of a triforium with arches formed of very flat segments of circles, and the string under the clerestory rising in the same line, and forming, as it were, a label to the arch below.

The gateway to the bishop's palace, with its steep and picturesque roofs; the palace itself, with its valuable remains of Romanesque work at the back; a portion of a Romanesque house near it; and a fine fourteenth-century gabled house in the Rue S. Véronique, with three pointed and canopied windows in its first floor, are the principal features of interest after the cathedral and S. Étienne. There is, too, a great

[1] See the Illustration of a Wheel of Fortune in *Les Arts Somptuaires*, Vol. II., taken from a MS. in the *Bibl. Imp.*, No. 6877.

store of fine timber houses, one of which, in the Rue S. Thomas, is particularly noticeable for the elaborate filling in of encaustic tiles between all the timbers.

From Beauvais I made an excursion of some ten or fifteen miles, to see the abbey church of S. Germer. It is a church little known, I suspect, to most English tourists, but of very rare interest, and equal in scale to our churches of the first class. The drive thither among woods and low undulating hills is pleasant. The church consists of a nave and aisles of eight bays, transepts, and an apse of seven sides, with an aisle and two chapels on either side. The place of the central chapel at the east is occupied by a low passage of three bays, leading to a grand Lady-chapel of four bays, with an apse of seven. The whole of the nave and choir are of fine style, in transition from Romanesque to pointed. Externally, hardly any but round arches are seen, but internally the main arches are pointed. I know few things much more striking than the treatment of the apse. The main arches have their soffits composed of a very bold round member, with a large chevron on each side; and the effect of this, in connection with the acutely pointed arches, is strikingly good.[1] Above this is the groined triforium, opening to the church with an arcade of semicircular arches, subdivided into two, and supported on coupled detached shafts. Immediately under the rather plain clerestory windows is a corbel-table, and in each bay square recesses, now blocked up, but which look as though they had opened to the roof of the triforium. The groining-ribs of the apse are

[1] This work recalls to mind the work of the same character at Glastonbury.

large, and profusely adorned with sculpture. The aisle round the apse is all built on the curve (as is usually the case in early work), and the groining, constructed in the same way, has those ungraceful and difficult curves which result from this arrangement. Very good low metal parcloses divide the choir from the aisles. In the nave some of the capitals appear to be of very early date (especially along the north wall, where the acanthus is freely used); the whole of the triforium is stopped up, but the design of this part of the church seems to have been similar to that of the choir, with the exception of the chevron round the arches. The groining, too, save of the two eastern bays of the nave, is of later date. At present the only steeple is an eighteenth century erection over the crossing; but there was evidently an intention originally to build two western towers. An altar of the same date as the church, which remains in it, is of much interest, as from its rather ornate character it seems probable that it was never intended to be covered with a cloth. It is figured at p. 180 of M. de Caumont's *Abécédaire*.

The exterior affords many features of interest. It is, as I have said, almost entirely round-arched, and the choir affords a good example of the triple division in height, rendered necessary by the groined triforium and the projecting chapels of the apse. The clerestory and triforium are each lighted with one window in each bay, whilst the chapels have three windows, — a wide one in the centre, and a much smaller one in each side. There are no flying buttresses to the clerestory, but small quasi-buttresses, formed of three-quarters of a shaft, finished under the eaves with a conical capping.

The eaves cornice all round the church, of intersecting round arches, resting on corbels, is so similar in its character to some of the work in the beautiful chapter-house of S. Georges de Boscherville, that I can hardly doubt that they were executed under the same influence, if not even by the same workmen.

The feature, however, which lends the most interest to the building and aids so much in its picturesque effect externally, is the grand Lady-chapel,[1] said to have been built by the Abbot, Peter de Wesencourt, between the years 1259 and 1266. In plan, disposition and general arrangement it appears to be as nearly as possible identical with the destroyed Lady-chapel of S. Germain-des-Prés at Paris, built by the celebrated Pierre de Montéreau, between the years 1247 and 1255. Pierre de Montéreau built also the S. Chapelle at Paris, between 1241 and 1248, and died on the 17th March, 1266. A comparison of the design of these three buildings has induced me to believe that in this Lady-chapel of S. Germer we have another genuine work of this great architect, for it was built before his death, and is identical in many of its features with work which we know to be his. The plan of all these buildings is identical.[2] They all had two staircase turrets and a large rose-window at the west end, a parapet above the rose-window, and a smaller rose in the otherwise plain gable. The design of the window tracery, the gables

---

[1] It is sometimes called also the "*Sainte Chapelle*" of S. Germer: I know not, however, on what grounds. M. Viollet-le-Duc does not mention it in his list of S. Chapelles.

[2] There is some reason for believing that the Lady-chapel of S. Germain-des-Pr´s was groined with sexpartite vaulting: if so, it differed from the other chapels in this respect.

over the windows, the detail of the staircase turrets, buttresses and parapets, are all so similar that my suggestion really scarcely admits of a doubt. The main differences are, that at S. Germer the original western rose-window is perfect, whilst in the S. Chapelle it is a flamboyant insertion, and that the chapel is of one story in place of two. In this last point, and in its complete separation from the church, it agrees entirely with the destroyed chapel at S. Germain-des-Prés. The passage between the apse and the chapel is of three bays, with a doorway at the side, but, so far as I could see, no trace of an entrance from the apse. It is groined: the windows (of four lights) are much elaborated with mouldings, and have trefoiled inside arches: and an ascent of six steps leads from it under a fine archway into the chapel. There is a north doorway in the chapel, and the whole is groined. The dimensions appear, as nearly as I can make out, to be precisely the same as at S. Germain, but less than in the S. Chapelle, being about twenty-seven feet six inches in the clear between the groining shafts, and between seventy and eighty feet in length. The original altar of stone, supported on a trefoiled arcading, remains fixed against the east wall. This is six feet five and a quarter inches long by three feet three inches high. In the museum at the Hôtel Cluny, at Paris, one of the most valuable relics is a stone retable, painted and gilded, formerly in this chapel. I have not its dimensions, but it is of much greater length than this altar, and I have no doubt, therefore, that the principal altar stood in its proper place under the chord of the apse, and that the retable belonged to it. This arrangement was not uncommon; it was identical with that of the altars in the S. Chapelle, the same arrangement existed originally at Amiens; and we have an instance of it in England in the choir of Arundel church.

The retable has subjects from the life of our Lord, and illustrative of the legend of S. Germer. In the centre is the Crucifixion, SS. Mary and John; to the right of the Virgin is the Church, and to the left of S. John the Synagogue; then come figures of SS. Peter and Paul, the Annunciation and Salutation, S. Ouen (uncle of S. Germer) healing a knight, a noble speaking to a pilgrim, and S. Germer asking Dagobert to allow him to leave the court, in order to found his abbey. The whole of the figures are painted and gilded in the most sumptuous and yet delicate fashion, and though much damaged, are still sufficiently perfect to be intelligible.

M. de Caumont has given a drawing in the *Abécédaire*[1] of what seems to be a remarkably fine shrine, of twelfth or thirteenth century character, still in the possession of the commune of Coudray, S. Germer. I believe this is within a few miles of S. Germer, and it ought not to be missed by ecclesiologists who take this route. It has an arcade of four trefoiled arches on each side, and one at each end, and has a steep roof with a fine open cresting at the ridge.

Of the other buildings of the abbey very slight traces now remain. Close to the west end there is, however, a very simple gate-house, and the modern conventual buildings appear to be now used for a school, superintended by nuns.

S. Germer is certainly one of those churches which no

[1] P. 365.

ecclesiologist who goes to Beauvais should on any account miss seeing. Its rare scale, dignity, and architectural interest, and its secluded situation afford attractions of the highest kind, and I am confident that no one who takes my advice in this matter will come back disappointed.

III

From Beauvais I made my way to Compiègne, where I found but little of much interest. The principal church is in size, plan, and general design, decidedly conspicuous; yet it is remarkable how little there is in it to detain an architect beyond the general effect. The bulk of the structure is of good uniform first-pointed character. It consists of a nave and aisle (fifty-three feet in width) of six bays, transepts, and an apsidal choir, the lower part of which has been modernized and has a very badly planned flamboyant aisle round it; and there were intended to be two western towers. The groining of the nave is flamboyant. The best feature is the apse, which has a glazed triforium of two lancet windows in each bay, and a clerestory of large single lancets. It is, I think, characteristic of many French churches of this fine scale, that they afford much less matter for study and description than our own churches of one-fourth the size and pretension. Their details are so uniform, and their planning so regular that a description of one bay is, in fact, a description of the whole church, and there is nothing in the shape of monumental effigies, screens, brasses, or other similar relics, to give a special interest to each part of the building. When we lament the general scarcity of examples of groining in our English churches, we ought not to forget that it was, in part at least, to this that we may attribute the extraordinary variety of their character; for it is undoubtedly very much more difficult to obtain those picturesquely irregular effects which charm us so justly in English examples, when groined roofs are used, than when their place is taken by roofs of wood. The points of support must be much more equally spaced, the piers more regularly planned, and each portion more exactly a reproduction of every other portion; and it has sometimes struck me as possible that we owe the much greater variety of designs in the treatment even of our groining, as compared with the French, to the great love of change and variety which our architects had imbibed in dealing so largely with wooden-roofed buildings. In this respect indeed, they sometimes ran into excesses for which they had no example, and happily, no imitators on the Continent; but on the whole, we have undoubtedly reason to be grateful for a feature in our national art which helped to place it in so high a position when compared with that of other countries.

Another church, dedicated to S. Antoine, is of large size and late flamboyant style. It has a fine font (now disused) of the same character and material as the well known fonts at Winchester, East Meon, and Southampton; the bowl of which is no less than three feet nine inches square. The floor of the nave of this church is boarded, and fitted up with very smart chairs, whilst the aisles have tiled floors and common chairs, and there is a rail fixed between the columns to shut in the select occupants of the smart chairs. It is a mistake, therefore, to suppose that the introduction of chairs will necessarily secure the annihilation of the pew system. Here, too, I saw a *"mandement"* of the Bishop of Beauvais, Senlis and Noyon, dated Dec. 8th, 1856, ordering the adoption of the Roman liturgy, in place of the local uses, of which he says there were no less than nine in his diocese, so that it often happened that the same priest " chargé de deux paroisses, trouve dans l'Église ou il va célébrer une première Messe une liturgie différente de celle qui s'observe dans la paroisse où il réside:" — "le chant, les cérémonies, la couleur des ornemens, les usages, tout est changé." The Bishop interdicted, among others, the Missals of Beauvais, Noyon, Senlis, Amiens, Meaux, and Rouen, and his order took effect from Whitsunday, 1857.

Of less distinctly ecclesiastical edifices Compiègne retains some remains. A cloister in the Caserne S. Corneille is a good example. The arches have no tracery, and the piers have buttresses to resist the thrust of the groining. This is very simple but good work, though late in the fourteenth century. The old Hôtel-Dieu, too, has a characteristic gable end towards the street, divided by a central buttress, and with a pointed archway below and a large window above in each division.

The very picturesque front of the Hôtel de Ville has been recently very carefully restored, but so completely, that it looks almost like a new building. The effect of the front is very good, though the belfry tower rises awkwardly from behind the parapet of the building. There is an illustration of this building in M. Verdier's *Architecture Civile et Domestique*, which will enable your readers to understand the character of this picturesque though late building better than any description that I can give. The roof of the main building, as well as that of the turrets at the angles and the belfry, is covered with slate: and it is worth notice how much the effect of these roofs depends upon the thinness of the slate, its small size and the sharpness and neatness with which it is cut. Foreign slating is in truth just as good in its effect as ours is generally bad and coarse.

The château of Pierrefonds ought to be visited from Compiègne. The ruins must be interesting, and I believe the site is very picturesque. It is a fashionable place of resort, and at a distance of some three hours through the forest from Compiègne. M. Viollet-le-Duc's description of the buildings is known probably to most of your readers.

From Compiègne I made my way to Soissons. It was here that on this journey I came first on the grand style which distinguishes the buildings of this part of France. Laon, chief in grandeur, both natural and architectural, Noyon, S. Quentin, Meaux, and Soissons, are magnificent illustrations of the main features of the style: whilst smaller churches, remains of abbeys, such as those of Ourscamp (near Noyon) and Longpont (near Soissons), and of castles, such as Coucy-le-Château, enable us to appreciate all its varieties. It is to be hoped that the stream of English travellers will for the future set more in this direction than it has hitherto done, since it is now possible in going to Strasbourg to take the railway through this country to Rheims, and in so doing to make acquaintance with a group of churches, which impress me more and more each time that I see them. They are remarkable evidence also of

THE SOUTH TRANSEPT AT SOISSONS

the wonderful vigour of the age in which they were built: for they are all of very nearly the same date — the end of the twelfth and early part of the thirteenth century, and conceived on the grandest possible scale. Indeed, France, under Philip Augustus, affords a spectacle such as perhaps no other country in the world can show. For if we think of the wars which characterized his reign, it is almost incredible that it should nevertheless at the same time have been possible to found such cathedrals as those of Paris, Bourges, Chartres, Amiens, Laon, Meaux, Soissons, Noyon, Rouen, Séez, Coutances, Bayeux: yet such was the case, and some of them were completed in but a few years with extraordinary energy.

Few things are more impressive than the cathedral of Laon, even in its present state: and what must it not have been with its central steeple and the six towers and spires which once adorned its several fronts, rising, as they all did, from the summit of a mighty hill, seen on all sides for many a long mile by the dwellers in the plain which stretches away from its feet! And yet, magnificent as is the cathedral of Laon, it is one only among many; and such a city as Soissons, inferior as it is in situation, affords nevertheless in its architectural remains, matter of almost equal interest.

The general view of Soissons, obtained from the distance, is striking only for its architectural character. The effect is mainly attributable to the fact, that in addition to the cathedral, with its lofty south-west steeple, the town also contains the west front, with two towers and spires, of the ruined abbey of S. Jean des Vignes. It is to this ruin that the eye first turns in anticipation of discovering the famous cathedral of the city; but a little acquaintance with the details of the two buildings leaves no room to doubt that the cathedral, with its lonely steeple, is nevertheless by very much the most interesting and noble example of art which the city contains.

Let us at once, then, bend our steps thither. We shall find a church, the greater part of which dates probably from the end of the twelfth or the first years of the thirteenth century, whilst its plan is very remarkable, and its details in some parts of exquisite beauty. In plan it consists of two western towers (one of which only is built), nave and aisles of seven bays, transepts (of which more presently), a choir of five bays, and an apse of five sides; chapels are obtained between the buttresses of the choir, and the apse is surrounded by an aisle and five chapels; these chapels are circular in plan at the ground line, octagonal above, and are groined with a vault which covers the aisle also; this is a mode which is seldom satisfactory in execution, and a falling off from the structural truth of those plans in which the groining of each chapel is complete in itself, and distinct from that of the aisle. The south transept is finished with an apse, and has a small circular chapel of two stages in height attached on its south-eastern side. The north transept is square-ended and of later date.

It is impossible to examine Soissons cathedral without having recollections of several other churches forced upon the mind. At Noyon, for instance, we have a grand example of a church of the same date, both of the transepts of which are apsidal; but the south transept of Soissons has a great advantage over its neighbour, in that it has an aisle round the transept opening with three arches, supported upon slender and lofty shafts, into each bay, both on the ground level and in the triforium. Indeed there are few fairer works of the period than this south transept of Soissons; for whether we regard its plan, general scheme, or detail of design and sculpture, all alike show the presence of a master hand in its conception and execution; — the same hand, I suppose, as is seen at Noyon, but at a slightly later period. Then, again, a comparison of Soissons with Meaux will show so great a similarity of plan, dimensions, and design in their eastern apses, that it is difficult to avoid the conclusion that they were the works of the same man, and at about the same time. And each of these churches has nevertheless some one special feature of its own, wherein it is unique and unmatched; Soissons has its exquisite south transept, Noyon its western porch, and Laon its cluster of steeples, by which every one who has seen them must especially have been struck.

One of the features which most marks the churches of this school is the fourfold division in height of the main walls. There is first the arcade, then the triforium[1] (which is large, groined, and lighted with its own windows), then a blank arcade which is analogous to the triforia of our English churches, and astly the clerestory. I cannot say that this arrangement is ever pleas-

---

[1] These groined triforia are called tribunes by the French antiquaries. At Montierender, where both occur, the upper stage is more than usually similar to our English triforia; and in all these cases it would perhaps be best to accept the French terminology as being substantially correct. The tribune is, in fact, a second stage of the aisle.

ing. The clerestory always looks disproportionately small and dwarfed, and the blank arcade below it rather unmeaning, whilst all the divisions have the appearance of being cramped and confined. At Soissons it occurs in the south transept, but not in the nave — where we see the usual triple division. Some of the capitals here are well sculptured, though generally very simply, and in the transept they are often held with iron ties (as in Italian examples) to resist the thrust of the groining. I should notice that the whole of the walling in this transept is circular on plan; this is generally a mark of early date, and though it gave rise to some complexity in the arches and groining, it undoubtedly often produces a very charming effect. The windows of the three eastern chapels are full of richly-coloured early glass, rather rudely drawn and executed; some of it, I suspect, came from the clerestory, the eastern portion of which is still full of similar glass. The clerestory has large lancet windows and flying buttresses of two stages in height, with the arches supported upon detached shafts, and a passage behind the lower order on a level with the sill of the clerestory windows.

On the exterior, one of the most noticeable features is that the ridge of the south transept roof rises no higher than the eaves of the rest of the church. Yet such is the care with which the design is managed, that this smallness of scale is not noticed, until from a distance a general view of the building is obtained, when it looks undoubtedly very lop-sided.

From the cathedral one goes naturally to the ruined but still imposing church of the great abbey of S. Jean des Vignes. The west front of this church is exactly in a line with that of the cathedral, at a distance of about a furlong; and standing on higher ground, and still retaining its two towers and spires, it produces a greater effect in the general views of the city. It is now the centre of the arsenal, with powder-stores, piles of shot, and various other preparations all around it, which afford subject for rather gloomy forebodings, in case Soissons should again suffer (as it has so often already suffered) the danger of a siege. The remains of the church are almost confined to the steeples and west front. The lower portions of these date from the thirteenth century, but the upper portion is all of a very ornate and rather late middle-pointed style; they are very pyramidal in their outline, and have a rather heavy arrangement of pinnacles at the base of the spires. The belfry-window of the north-west tower has a very large stone crucifix contrived against its monial and tracery; there is a canopy in the tympanum over the head of our Lord, and the tracery seems to have been designed with a special view to the introduction of the figure. The spires are crocketed on the angles, scalloped on the face, and pierced with alternate slits and quatrefoils. The sculpture of this front is not of very good character. From the south of the south-west tower extends a remarkably fine portion of the domestic buildings of the abbey, two stages in height, and eight bays in length. Its south end has the favourite French arrangement of a central buttress between two large circular windows, with two lancet windows in the gable. On the west side each bay has a fine simple pointed window: whilst on the east side the lower part is concealed by the cloister, and the upper stage has a row of plain circular windows, similar to those at the south end. The steep-pitched roof still remains, and the whole building is a very fine relic, even among the relics of this kind in which France is so peculiarly rich. The remains of the cloister are in a very dilapidated state. Drawings which I had seen of it had prepared me for earlier and better work than I found. I imagine that it is not earlier than *circa* A.D. 1300. The sculptured foliage is in exact imitation of nature, very pretty, and no more. It is, however, singularly instructive, as it illustrates just the kind of work which our English carvers are most prone to introduce just now, and which is generally (as it is here) very ineffective for want of due architectural subordination. The windows of this cloister are of four lights, with geometrical tracery; but the chief peculiarity is the treatment of the buttresses, which are angular on the face, and above the springing of the windows crocketed on the angles. Had the sculpture been fifty years earlier in date, it would, I have no doubt, have been a singularly beautiful cloister. A doorway which opened from the cloister to the church is peculiarly flat in its mouldings and sculpture, but remarkable for the still existing traces of painting over its whole surface. The foundations of the east wall show that the church was not of any great length from east to west.

The church of S. Léger is the finest edifice after these of which the city can now boast. Anywhere its transepts and choir would be of great interest for their early thirteenth-century date, and their good architectural character. The church consists of a nave and aisles of six bays (of which the four western are Renaissance), transepts of two bays in depth, and a choir without aisles, which has one bay of sexpartite groining, and an apse of seven sides. The detail is very much the same as in the cathedral. The clerestory windows in the apse are lancets, and in the rest of the church of two lights with tracery, consisting of a cusped circle within an enclosing arch. In these Soissonnais churches the label generally has a ball or four-leaved flower at intervals. There is a procession path or passage, with openings in the buttresses, round the church outside the clerestory windows, dividing the church very markedly into two divisions in height, and recalling to memory the very similar arrangement in the church of S. Elizabeth at Marburg. The transept has fine angle pinnacles and a large three-light window with early tracery, whilst the cloister is somewhat similar to that of S. Jean des Vignes. Stepped gables are a favourite feature here even in early work. The aisles of S. Léger are so finished, as is also an early building by the side of the cathedral.

The church of S. Pierre, which is desecrated, has a west front of much interest. It has a nave and aisles, three western doorways (whereof the central is pointed, the others round), and a single wide, round-arched window over each door. The detail is peculiar, — of late Romanesque character, and effective. Only two bays of the nave remain. The labels and string-courses have a dogtooth enrichment, whilst the cornice above them is adorned with a regular acanthus-leaf. The shafts of the west door are fluted; and in this, as in the quadruple arrangement in height, which I have already noticed as a frequent characteristic of the Soissonnais churches, I suspect we may trace the influence of the grand church of S. Remi at Rheims.

Of domestic buildings there are but few traces in Soissons. The best are: a building near the west front of the cathedral, with stepped gables, central buttresses in the end, and good simple three-light windows in each bay; — a house in the Cloître S. Gervais, near the north transept of the cathedral, with a steep unpierced gable and three two-light windows in the stage just below it, and an unpierced ground story; — and an old hospital near the cathedral, of good early-pointed work, without groining, but with transverse arches from column to column, — the capitals being carved, and the arches quite square in section.

From Soissons, an excursion ought to be made to the abbey of Longpont.[1] I was not aware at the time I was there that it was in this neighbourhood, but I believe that it is only some eight or ten miles distant, and that the church is of rare interest and grandeur. I regret extremely my inability to give any notes of it.

A walk of a mile across meadows took me to the remains of the great abbey of S. Médard. These are very slight and consist of some remains of crypts, in which are preserved portions of buildings or monuments which have been dug up from time to time. An old view of S. Médard shows it surrounded by fortified walls, enclosing a vast range of buildings and two or three churches. Of all this nothing now remains, beyond a modern house, converted into an asylum for deaf and

---

[1] The abbey church of Longpont was dedicated in A.D. 1227, in the presence of S. Louis. Its value as a dated example is therefore considerable, independent of its high architectural interest.

dumb, in one portion of which remains an old vaulted apartment, now used as the chapel of the institution.

From Soissons, I made my way across country to Château Coucy. . . . and from Coucy, I made a considerable détour to visit the abbey of Prémontré. The situation is very striking, in a narrow valley, closed in on all sides with steep, thickly-wooded hills, and with only a few dependent cottages leading up to the gate of the abbey. This was the chief house of the Premonstratensian Order, which established as many as thirty-five houses in England. The abbots of the order were bound to meet once a year at Prémontré, and as there were as many as a thousand abbeys belonging to them, the wild valley must then have presented a singular contrast to its present deserted state. Until lately the buildings have been used as a glass manufactory: but they have just been purchased by the Bishop of Soissons (who seems to have a great character for piety and liberality among the people) for an orphanage. I saw the nun who holds the post of superior of the institution, and obtained permission to search for remains of the old buildings: she seemed much surprised at my demand, and with some reason, as the only traces left of them are a portion of (I think) a crypt under the church, which has fallen with its groining, and is left a confused mass of stones, just as it fell. On my way from Prémontré, I passed, between Anizy-le-Château and Laon, a very interesting example of a village church at (I believe) Chalvour. It is cruciform, with a good central gabled tower. The chancel has single lancet windows to the east and south, and the south transept a large boldly-cusped circular window, and a small projection on the east for the altar, also lighted with a circular window. The chancel, tower, and transepts, are groined: the nave (with its aisles) is of inferior work. Altogether, this is a very characteristic thirteenth century church, of bold and vigorous character, and severely simple in all its details.

An ascent of about two miles leads up the side of the mountain, on which Laon is perched, to the western extremity of the city. And here I must pause, trusting another time to say somewhat of the architectural glories of the place, upon which I suppose I can scarcely descant too enthusiastically.

IV

The two great architectural attractions of Laon are the cathedral and its subordinate buildings, and the fine church of S. Martin. They are situated at the two extremities of the long narrow ridge on which the town is built, which towards the east falls precipitously on three sides almost from the very walls of the cathedral down to the broad vast plain which extends as far as the eye can reach, and from all parts of which the grand mass of the building, with its almost unrivalled cluster of steeples, is seen standing — just as our own glorious Lincoln — on the very spot of all others fitted for a diocesan throne.

I know no church which is altogether more calculated to leave a lasting impression on the mind than the cathedral. What is wanting in grace and delicacy is amply atoned for in force and majesty; and the completeness of the plan, the short period which seems to have elapsed between its commencement and completion, and the almost entire absence of later additions or alterations, combine to make it in every respect of the utmost value to the architectural student. The stern, solemn majesty of its art is just what we modern men ought to endeavour to impress ourselves with; but whilst I believe that all students would be enormously benefited, they must not come here under the impression that they are to see work which is pretty and attractive in the same sense or degree as S. Ouen at Rouen, or Cologne cathedral.

In plan this church has the remarkable peculiarity of a square east end, and consists of a nave and choir respectively of eleven and ten bays in length, transepts with an eastern apsidal chapel to each, a small cloister on the south side of the nave, and sacristies formed in the angles between the transepts and choir. The groining is sexpartite in the principal vaults, and quadripartite in the aisles; there is a large vaulted triforium, and the fourfold division in height to which I have already referred as a characteristic of many of the churches of this district. But the most noteworthy feature is that the three principal façades — on the west, north, and south — were each intended to have two towers and spires, whilst a lantern crowned the crossing. No less than four of these towers and the lantern still remain (though without their spires, shown in an engraving by du Sommerard), as well as the lower portion of the others. On the east and north the cathedral is enclosed with extensive ranges of coeval buildings belonging to the bishop's palace, including the small private chapel, to which I must recur again.

Let us hear what M. Viollet-le-Duc says about the

characteristics of this cathedral of Laon:[1] — "La cathédrale de Laon conserve quelque chose de son origine démocratique; elle n'a pas l'aspect religieux des églises de Chartres, d'Amiens ou de Reims. De loin, elle paraît un château plutôt qu'une église; sa nef est, comparativement aux nefs ogivales et même a celle de Noyon, basse; sa physionomie extérieure est quelque peu brutale et sauvage; et jusqu'à ces sculptures colossales d'animaux, bœufs, chevaux, qui semblent garder les sommets des tours de la façade, tout concourt à produire une impression d'effroi plutôt qu'un sentiment religieux, lorsqu'on gravit le plateau sur lequel elle s'élève. On ne sent pas, en voyant Notre Dame de Laon, l'empreinte d'une civilisation avancée et policée comme à Paris ou à Amiens; là, tout est rude, hardi: c'est le monument d'un peuple entreprenant, énergique et plein d'un mâle grandeur. Ce sont les mêmes hommes que l'on retrouve à Coucy-le-Château — c'est une race de géants."

I am disposed to think that M. le-Duc scarcely values the architecture of Laon sufficiently highly, and that he is mistaken in his idea of the democratic character imparted to it by the turbulence of the citizens at the time of its erection. It appears to me that the peculiarity of its character is derived much more from some connection with German art, and I believe that the churches throughout this part of France show many evidences of such a connection. The planning of the towers of Laon is very German; I need hardly adduce examples from the Rhine district, where, as we all know, the steeples are treated as so many great turrets, nearly similar in size, height, and design, whilst the crossing

[1] *Dictionnaire*, Vol. II. p. 309.

is often marked by a low lantern. The grand cathedral at Tournai in this respect resembles very strongly that of Laon; and if we were coming from Germany into France, we might at Andernach, Coblentz, Trèves, and Châlons-sur-Marne (in the church of Notre Dame), see a regular sequence of buildings by which we should arrive without any very great or sensible break at Laon. The groined triforium is another well known German feature, and though the apse is a very general termination to German churches, it is yet not impossible that its absence at Laon may be an evidence of Germanic origin, as we do meet there with some examples of the same kind. In one particular feature I am able to trace a most singular coincidence with a German example, to which, however, I do not wish to attach very much weight, though it is undoubtedly curious. The steeples at Laon are very fine compositions — I should hardly speak too strongly of the steeple of the south transept, were I to say that it is the best-designed steeple in France, — marked by turrets at the angles, which are either octagonal or square in plan with shafts at their angles, and very beautiful in their effect. In the west front one of the stages has, in these open turrets, large figures of oxen and other animals looking out from between the shafts on the city roofs far away below, — a quaint conceit, which one would suppose to be a purely personal and peculiar device, and of which nevertheless there is an almost exact repetition in the very similar steeples of the grand cathedral at Bamberg.

My belief is, that as we can trace a stream of Italian art coming to the south and south-west of France, and thence working on to the north in gradual and steady development, so we may also see the same thing here. Italian art first spread down the Rhine, and thence spread right and left, and in these border provinces of France influenced to a greater extent than is generally supposed the French architects. On their part there was a peculiar skill and art displayed which soon enabled them to develop from the germ which they received; but the Romanesque work out of which they developed their buildings was of a different order from that which was the ground-work on which the architects of Poitiers, Bourges, and Chartres had to work; the latter having in Italy a Byzantine origin, whilst that of the Rhine churches was rather Romanesque. Something therefore of the magnificent character of the best early French Gothic is owing to Germany, and it was the situation of the Île de France, the meeting point as it were of these two developments, which made it the centre from which the best Gothic architecture of the world naturally sprang. But whatever was the history of Laon cathedral, no one can doubt the excessive grandeur of the result. No doubt the magnificence of the situation, which recalls forcibly some of the most interesting of Italian cities, such as Siena and Perugia, has something to do with the colouring of memories of Laon; but in the church itself there is but one point on which it is possible to feel that there is any serious shortcoming, and this, as an Englishman, I am almost afraid to say is the absence of an eastern apse. It is only when one travels from church to church finished with apsidal choirs, that the eye sees the whole evil of the square east end as the termination of the vista in a large church. But there can be no doubt that there is less completeness and unity of effect, fewer fine effects of light and shade, and altogether less skill and architectural ingenuity in the English plan than in the other: and though I should be sorry to see the apse commonly introduced in small churches, yet I think it fortunate that attention has been a good deal drawn to this matter of late years, and that men have not been slow to recognize the advantage of importing this one foreign practice at any rate into our own country. Both externally and internally the east end of Laon is deficient in effect, and gives the impression of being low and awkward in proportion. There is an eastern triplet which comes down very near to the floor, and a large rose window over it; an arcade of open arches, flanked on either side by a pinnacle, conceals the lower part of the gable. This elevation is indeed the worst thing in the whole church, and contrasts unfavourably with that of the north transept. This is perhaps a little later in date and owes much to the irregularity of outline caused by the completion of one only of its steeples. It has the peculiarity of two double doors; and the large rose window composed of eight octofoiled circles surrounding a ninth, is of rare beauty. It is to be prized the more, too, because in the fourteenth century there was a plan for its removal, of which we have curious evidence: one of the side jambs and part of the arch of a large middle-pointed window having been inserted by cutting away the wall close to a buttress in such a way as to disturb very little of the original work, and yet to afford us a very curious evidence of the way in which alterations of this kind were made by the mediaeval masons, without the introduction of a single shore or support of any kind. Fortunately the alteration was stopped just where it ought to have been, after it had afforded evidence of the customs of the masons, but before it had destroyed a perfect first-pointed façade; and I suppose that by this time we have outlived the rage for middle-pointed work so far that it would be difficult indeed to find any one so wrong-headed as not to be grateful for the stoppage of the alteration at the point at which we see it now. Of the western façade I can say but little. It has been my fortune to see it twice, but an evil fate has so covered it with scaffolding at one time, and taken down and rebuilt so much at another, that I have only been able to guess at its general effect. The western doorways are adorned with sculpture, and this is almost the only place in the church in which figure sculpture still remains; but the whole exterior of the church is remarkable for the fine architectural character of the sculpture of foliage, which is used with special lavishness along almost all the string courses. I hardly know any finer work of its kind, but it is altogether conventional in its treatment, and arranged with very particular reference to architectural effect, the foliage in each bay being very nearly identical in its design. A peculiarity in the external effect of the church is the lighting of the triforium with separate windows, so that we have three heights of windows in the elevation belonging to the aisle, triforium, and clerestory.

Of the various steeples which adorn the church, and whose character is generally very similar, the most beautiful is, I think, that of the south transept. The lower stages are lighted with couplets of lancets, and have buttresses at their angles; above the roof line square pinnacles are set diagonally at the angles, and in the topmost stage the tower is an octagon in plan with octagonal angle pinnacles resting on the square pinnacles below, and lighted by lancet windows of very light proportions. The octagonal pinnacles are composed entirely of shafts supporting arches, and are of two stages in height; and within them are contrived some newel staircases of exquisite design. They consist of a series of delicate shafts — one on each step, supporting another above: the capitals of these shafts are all well carved and with great variety: the effect of this winding cluster of shafts, seen through and behind the shafts of the pinnacles, is a great lesson in the beauty of shafts and the value of scientific construction. Much of the beauty of the design is owing to the very light and airy character of these angle pinnacles, and it is much to be deplored that the spires shown in du Sommerard's view no longer exist.

The small cloister on the south side of the nave is one of the features to which it would be unpardonable not to refer. It forms only one side of the enclosure, the east and west ends being occupied by the chapter room and a groined chapel projecting from the south wall of the nave, whilst the wall of the aisle forms the north side. The merit of this cloister is, therefore, not its extent, but the beauty of its design. The windows are of two lights, and above these is a quatrefoil opening enclosed within a circular moulding, round which are pierced sixteen small circles. The tracery was glazed, though the lower part of the windows appears to have been always open as it is at present. The whole design is a very good example of plate tracery. The outer wall of the cloister abuts on the street, and though only pierced with small square windows, is yet so skilfully buttressed and finished with a cornice so finely sculptured, as to be a very successful architectural feature. At the angle of this wall near the south transept doorway, a buttress is brought out from the transept, and against it is placed, standing on a corbel under a canopy, a grand angel which now holds a sundial; and though the dial is not old, I suppose, to judge by the position of the hand, that it takes the place of one coeval with the fabric. The angle of this buttress, coming forward rather awkwardly in front of the door, is cut back in a very skilful manner, and has two recessed shafts with capitals and bases, affording a capital example of angle decoration.

There is not much of which I need make special mention in the interior. The main columns are generally plain cylinders, with very large capitals from which the groining shafts rise; these are banded very frequently in their height with bad effect. There is the fourfold division in height to which I have already adverted, and considerable matter of study in the sculpture of the capitals, which is however in some cases rather too rude and early in its character.

There is some very fine early glass in the eastern windows of the choir. In the transept there are two arches across next the wall, supporting a floor on a level with and connecting the triforia, the spaciousness of which is quite wonderful. They are groined throughout, and the views of the church obtained from them are very good. I found some middle-pointed screens dividing the several bays of the triforium in the nave, and there was a good deal of thirteenth century glass lying on boards, and about to undergo restoration. Considerable alterations were made in the last century by the insertion of chapels between the buttresses of the choir, but these do not detract much from the general effect of the church, which exhibits a degree of general uniformity hardly to be paralleled save at our own Salisbury.

I think it admits of a fair doubt whether such a cluster of similar great steeples at regular intervals around one building, as we have here, could ever be perfectly satisfactory; but of the beauty of their design, taken separately, there cannot be two opinions. It is possible that if the central lantern had been carried up to a great height, whatever defect there is might have been rectified, but there is no sign of any such intention.

To the east and north of the cathedral are very large remains of buildings of the same date as the cathedral, and fairly perfect in their external effect. Towards the interior they all rest on open arcades, whilst on the exterior the outline is well and picturesquely broken by a series of turrets projecting from the walls of the great hall of the palace, said to have been built by Bishop Garnier in A.D. 1242.

The bishop's chapel, a groined building with nave and aisles, and of two stages in height, still remains. It is of slightly earlier date than the cathedral, is covered with a roof of one span, and has a very small apse at the east end.

There seems to have been a communication directly from the bishop's palace to the eastern part of the cathedral; and if the people of Laon were as turbulent as they are said to have been, the bishops were wise so to place their palace, and so to connect it with the cathedral as to enable themselves to stand a siege if need be.

After the cathedral, the church of S. Martin, at the opposite end of the town, is the principal architectural relic still left in Laon. Like the cathedral, it is remarkable for its square east end. It is cruciform in plan, and consists of nave and aisles, choir without aisles, and transepts with chapels on the east side. Two towers are placed in the angles between the transepts and nave. The general foundation of the fabric is Romanesque work, but the choir and transepts are of a rather ornate early first-pointed, much more German than French in its character, and the western façade is one of the best examples that I know of a middle-pointed front to a church of moderate pretensions. The early-pointed work at the east is remarkable for the very heavy character of its mouldings and string-courses, the use of both round and pointed arches, and the very ingenious arrangement of the chapels in the east wall of the transept, and of the buttresses above them. Three chapels are formed under two bays of vaulting, so that the vaulting shaft and buttress come over the point of the arch. The church is well groined. The steeples are poor in character and rather insignificant, but they appear never to have been completed, and in the neighbourhood of the cathedral it was dangerous to venture upon any but the most careful and noble work.

The west front is very ornate, and is marked chiefly by the fine octangular pinnacles at the angles of the clerestory and by the large sculpture of S. Martin in a quatrefoil which fills the gable. The three western doorways are composed of a succession of small reedy mouldings, and against the buttresses beyond the central doorway are figures of saints considerably mutilated.

Almost the only other interesting church is a small building attached now to an educational institution for boys. A priest told me it had belonged to the Templars, and at any rate it is an octagonal building with a small chancel on its eastern side, and a smaller circular apse. At the west end there is a small porch. The whole is in a late Romanesque style, and very small, the external measurement of each side of the octagon being only about eleven feet.

Here and there are to be seen remains of houses and gateways, but there is nothing of sufficient interest to require a special note here, and the only other building I need mention is the very curious church at Vaux-sous-Laon, a village at the foot of the hill below the citadel and cathedral. This has a western porch or narthex, nave and aisles of five bays, transepts and low central steeple, and a choir and aisles of three bays, groined, and both loftier and wider than the nave. The east end is square, and has a triplet and a large rose window above, very similar in design to the east end of the cathedral. The columns are cylindrical, with simply carved caps of bold design. The choir is all first-pointed, the nave of earlier date and much simpler character and not groined.

I must conclude this brief notice of Laon and its buildings with just mentioning two of the existing buildings in the neighbourhood which ought to be seen and examined. These are the magnificent granary of the abbey of Vauclair near Laon, and the still more interesting hospital for lepers of Tortoir: both of these are figured by M. Verdier in his *Architecture Civile et Domestique*, and appear to be of rare beauty and interest.

V

The cathedral of Rheims is most unquestionably a very noble, I might almost say, a perfectly noble, piece of architecture, and nevertheless it seems to fail in producing so great an effect on the mind as many other French churches of smaller dimensions and less architectural pretension. The truth is, that it is a work conceived and executed at two periods and by two (if not more) architects; and though the ground-plan, some portion of the walls, and a little of the sculpture, of the first architect have been preserved, the general aspect of the church at the present day savours more of the later artist than of his predecessor. It was in the year 1212 that Robert de Coucy (a friend of Wilars de Honecort) commenced the erection of the present cathedral, and it was after his death and from *circa* A.D. 1250 to *circa* A.D. 1300 that the whole of the upper portion of the building, the western portion of the nave from the ground, and the elaborate western façade were in course of erection. There remains to us, therefore, little of genuine first-pointed work, for it has been clearly shown by M. Viollet-le-Duc that the lower stage only of the building was the work of Robert de Coucy. He seems indeed to have contemplated a building of greater height and grandeur than the present, since his work is remarkable for the great size of the buttresses and the thickness of the walls, which were diminished at once, and abruptly, by the architect who followed him, and whose work is nevertheless amply solid and massive for the existing edifice.

It will be seen from what I have said, that we must not go to Rheims expecting to see a work of the best period of the thirteenth century. We shall find a small portion of sculpture in one of the doors of the north transept, and the plan and basement story of the building throughout, of this early date, but the bulk of the structure and almost the whole of the decorative features are purely middle-pointed work of the end of the thirteenth and early part of the fourteenth century. There is exquisite grace about most of this work, but an entire lack of that stern character which makes Chartres the grandest of French churches; there is prettiness where there should have been majesty; and in parts a nervous dread of leaving a single foot of wall free from ornament, which reminds one much more of the work of an architect of the nineteenth century than of one of the thirteenth. The west front, on which all the greatest efforts of the later architects of the church were lavished, can thoroughly please none but those who see in elaborate enrichment of every inch of wall the evidence of art, whilst I need hardly say that to those who have studied the best examples of architecture in whatever style, such elaborate ornamentation is in itself an evidence of weakness. There is a kind of sacredness about the simple breadth of wall and buttress which must be reverenced by all who would produce really grand work. But for this the later architects of Rheims had not the slightest feeling, and their work seems therefore to me to be more really allied to the debased art which followed it, than to the pure early work which had immediately preceded it. As at Laon, so here, the original design was to have a grand group of towers and spires, six for the three grand façades, and a seventh over the crossing. Some of these spires were, I believe, actually erected, and in lead; and whether this was the first intention or not it is certain that the plumber's work was in great request in this church and city, as there still remains a very fine flèche on the point of the apse roof of the cathedral, some good detail of lead work on the roofs, and a much modernized leaded steeple in the church of S. Jacques; whilst in the west front of the cathedral we see large gurgoyles of lead simulating enormous animals. The interior of the cathedral is very noble in its proportions (though the triforium might well have been more dignified), and is remarkable for the immense size of the capitals of the piers in the nave; they are very closely copied from natural foliage, and fail to satisfy me that such work is the best fitted for architectural enrichment. The decoration of the west end is not confined to the exterior, the whole inside face of the wall being divided into panels and niches filled with foliage and single figures. The stone imitation of hangings in the lower part of this wall ought to be recorded, though hardly without a protest.

On the south side of the cathedral is the archbishop's palace which still retains its thirteenth century chapel of two stages in height, and good, though simple, character. It is a parallelogram of five bays in length with an apse of seven sides.

And now that I have ventured to say so much in the way of criticism upon what I believe most Frenchmen consider their most glorious church, and without any attempt at a detailed account either of its general architectural arrangements or its sculptures (the latter exceedingly rich and suggestive), I must take my reader with me along the dreary dirty road which leads to the squalid quarter of the city in which still stands as a rival to the more modern cathedral the enormous church of S. Remi. The exterior, with the exception of the apse, has been much modernized, and presents accordingly but few features of much interest. The south transept has been all remodelled in flamboyant, whilst the nave is simple Romanesque, and the west end — recently almost entirely rebuilt — is a singular agglomeration of anomalous work, half classic or Pagan, and half Romanesque or Gothic and Christian. In the apse we have flying buttresses supported on fluted shafts, a clerestory of triple lancets, and a triforium also lighted with three-light windows. The proportions of the buttresses, roofs, and walls are however heavy and unskilful, and give evidence of the early date of this nevertheless very grand attempt. It is on entering by the transept, through a doorway covered with fine flamboyant sculpture, that we see how grand the attempt was, and how fine the internal effect. I think I know no church whose whole interior gives a greater idea of spaciousness and size, whilst the beauty of the design of the apse and the aisle and chapels round it is extreme. And indeed the appearance of size does not belie the facts, for the dimensions of the building are singularly fine. It has a Romanesque nave and aisles (groined with a pointed vault) of thirteen bays, transepts, and a choir of three bays with an apse of five. Round the apse is the procession-path aisle, and opening into this a series of chapels, whereof the five eastern are very noticeable. The Lady-chapel is of three bays in length, with an apse of seven bays, whilst the other four are very nearly circular in plan, and each of the chapels opens into the aisle with three arches supported on delicate detached shafts. The groining of each of the four smaller chapels forms a complete circle in plan, with eight groining ribs, whereof two are supported on the columns opening into the aisle. Each chapel is lighted by three windows, recessed so much as to allow of openings being pierced in the groining piers to admit of a passage all round the interior. This arrangement (as well as the beautiful planning of the chapels) is a distinct feature of the churches of Champagne. The chapels of Notre Dame, Châlons-sur-Marne, are similarly planned, and in those of the cathedral at Rheims it is clear that Robert de Coucy had the same plan in his eye, though he gave up the triple-arched entrance from the aisle; whilst at S. Quentin we see an almost similar plan at a rather later date. The whole of the nave retains the original very simple Romanesque arcades, and lofty groined triforia; but its groining throughout is fine early-pointed work and of grand dimensions, the width in clear of the vault being about forty-five feet. It is a curious fact that in this nave the triforium compartment is absolutely more lofty than that below it which contains the arch opening into the aisle. In the choir there is a sort of fourfold division in height such as I have described at Soissons and Laon, an arcade of pointed arches being introduced between the clerestory and the triforium; but as this arcade is in part a continuation of the lines of the clerestory windows, and as there is no string-course to divide the stage in two, the effect is better than in other examples of the same arrangement.

There is much matter for careful study in the interior; among other things may be noticed the remarkably fine and large corbels supporting the groining shafts in the eastern part of the nave, adorned with figures of the prophets bearing scrolls and still retaining traces of their old colouring; and again, the very beautiful sculpture of some of the early capitals near the western end of the nave, and on either side of the great western doorway. In the windows of the apse are some small remains of fine early glass.

Among the other architectural remains in Rheims is the church of S. Maurice, consisting of a Romanesque nave and aisles, and a lofty groined flamboyant choir, the west front of good character, having small buttresses supported on shafts on each side of the central door, and separating the western triplet of broad lancets above the doorway. The rest of the church is very uninteresting.

There is also the church of S. Jacques, whose west front has the unusual feature of a sham gable on either side of the real central gable.[1] These gables are above the aisles, and completely conceal their roofs and the clerestory. The nave is of early-pointed date, but very much altered; only the two eastern bays appearing to retain the original triforium and clerestory,—the latter a lancet with internal jamb-shafts, which are continued into the triforium and form a portion of the arcades of four pointed arches which occupy each bay,—an arrange-

[1] The arrangement of these gables recalls to mind the very similar arrangement at Salisbury and Lincoln.

ment very similar to that of the clerestory of S. Remi. These two bays are groined with a sexpartite vault, which is slightly domical in its longitudinal section. The alternate piers in the nave consist of coupled columns of very solid character, and with very deep capitals. Some of these columns are regularly fluted. The rest of the nave has been much altered in the fourteenth century, whilst the choir is flamboyant, with aisles of Renaissance style, but groined in stone. The crossing is surmounted by a very large flèche of timber covered with lead, almost completely modernized, but showing still some large three-light windows of middle-pointed style.

The *Maison des Musiciens*, in the Rue de Tambour, is a well-known example of excessively good domestic architecture of the thirteenth century.

From Rheims I made my way by railway to Châlons-sur-Marne, where I was rewarded by the sight of one of the most interesting churches I have ever seen, that of Notre Dame, and of a cathedral of inferior interest. It was the more gratifying to find such really fine work just on the extreme borders of the country to which French influence extended, and beyond which to the eastward the churches appear to be entirely German in their style.

The points of resemblance between Notre Dame de Châlons and the church of S. Remi at Rheims are too obvious to be overlooked. The planning and the general design and detail of their chevets are precisely similar, though the scale of Notre Dame is considerably smaller than that of S. Remi. The former church has however the great advantage of being of the same character throughout, wonderfully little damaged by time, and singularly fortunate among French churches in being under the care of a priest, M. Champenois, whose zeal and enthusiasm for his beautiful church is equalled by the care and skill with which he has himself carried out its restoration. It is the most conservative restoration I have as yet seen in France; it could not be more conservative, and hence it is impossible that it could be better. M. Champenois feels that every stone is a deposit entrusted to him, and I would that we saw signs of such zeal as his rather oftener in the French clergy. Unfortunately, it seems to be too generally the case that they take no interest whatever in the churches which they serve. They have been taught to look to the government as the owner and restorer of all religious buildings, and they have ceased to concern themselves about either the security of their fabrics or the character of their fittings and decorations. Fortunate indeed is it for us in England that the State is not so careful for us as it is in France, for then we should see here, just as we do there, a people utterly careless of the noble buildings which surround them, in place of — as we do here — a people whose love for their old monuments is enhanced and in part created by the fact that they are themselves perpetually invited to help in their restoration and repair.

The church of Notre Dame consists of a nave and aisle of seven bays in length, transepts, and a very short apsidal choir (an apse of seven sides), with an aisle and chapels planned like those of S. Remi, beyond it. There are four towers, two at the west ends of the aisles, and two in the angles between the transepts and the choir.

The triforium throughout is large, lofty, and groined. As at S. Remi, the external effect of this church is much inferior to the internal effect. It is rather too heavy and ungainly, and savours much of the character of German Romanesque work. The four towers have the defect of being almost exactly alike, of four stages, richly adorned with round-arched arcades, and rising hardly at all above the level of the ridges of the roof. The south-west tower retains its fine leaded spire, with four tall pinnacles at its base, and a cluster of eight spire-lights about midway: it is an exquisite example of lead-work, and still more precious to us as affording evidence of the extraordinary extent to which decoration was sometimes carried in the Middle Ages. The pinnacles at the base still retain distinct traces of decoration on the lead, each side having a large crocketed canopy, below which is a gigantic figure, in one case of an archer with a bow. The whole is done in white and black only, the ground being the dark lead on which the white lines seem to have been marked by a process of tinning or soldering. It is a kind of decoration which we may well attempt to revive. A spire very similar to the other has recently been erected on the north-west tower, and the western front is now therefore quite in its old state, and singularly well does it look. I almost doubt whether the addition of similar spires to the two eastern towers, for which the Curé is now collecting funds, will really improve the look of the church. With four steeples, it is well that two at least should be pre-eminent, which is the present state of the case; whilst the completion of the others would reduce all to the character of mere turrets — a result not to be desired. The variety of string-courses and cornices throughout the exterior of this church, all filled with sculpture of foliage, gives a very ornate character to the external detail.

The principal entrance is by the south door of the nave. This has been cruelly damaged, indeed nearly destroyed, but what remains is of great interest, owing to its very close resemblance to the noble western doorways of Rouen cathedral; the doorway is double, with eight shafts in each jamb, the alternate shafts having figures in front of them, as in the west doorways of Chartres; whilst the tympanum is similar also, having a figure of our Lord, surrounded by the emblems of the four Evangelists. Portions of archivolt enrichments and other sculpture have been dug up in the neighbourhood of this doorway and carefully preserved, and they appear to me, by their vigour and grandeur of character, to be undoubtedly the work of the same artist, and possibly portions of this once magnificent but now woefully mutilated entrance.

It is in the interior, however, of this church that the effect is finest and the architecture most noble. The whole is very uniform in character throughout, marked by great solidity of construction and proportion, and by the boldness and distinctness of all its architectural detail. The triforium throughout opens with two arches enclosed within another, the spandrels being unpierced, and throughout the church it is groined; nor must I forget to say, that at the present day the spacious area it affords is turned to some account; for, when I was there, on one side they were making the organ pipes, on the other constructing the organ, and in another part the carpenters were busy upon the organ case; and the

Curé assured me that he not only had the satisfaction of seeing everything executed in the best possible way, but at the same time there was no inconvenience, and no want of reverence, on the part of the workmen. The clerestory consists throughout of lancet windows, the lower portions of which are filled in with an arcade in the manner I have described in the choir of S. Remi, at Rheims. The sculpture throughout this church, though almost entirely confined to foliage, is very instructive, and at the same time a little puzzling; for we see almost side by side work of the best Byzantine character — almost rivalling the sculpture we see in Venice — and distinctly thirteenth century French work, whilst the building itself shows no corresponding diversity, and I can only suppose, either that the sculpture was in hand much longer than the building of the church, or that two sets of sculptors were at work, the one educated in a Byzantine school, the other influenced by the more developed school of the Île de France.

I have said enough, I trust, to induce others to examine carefully this very interesting church; it is valuable as being a little in advance of the most perfect period of the French pointed style, and as being much more instructive, therefore, than a building which, like the cathedral at Rheims, is in the main a little after the most perfect period, and full, therefore, of symptoms of decline, instead of promise of advance.

From Notre Dame to the cathedral it is a descent from the finest early first-pointed to commonplace middle-pointed, full of German character in its detail. The west front and the whole of the apse have been much modernized, and the finest remaining portion of the exterior is the north transept front. The windows are geometrical middle-pointed of four lights, and the flying buttresses on a large scale, double, and surmounted by pinnacles. There is some good stained glass of late date in some of the aisle windows.

Another church, dedicated, I think, to S. Alpin, has a nave and aisles of six bays groined, without a triforium, and of the same date as Notre Dame. There are transepts and a central tower, and a choir in flamboyant style, and of a most unusual plan; the two arches east of the tower diverge from each other, so that the width of the choir gradually increases up to the point at which it is finished with an apse of three sides. An aisle surrounds the whole, the windows of which retain some very rich stained glass. This choir is the most remarkable example that I have met with of a very late revival of, perhaps, the earliest type of chevet. There are a great many altars in this church, pews throughout with doors, and no sign whatever of any improvement. In Notre Dame, where pews had disappeared and everything was being restored, all the side altars had disappeared, and there was only one altar left besides the principal altar in the choir.

And here I might well conclude these notes of French architecture. From Châlons I went to Toul, and thence by Metz to Trèves, and I found, as might be expected, nothing but German work. At Toul there are two churches, the cathedral and S. Gengoult, both of some interest, and with good cloisters; but it is very remarkable how we find here, not only German detail, but the favourite German ground-plans also; S. Gengoult is a cruciform church, with an apsidal chancel, and a small apsidal chapel on each side opening into the transepts; whilst the cathedral has an apsidal choir without aisles, and a square-ended chapel on each side opening from the transepts. The window tracery in S. Gengoult is perhaps the ugliest ever devised even by German ingenuity, and yet of early geometrical character (*circa* A.D. 1300), and still retaining much very beautiful glass of the same date. The nave of the cathedral has been recently seated with very smart fixed open seats, of the kind which might have been erected fifteen or twenty years ago in England.

Of Metz I can say but little more than of Toul. The cathedral is undoubtedly magnificent in its scale and general proportions; but its detail throughout is miserably thin and meagre, and the church appears to me to be utterly undeserving of the praise I have heard bestowed on it by some English authorities. Of course, however, the degree of admiration felt for such a building depends very much upon the standard of perfection which each man sets up for himself. If he comes to Metz strongly possessed with a sense of the noble character of German Gothic, of course he will admire this extremely German edifice; if, however, he have the slightest feeling for early French art, I imagine that he will turn away with disappointment and sorrow from this church, so vast, and yet, as compared with fine French churches, so tame, poor, and weak.

The best of the other churches in Metz is that of S. Vincent, a work of better style than the cathedral, and with a well-planned German east end, showing undoubtedly marks of the same hand as (or at least of imitation of) the famous Liebfraukirche at Trèves.

NAVE AND TRANSEPT, THE NEW CATHEDRAL, SALAMANCA

From Metz I made my way by Sierck (whose small church has a groined roof forty feet in clear width) to Saarburg; here the church is noticeable for a tower oblong in plan, and roofed with *two* thin octagonal spires which unite together at the base; and from Saarburg I went to Trèves.

Trèves well deserves a long notice. Its churches are full of interest, the cathedral for students of early art, and the Liebfraukirche, as being (I think) the most beautifully planned thirteenth century church in Germany. The close juxtaposition of these two churches is singularly effective in all points of view. Then there are the very fine Roman remains, and finally a really enormous number of houses of the thirteenth and fourteenth century, all in very fair preservation. From Trèves, by the interesting abbey of Laach, I reached Cologne, and at once made my way to the cathedral, anxious to see whether the opinions which have grown on me more strongly the more often I have visited it would remain unshaken now that so great progress has been made in the new work. It is impossible to overrate the excellence of all the new constructions; nor are they obviously open to any hostile criticism in regard to their conformity with the general character of the old work; but it is at the same time useless to conceal the fact, that the work is of a poor kind, and that it certainly does not improve as one sees more of it. The only comfort is that the interior will be much finer than the exterior, and that it is worth while therefore, to put up with some shortcomings in the latter in order to obtain what will, no doubt, be the sumptuous effect of space, height, and (I hope) colour, which the former promises to afford. It is much more difficult to spoil the interior than the exterior; it must of necessity be simple and uniform, and it admits of less attempt at enrichment with such crockets and pinnacles as cover the exterior. The south transept front, which is the most conspicuous portion of the new work finished, is, I think, thoroughly unsatisfactory. The crocketed gable over the great window, repeated again just above up the roof gable, is perhaps the most unhappy repetition of a leading line that could have been hit upon. If a gable was necessary over the window, it should have been different in its pitch from the other; and then again, however much the old architect indulged in reedy mouldings and endless groups of crockets, it does seem to be a sad thing that a nineteenth century artist should feel bound to emulate his enthusiasm for such worthless things. I grant at once, that he has done no more than follow precedents. In the old west front of the cathedral, there is scarcely a moulding three inches in diameter, whilst the central doorway between the steeples is very small, and made up of a repetition *usque ad nauseam* of orders of reedy mouldings and small flowers, and admits not for one instant of comparison with any good examples of French doorways; and, it is indeed very striking how, as one comes fresh from French churches, all this work looks thin, petty, and wanting in expression.

    In the sculpture of foliage in the new works, the system seems to be to take sprigs of two or three leaves and fasten them against a circular bell, with no evidence of any kind of natural growth, and no proper architectural function to perform. They seem to require a piece of string or a strap round them to attach them to the bell.

The copying of the foliage is perfectly naturalesque, even to the marking of the fibres on leaves which are to be elevated to a great height in the building. I have heard all this sculpture so often referred to in terms of the highest praise, that unpleasant as it is to criticize work executed at the present day, I feel that I am bound to express my dissent from those who so speak of it. The whole work is so famous that all the world is interested in it. English tourists, year after year, going in great numbers on their travels, admire thoughtlessly everything that they see, and architects even seem to me to follow in their wake, forgetting that our true function is not simply to admire the work, because it is a vast and noble enterprise, but to weigh and compare it with the most perfect work we can find, and to endeavour, if the faults we see in it are great, to point them out by way of warning for ourselves and others. Indiscriminate admiration of such a building does enormous mischief, just as a wild enthusiasm for the fourteenth century work which we see throughout Germany would be fatal to the eye and taste of the enthusiast.

Undoubtedly the architect of Cologne has had an office of enormous difficulty. The national enthusiasm, which has raised the funds hitherto expended, must have needed very cautious treatment. It would probably indeed be indispensable that the steeples, if ever completed, should be built exactly on the old plan so curiously preserved and discovered, but the elevation of the transepts, on which so very much of the external effect of the whole church depended, was just one of those points on which the architect might have ventured (one would have thought) to step out of the old path a little, and — just as the old architect when he wanted a perfect ground-plan went to Amiens for his example—he might at this day have gone to Chartres or Amiens, Rouen or Paris, and grafted something of their grace and grandeur on the otherwise merely German conception of façade which he has given us. That this might have been done without detriment to the old portions of the building is I am sure unquestionable; and that if well done it must have resulted in great gain and increased beauty is equally certain. If (as we all, with insignificant exceptions, admit) it is well for us to study early French art as well as English, surely some attention to it must be even more necessary in Germany, whose national art was inferior, in the thirteenth and fourteenth century, not only to that of France, but almost as much to that of England.

SOME CHURCHES OF LE PUY EN VELAY AND AUVERGNE

(From the *Transactions* of the R. I. B. A. 1889)

IN the course of last autumn,[1] after having spent three weeks in climbing Swiss mountains, I was able to devote a few days, on my way home, to a district which, as far as I had been able to gather from books, appeared to contain a mine of interest for the architect, not less than for the geologist and the lover of natural scenery. From Lyon I went by Monistrol to Le Puy, which was the grand object of my tour; thence by Brioude into Auvergne, and through Issoire, Clermont-Ferrand and Nevers, to Bourges and Paris. I was so much struck by what I saw, that, though I am well aware that my visit was too hurried to be at all exhaustive, I think I cannot do better than give you the results of my journey, in the trust that what was full of interest, novelty, and instruction for myself, may be of some use also to others who have not been able to make this journey for themselves. The complete-Gothic architecture of Velay and Auvergne is not, it is true, to be compared to the best work in the north of France. I am not, however, going to tell you about it, but about an

[1] The autumn of 1860. The original paper, which has undergone considerable revision since it was read on 7th January, 1861, will be found in the First Series of *Transactions*, 1860-61, pp. 97-119. — A. E. S.

earlier style, which, as I hope to show, has special value as illustrating, among other things, the way in which French Gothic was developed from Romanesque and Byzantine buildings; and our attention will, therefore, be almost entirely devoted to buildings which are either Romanesque or Romano-Byzantine in their character, or belonging to the period of transition from those styles to first-pointed. The complete-Gothic buildings are comparatively few, and have no special value; and I shall, probably, not have time now to refer to them even in the most cursory manner.

I will begin with Le Puy, the ancient capital of Velay. The city is crowded up the side of a volcanic rock, one end of which is crowned by the picturesque mass of its Eastern-looking cathedral. It consists of a network of narrow streets not passable by carriages, and reminds one forcibly of some such city as Genoa. Above the rock on which the cathedral is perched rises another, called the *Corneille*, on which are some old fortifications, and which has just been crowned by a monstrous image of the Blessed Virgin, made of the metal of guns taken at Sebastopol, to whose charge I may fairly lay much of the imperfection of my account of the buildings beneath her feet; for I had the ill-luck to arrive at Le Puy only three days before the inauguration of this statue, and I found the whole city so entirely occupied with the preparations for the fête, that it was with the greatest difficulty that I examined the cathedral at all, and into some portions of it I was quite unable to penetrate; whilst the only condition on which I could obtain rooms at an inn was that I should not stop for more than two days, and should make room for some bishop, prince, or cardinal (of whom there were a legion on the road), before the great fête-day. I had to work very hard, therefore, to do as much as I did, and I make no doubt that a more leisurely and uninterrupted examination would have enabled me to discover and do much more. Separated from the great volcanic rock I have already mentioned by one or two furlongs only, is the smaller, but even more striking rock, called the *Aiguille de S. Michel*, and crowned with a little chapel dedicated to that Archangel. It rises, in the most abrupt and precipitous manner, to a height of about 265 feet. The distant background includes a series of truncated conical hills, evidently ancient volcanoes, and from almost every point of view a landscape of the most picturesque and extensive description is seen. Rarely have I enjoyed a more charming ride than that which, for the last twenty miles into Le Puy on the road from S. Étienne, made me generally acquainted with the remarkable physical formation of this mountain district; beautiful throughout, it was at its best just when, some twelve or fifteen miles before I reached the city, I first saw the "angelic" church, as it is styled, standing up boldly on its rock, the centre of an almost matchless landscape.

The story of its claim to this style of "angelic" is this. Bishop Evodius, at the end of the sixth century, on being made first bishop of Le Puy, wished to construct a church; the Virgin, who had before shown to S. George the place where she wished one to be built, appeared to a sick woman on the Mount surrounded by a crowd of angels, and desired her to tell Evodius to proceed at once with his work. After much prayer he went to Rome, and the Pope sent back with him an architect and senator named Scutarius, under whose auspices the church was soon built, and whose tombstone is still to be seen near the transept door. Evodius and Scutarius then started for Rome again, but on the way met two old men, who gave them two boxes of relics, and desired them to return to Le Puy, saying that as soon as they arrived with the relics before the church the doors would open, the bells would ring of themselves, the whole interior would be bright with torches and candles, and they should hear divine melodies, and smell the sweet perfume of the heavenly oil which had served for the consecration of the church by the angels. Everything happened just as had been foretold, and Evodius felt it unnecessary again to consecrate his church, which from that time to the present day has been called the "angelic" church. No doubt you all know how curious a parallel to this legend the history of our own Abbey of S. Peter at Westminster affords.[1] But in searching

---

[1] I give an extract from "La Estoire de Seint Edward le Rei," MS. Bibl., Publ. Cambridge. Ee iii. 59:

"Seint Pere, du ciel claver,
"Va sa iglise dedier,
"Des angeles mut grant partie
"Li funt servise e grant aie.
"Li angele chantent au servise,

"La nuit quant dedient l'iglise
"Tant ja du ciel luur
"Ke vis est au peschur,
"Ke li solailz e la lune
"Lur clarté tute i preste e dune."

This is the rubric descriptive of the illustration, whilst in the poem itself is the following passage:

"E cist si tost cum arive
"Entrez est en sun muster;
"Li airs devint lusanz e clers,
"N'out en muster tenegre ne umbre;
"Atant des angres grant numbre,
"Ki s'en venent a sum servise
"A dedier cele iglise.

"Tant ja partut odur,
"Ke vis est a cel pescur
"Ke li solailz la lune
"Sa clarté tute preste u dune
"Angles pu cel avaler
"Regarde e puis remunter;
"Teu joie a, ke li est vis
"Ke raviz est en Parais,
"Pur l'avisium k'apert."

for information about the churches of Auvergne, I came upon a continuation of the Le Puy legend, to which the Westminster story affords no such parallel. This second legend tells how, when the seraphic basilica of Le Puy had been thus dedicated, S. Anne descended from heaven to visit the palace of her daughter. Not content with this human work, she seized the hammer of the master-mason, and, taking wing, descended on the summit of a hill, and, turning towards Auvergne, which to her mind offered no church worthy of the Queen of Heaven, she threw the hammer, saying as she threw it, "On the place where the hammer falls a church shall rise." The hammer fell on the right bank of the Allier, and immediately there rose from the soil like a flower the church of Les Chases, which was dedicated forthwith to S. Mary.[1]

Let us now leave legends, and direct our attention to the ground-plan of the cathedral. Its architects have ingeniously contrived to cover the whole of the summit of the rock on which it stands. It consists of a nave with aisles, transepts, a choir, and choir-aisles, and a steeple at the east end of the north choir-aisle. To the south of the cathedral is the modern bishop's palace, whilst to the north are the cloisters, two grand halls, some ruins, and to the north-east a chapel dedicated to S. John and other buildings. There are entrances in the east walls of each of the transepts, but these were rather intended, I suppose, for the exit than for the entrance of the people, and the mode in which they were admitted forms one of the most striking features

[1] *L'Auvergne au Moyen Age*, by M. Dominique Branche. Clermont-Ferrand, 1842.

of the whole scheme. I said that the church was built on a rock, and its western face, forming one of the principal streets of the city, is so steep as to consist alternately of steps and inclines, until, at a short distance in advance of the west front, it is changed to an almost interminable flight of steps. The grand west entrance is an open porch, like an enormous crypt, beneath the three western bays of the nave and its aisles, whose walls and piers it reproduces in its plan. The steps [1] formerly rose in a straight line, until they came up in the very centre of the church, in the fifth bay of the nave, and in front of the roof-loft, and of the miracle-working image of the Blessed Virgin, which, brought from the East and given to the church by S. Louis, was, until its destruction in A.D. 1789, the greatest attraction for pilgrims in France.[2] This singular entrance, and the mode of exit by the eastern doors of the transepts, gave rise to an old saying, "In Notre Dame du Puy one entered by the navel and went out by the ears." Unfortunately, however, the central entrance has been diverted, and after ascending a hundred and two steps, and arriving at the Golden Gate, as it was called, the passage branches right and left — on the left ascending into the cloister, and on the right winding round the south side of the church, until the hundred and thirty-fifth step lands the weary pilgrim in the south

[1] The steps are arranged in successive groups of eleven, with platforms between them.

[2] As evidence of the popularity of Notre Dame du Puy this may suffice: — in Amiens cathedral, until A.D. 1820, there existed a series of pictures given by the "Confrèrie de Notre Dame du Puy." A similar confrèrie existed at Limoges. — G. E. S. There is an image and a devotion of N. D. du Puy at Estella in Navarre, carried thither by French pilgrims. — G. G. K.

aisle, near the transept.[1] This, then, is the general scheme of this most singular church. Let me now go on to describe it in detail, beginning with the oldest portion. This comprises the choir, the transepts, and crossing, and the two easternmost bays of the nave. The choir is completely modernized, and I am unable to say whether any portion of the internal arrangement is old. It presents the peculiarity of a square exterior and a circular interior. This is a not uncommon arrangement in the earliest Italian examples of the apse, and is seen at St. Mark's, Venice, and elsewhere. The arches opening into the choir-aisles are old, and I believe that we may venture to say that the original plan must have been very nearly the same as that of the church of S. Martin d'Ainay, at Lyon, in which the choir-aisles are shorter than the choir, and all are terminated with apses.[2] I shall have other occasion to point out that at a later date the architects of Ainay and of Le Puy must have been the same. The date of the foundation of Ainay is some time in the ninth century, and it was carried on until the end of the eleventh; but the apse and capitals of the columns of the crossing — for the columns themselves are Roman — cannot, I think, be later than about A.D. 940 to A.D. 1000, which latter would, I think, be the date generally accepted for this portion of the work at Le Puy. To proceed with my notice. The crossing is surmounted

[1] The passage to the right is evidently modern, that to the left looks as though it were ancient, but a protest against the removal of some ancient work, in the course of constructing it, which I have found in the *Bulletin Monumental* [A. de Caumont], seems to show that it is not so.

[2] S. Martin d'Ainay, at Lyon, is a parallel triapsidal church, with a central dome, and a western tower of unusual and picturesque outline, adorned largely with inlaid tiles and bricks.

by a quasi-dome, carried up as an octagonal lantern, much of which has been modernised in restorations, whilst much is quite new; though the universality of the raised central lantern in the churches of the district makes it probable that it is, to some extent, a proper restoration.[1] The transepts are covered with barrel-vaults, strengthened by tranverse ribs of a square section below them; the small apses in their end walls have semi-domes, and the tribunes which cross them are groined with quadripartite vaults without ribs. The whole of the nave is covered in the same way as the crossing, each bay being divided from the next by bold transverse arches, and having a quasi-dome, supported by arches across the angles of each compartment, and all of them, in truth, being not domes, but eight-sided pointed vaults, springing from the octagonal bases thus contrived. There are no pendentives, properly so called, and the construction is, I should say, that of men who desired to erect domes, but had no knowledge whatever of the way in which they were constructed in the East; or — to take a more favorable and, perhaps, juster view — of men who, desiring to give a small building the greatest possible effect of space, to roof it with stone (not knowing anything yet about flying-buttresses), and to light it from a clerestory, actually solved all these points in a successful way. Where this kind of roof was first attempted I am quite unable to say. Certainly the central lantern at Ainay is so identical in character with some of those at Le Puy, that the same

[1] At present the exterior of the lantern is covered with a domical roof; but an illustration that I have seen shows it finished with a low-pitched tile roof, and without any of the inlaid mosaic which is now upon it.

workmen must have executed both; but there seems to be no other example in the same district as Ainay, whereas at Le Puy, and in Velay and Auvergne, everything is more or less roofed on the same principle. The second portion of the cathedral at Le Puy consists of the third and fourth bays of the nave, and the third portion of the fifth and sixth bays.[1]

The latest portion is of early pointed character, and not later in date than *circa* A.D. 1180 to 1200, and it was at the same time that this was erected that the greater part of the enormous substructure forming the porch was also completed. The aisles throughout the church are vaulted with quadripartite vaults, the three western bays alone having ribs. In the two western bays there are engaged shafts both in the porch and above it in the nave, but the rest of the piers are of the simplest plan, large and generally cruciform in their section, save at the crossing, where the arches are carried on coupled detached shafts. There is much elaborate sculpture introduced in the capitals of the pilasters and columns of the nave, but it is nowhere of any very high merit, and is so inferior in delicacy and beauty to the sculpture of the same age to be seen on the banks of the Rhone, that I should attribute it to a native school of sculptors acquainted, probably, with none but inferior Roman sculpture, from which they endeavoured to develope a style for themselves. A clerestory of wide and rude round-headed windows, one in each compartment, lights the series of domes in a very effective manner.

The arches across the nave are very bold, and, in the

[1] The division of the building into work done at various epochs is beyond question, though there may be some question as to the date I assign.

wall above them, an opening is pierced under each of the cupolas. As is generally the case, however, in churches covered in this way, very little is seen of the real vault in any general view of the church, these transverse arches only, with the quasi-pendentives above them being seen. The pendentives are true semi-domes, constructed in alternate courses of dark and light stone, and the difference between their plan and the square angle in which they are placed is skilfully concealed by detached shafts, with capitals placed under the pendentives.

I think you will agree with me that considering its early date (no part probably later than *circa* A.D. 1150 or 1180), it would be difficult to find a grander or more nervous scheme, or one which, with such small dimensions, conveys nevertheless so great an impression of size and importance. The choir-aisles were altered at various times. That on the south has been rebuilt in second-pointed of poor character, and is now a mere passage-way to the modern sacristy, and that on the north was probably interfered with not very long after its first construction, when the great steeple which now abuts upon it was commenced. M. Mérimée,[1] in his very interesting description of the church, suggests that the base of the tower was originally a baptistery, but I see no reason whatever for this suggestion and it is impossible to doubt, when we carefully examine the whole design, that though the steeple was long in building, the main feature in its design was from the first just what we now see it to be. Moreover, the chapel of S. Jean close by is said to have been the baptistery for the whole city until within the last sixty

[1] Mérimée, *Notes d'un Voyage en Auvergne*, p. 226.

years. The design of the steeple is very bizarre and unusual. It consists of a long series of no less than nine stages on the exterior, and it diminishes rapidly in diameter, and is, perhaps, on the whole, more curious than pleasing in its outlines. If you look at the ground-plan you will see that its construction is most remarkable. The internal diameter of the tower at the base is twenty-four feet six inches, but this is reduced to only twelve feet by four detached piers, one foot ten and one-half inches square. These piers are carried up from the base to the very summit, detached in the three lower stages, and forming part of the thickness of the wall in the portion above. The highest stage of the steeple, twelve feet in internal and sixteen feet in external diameter, is therefore, as nearly as possible, carried up on these four piers, and the rapid decrease in the external dimensions, from thirty-six feet to sixteen feet, was only rendered possible by this very ingenious mode of construction. So far as I know there is only one other example of the same scheme, viz. in the steeple of the cathedral of S. Étienne at Limoges. Here, however, the base is the only portion remaining of the original work, and the columns are cylindrical in place of being square, but it is evident that the intention was the same as at Le Puy. The steeple at Limoges is probably the first in point of date. M. Viollet-le-Duc dates it at about A.D. 1050, but the Abbé Arbellot, in a learned paper on the cathedral, in the *Bulletin* of the *Société Archéologique et Historique du Limousin*, maintains that it was certainly built before A.D. 1012, when the Bishop Arnaud de Périgeux, after assisting at the consecration of Bishop Gerald at Poitiers, accompanied him to Limoges, and put the cords of the bells into his hands. The lower part of the steeple at Le Puy may, I think, safely be referred to the end of the eleventh century, and its completion to the end of the twelfth, whilst the planning appears to me to be thoroughly characteristic of a Byzantine artist, the construction of the piers in the lowest stage being almost identical with that of the main piers under the domes of S. Mark's, Venice, and S. Front, Périgueux.

The arrangement of the belfry stage, with its gable on each face, is very noteworthy, and is, perhaps, one of the earliest examples of a type which was developed afterwards into the well-known arrangement of the belfry of the south-west tower at Chartres, and this, with the influence of the churches of the Rhine,[1] developed in almost all subsequent modifications of the spire with its gabled spire-lights; one of the windows under this pediment is planned in a most ingenious manner, presenting externally a semi-dome pierced by two pointed arches; another window is pierced with a trefoil head, the diameter of which is much larger than that of the light it surmounts. This is a favorite form of cusping throughout this district. I have seen it in Lyon, at Vienne, often at Le Puy, at Brioude, at Notre-Dame-du-Port, Clermont, and in the south porch at Bourges; and there can, I think, be little doubt that it is somewhat Eastern in its origin, and analogous to the horseshoe form of arch.

The cloister on the north side of the church appears to be in part coeval with the earliest,[2] or, perhaps, the

[1] See Viollet-le-Duc (*Dictionnaire*, art. "*Clocher*," pp. 312-18) for a reference to this influence of the Rhine churches.

[2] M. Viollet-le-Duc considers the earliest part of the cloister to date from the tenth century; M. Mérimée thinks the eleventh century more likely.

second portion of the fabric, and in part with the later additions to it. It consists of a simple arcade of round arches on rather solid piers, with a detached shaft on each face. The capitals are all richly sculptured, some with figures, some with foliage. The spandrels of the arches are filled in with a reticulation of coloured stones; above the arches runs a band of similar ornament, and above this again a carved cornice, which in the later part of the cloister forms a sort of frieze. In this portion the arches have sculptured key-stones, a peculiarity which I hardly remember to have met with before in work of the same date. On the south side there are two fluted shafts and one spiral; all the rest are circular, but noticeable for their very considerable entasis. The groining is all quadripartite without ribs, and executed with rough stones, set in concrete, on a centring of boards. The cloister was surrounded on all sides with buildings. On the south is the cathedral; on the east, and opening to the cloister by an arcade of open arches, is a large hall covered with a pointed barrel-vault. This was originally called the choir of S. André, and in it masses in commemoration of the dead were said, and services held on the feasts of the Invention and Exaltation of the Cross, and on the feasts of S. Andrew and S. Eustachius. It was also called "cæmeterium," being used for the burial of the clergy, and is now called the chapel *des Morts*. On the wall are still to be seen remains of a painting of the Crucifixion, with many prophets and angels, S. Mary and S. John, the sun and moon, etc. In the northern gable of this building is a fine cylindrical chimney, built in alternate courses of dark and light stone, and rising from a fireplace in a chamber over the hall, and of the same date as the hall. M. Viollet-le-Duc gives a drawing of the fireplace, which is of a not uncommon early type, the head projecting considerably on a semicircular plan. At the north end of the *Salle des Morts* is a passage leading to the cloister, and along the whole northern boundary once stood a vast range of building called the Maîtrise.[1] Nothing now remains of this save its undercroft, which was spanned by bold pointed arches of stone, on which the wooden floor rested. The Maîtrise was pulled down a few years since, and, not long before, a tower close by it, called the tower of S. Mayol, was also destroyed. It is described as an erection of the eleventh century, battlemented, but without machicoulis.[2] It seems to have served as part of the fortification of the church, which was also attended to in an alteration of the building on the west side of the cloister, in the fourteenth century. This building contained, below, a hall on a level with the church, which was the chapel of the Holy Relics; above was the *Salle des États* of Velay, with a stone barrel-roof, now both thrown into one room. Above these again was an open space under the roof, protected on the side towards the town by a magnificent overhanging battlement and machicolation of the fourteenth century, and quite open on the side towards the cloister save for the stone piers supporting the roof. The machicoulis are some of the finest I have ever seen, and project from the buttresses as well as from the walls. The only access to this stage of the building seems to

[1] The *Maîtrise* was, I believe, the school attached to the cathedral.
[2] Mérimée, *Notes d'un Voyage en Auvergne*, p. 232.

have been from the roof of the cathedral. Le Puy was, in the first instance, selected as a site for the cathedral because it afforded so secure a refuge from attack, and in later days it seems to have been not less necessary to provide against danger: for among other enemies the Lords of Polignac, whose magnificent castle is visible from the steeple of the cathedral, only some four miles distant, were the most conspicuous as they were also the most powerful. M. Viollet-le-Duc supposes, indeed, that the tower of the cathedral was meant in part for defence; but I see no evidence of this, and possibly he had in his mind the destroyed tower of S. Mayol, which, as well as the double wall of enceinte which formerly surrounded the whole cathedral, was no doubt a purely military construction. Fortified churches are by no means uncommon in this part of France. At Brioude is a painting showing the church entirely surrounded by a crenellated and turreted wall in A.D. 1636; and Royat, near Clermont, and the abbey church of Menat, also in Auvergne, still retains provisions for defence. The *Salle des États* contained formerly the archives of Velay, and in removing them a few years since (about A.D. 1850) portions of a hanging of blue wool, "semée" with fleurs-de-lys, and adorned with the armorial bearings of Jean de Bourbon, Bishop of Le Puy from A.D. 1443 to 1485, were found.[1] At the same

[1] It is very difficult to understand precisely where these hangings were found. M. Aymard, a distinguished antiquary at Le Puy, in the *Album Photographique d'Archéologie Religieuse*, speaks of the painting on the wall of the *Salle des États*, and then, in another place, says that the tapestries given by Jean de Bourbon served to decorate the *Salle des États* of Velay, and after the regrettable destruction of that hall the remains of them were preserved part in the cathedral and part in the museum. Possibly he refers to

time a curious painting on the east wall of the lower chamber was discovered under the whitewash. It represents four liberal sciences — Grammar, Logic, Rhetoric, and Music — as females seated with ancient worthies at their feet. Priscian sits below Grammar, writing; and two boys, with open books, are on her other side. Logic holds a lizard in one hand and a scorpion in the other, and Aristotle is arguing below. The inscription underneath is — "Me sine doctores frustrâ coluere sorores," and each figure has a corresponding leonine verse inscribed below. Rhetoric holds a file in her left hand, and Cicero sits at her feet. Music plays an organ, whilst Tubal, with two hammers, plays upon an anvil. There used — according to the "*Chronique des Médicis*" — to be a second painting here with figures of young demoiselles gorgeously clothed, and from the same chronicle it appears that Messire Pierre Odin, official of the Bishop Jean de Bourbon, who died in 1502, presented both: — "Il estait si grant orateur que, par son mellifère et suaviloquent langage, fust commis plusieurs fois estre ambassadeur devers le Pape à la requette du très-excellent et redouté Prince Louis XI. roy de France, lequel dudict Pape obtint grande louange et avoir, ce que il employa en divers façons et moyens en aulmosnes et à la décoration de cette saincte église du Puy." The picture has considerable merit; its detail is a mixture of Renaissance and Gothic, and the Gothic portion — as for instance, the chair on which one of the figures sits — is not Italian, and I should be inclined to suppose that it was the

the removal of the floor below the *Salle des États*, for the hall itself has not been destroyed.

work, therefore, of a French artist. Its date must be between 1475 and 1502. Louis XI. came to Le Puy on a pilgrimage in 1475.

The external side elevation of the church is best seen from the cloister, and, with a few words upon this, I will leave this portion of the building. Here, even more clearly than inside, the division of the building into work of different epochs is seen. The two bays nearest the crossing have large coupled windows in the aisle, with parti-coloured voussoirs and jamb shafts. The clerestory is very peculiar in its treatment, and undoubtedly very effective; the windows are of one light in each bay and round-headed and on each side of them above the springing there is a recess in the wall, in the centre of which a detached shaft is placed to carry the cornice. A similar recess and a smaller shaft occur immediately over the arch of the window, and the window-arch being built of alternately dark and light stone, and all the sunk panels being filled in with geometrical patterns, composed in the same way, an extremely rich effect is obtained. Recesses of the same kind in the upper part of the walls occur all along the eastern face of the transept at Le Puy; and between the clerestory windows of Notre-Dame-du-Port, Clermont; S. Paul, Issoire; and commonly in Auvergne. But so far as I can judge from the portion of the cathedral in which they occur, and from the early and simple character of the work itself, I am inclined to believe that it is earlier here than in any of the other examples. It would be of great interest to have some more positive evidence on this and other similar questions of date. But, so far as I have been able to discover, there is no such evidence, and we are left in doubt, therefore, whether this portion of the architecture of Velay came from Auvergne, or whether the reverse was the case; as also whether this external decoration of the fabric is coeval with its first erection, or is a subsequent addition.

The two central compartments of the nave have circular windows (sixteen feet in diameter) to light the aisle, and round-headed windows in the clerestory; and between the arches of the latter windows are small arched recesses. In the two western bays the clerestory is similar, save that the intermediate recessed arch is omitted. In both the voussoirs are counter-charged, and the wall from the springing up to the eaves is coursed with stone and lava. The transept gables are only noticeable for the courses of inlaid patterns with which they are enriched. All these patterns are formed with white stone and lava. The latter, indeed, forms the whole ground of the walls, and varies in colour from a greenish grey to black; and the patterns are formed with the darkest lava and stone. The cloister is similarly inlaid above the arches, but it has almost all been restored in a most injudicious manner. They have *struck* and *ruled* (I believe that is the technical phrase for this most abominable of inventions, is it not?) an enormous red mortar joint between all the stones,[1] and wherever this has been done the diaper appears to be formed with a chequer of black and red; wherever the cloister has not been retouched the diaper is black and white.

I have left, almost until the last, that which is after all the crowning wonder of this singular church — the

[1] M. Mallay, of Clermont, says that the mosaic work of the church of Notre-Dame-du-Port, Clermont, was all set in red mortar originally.

western porch. I have already referred to its position and plan. The majesty, I may say the awfulness, of this entrance, can hardly be exaggerated. It owes little to delicate detail or enrichment of any kind, for, though these have been, they are no longer; but it is the gloom and darkness, the simple, nervous forms of arch and pier, the long flight of steps lost in obscurity and crowded constantly (when I saw them) with a throng of worshippers, which constitute the strange charm of this strangest of entrances. I told you that in the nave the two western bays of the aisle alone had groining ribs; in the porch below it is only in the western bay that they are used, and this affords interesting evidence of the very gradual yet regular development of our art.

The spaces below the aisles in the third bay from the west form chapels — that on the right dedicated to S. Martin, and that on the left to S. Gilles. Before the last extension of the building these chapels were at the extreme west end. They have western doorways, which still retain the wooden doors. Each of these doors was of four divisions in height, covered with subjects carved in low relief. They are executed either in cedar or oak (I am uncertain which, for they are covered with paint), and the subjects, inscriptions, and borders are all obtained simply by sinking the ground three-sixteenths of an inch. The figures are, of course, only in outline, but it is still evident that they were carefully painted with draperies, etc., so as to be thoroughly distinct. There is some appearance of the ground having been painted with broad horizontal bands of colour, but the traces are so indistinct that it is difficult to speak positively.[1] The doors are hung folding, and those to the chapel of S. Gilles contain subjects from the early life of our Lord, whilst those in the chapel of S. Martin contain subjects from His Passion. The meeting-rail in the former fortunately contains an inscription of extreme value: "Gaulfredus : me : fct : Petrus : epi"; after which some letters are lost. If my reading of the last letter but one as "p" is correct, I think it leads to a most important inference. No one who looks at the design of these gates can doubt that they are thoroughly Eastern in their character; and, upon searching for the lists of bishops of Le Puy since my return, I was delighted to find that the first bishop of the name of Peter [2] was consecrated at Ravenna by Leo IX. in A.D. 1043, and died at Genoa A.D. 1053, as he returned from the Holy Land. Gates of the same description are said to exist in the churches of Chamaillères and of Lavoulte-Chilhac in the same district, whilst other evidence of intercourse with the East is afforded by fragments of *tissus* preserved at Monestier, at Pébrac, and at Lavoulte-Chilhac. These *tissus* are all extremely Eastern in their character, and very similar to the famous cope at Chinon described by M. de Caumont in the *Abécédaire*, and to the Le Mans *tissu* described by M. Hucher in the *Bulletin Monumental* (1846, p. 24). The date ordinarily attributed to them is the middle of the eleventh century, which exactly tallies with the return of Bishop Peter from the Holy Land. I dwell on this the more because, if the inference I have

---

[1] See further observations on this subject, page 223.

[2] The predecessor in the See, Stephen II., uncle of Bishop Peter I., was buried at Lavoulte-Chilhac.

drawn from the inscription be true, it gives the date also to the second portion of the construction of the cathedral, to which the chapels in the porch undoubtedly belong; and the result would be that whilst I should date the earliest portion of the church at about the end of the tenth century, or quite the commencement of the eleventh, the second portion would be dated at about A.D. 1050; and, finally, there is little doubt as to the whole having been completed in the course of the twelfth century.[1] These dates are, as in all such cases, of course only approximate; and it is pretty clear that there was seldom any long pause in the works, and the development in their architectural features is therefore very gradual.

The external elevation in the west front is similar in style to the clerestory on the north side, and mainly executed in alternate courses of lava and stone. The aisle-roofs are masked by walls with pediments. Throughout this part of the work you will observe that its early date is proved by the fact that the round arch is almost invariably used for ornament, and the pointed arch only where great strength was required. A great buttress, which had been built against this vast front, was removed during the recent restorations.

I observed before that there are doorways on the east side of both transepts — the "ears" referred to in an old saying. The south transept door is in itself remarkable for the peculiar form of the cusping of its arch, and still more for the magnificent porch built over

---

[1] A diploma of A.D. 1146 is dated from the "Ville d'Anis" (i.e. Le Puy) and fixes the date at which this "cité" received the name of "ville."

it. The date of this is the latter part of the twelfth century. It is open on the south and east sides, and abuts on the church on the west and north, occupying the re-entering angle between the transept and choir aisle. The arch is remarkable for a rib detached below the arch, and connected at intervals with it by columns, so as to have the appearance of being suspended. My impression is that the architect feared that his arch had not sufficient abutment, and hoped by bringing some of the weight on to the lower rims of the arch to remedy this defect. The whole detail of this porch is a very rich kind of pointed, full of half-Romanesque and half-Byzantine detail. The groining, in alternate coloured courses, is quadripartite, but has the very rare feature (in France) of ridge ribs. Above the porch is a room or chapel, to which I omitted to gain access. Over the door of the other (north) transept a great arch, thrown from the cathedral to the chapel of S. Jean, carries another chapel, lighted with a first-pointed triplet. This door is square-headed, and covered with rich though rude ironwork. The door-handles have a resemblance to one in the cathedral at Trèves made by Jean and Nicholas of Bingen, which struck me, and was remarked on also, I find, by M. Mérimée. The lintel of the door is deeper at the centre than at the sides of the door, pediment-like, and has figures of our Lord and the Twelve Apostles carved on it, whilst above, under a circular arch, is another figure of our Lord, with an angel on either side. The whole has been very much mutilated and all the figures are hacked to pieces. The ground was painted, and no doubt the figures were also, and the woodwork of the door was covered with linen or leather under ironwork.

The very ancient chapel of S. Jean is close to this door, and by its side is a fifteenth century archway. The chapel is arcaded on its south side and pierced with very simple windows. Some antiquaries assert that it is a piece of Roman construction, and it is not impossible, though I should be much more inclined to call it tenth century work. The chapel has a rude quadripartite vault, and its apsidal chancel is roofed with a semi-dome.

I must conclude my long notice of this church by some mention of the extensive remains of painted decorations still visible. During the late restorations of the cathedral, I understand from M. Aymard, the greater portion were destroyed. The vaults of the north transept and the semi-domes of its apsidal recesses are still, however, covered with paintings, though they are scarcely intelligible, owing to darkness and dirt. In one of them occurs a figure of our Lord giving the benediction in the Greek fashion, and it is one of the many evidences which may be adduced of the Eastern influence visible here in so many respects, though I am not disposed to lay so much stress upon it as some of those did who engaged in the controversy it occasioned.[1] In the

[1] See M. Aymard's *Album Photographique d'Archéologie Religieuse*, and a communication from the same gentleman in the *Bulletin Archeol.* vol. ii. p. 645. M. Aymard mentions one other example, a diptych, figured in Montfaucon (*L'Antiquité Expliquée*) vol. iii. p. 89, which dates from about A.D. 900. The hand at Le Puy is larger than life, and has a double nimbus round it, the inner yellow, the outer dark red; the hand is white and the ground within the nimbus dark blue. The Secretary of the Comité Historique des Arts et Monuments considers that this representation of the Greek mode of giving the benediction makes it certain that the work at Le Puy is Byzantine in its origin. But one may, I think, be allowed to doubt whether this conclusion is to be absolutely depended on.

western porch there are also extensive remains of painting; the soffits of the arches in the third bay from the west are all painted, and so too are the walls over the altars in the chapels of S. Martin and S. Gilles. The painting was executed on a thick coat of plaster, and the nimbi are of gold with lines incised on them. No doubt the whole church once glittered with gold and colour, and, seeing how fine its effect still is, we may, aiding the indications still left with our recollections of Assisi, of Venice, and of Padua, people the bare walls once again, and bring before our eyes an interior of the most gorgeous magnificence.

I may conclude what I have to say about the cathedral with a few words about the sacristy and its contents. The building itself is not more than a hundred and fifty years old, and most of its treasures have been lost. The most precious relic still left is a Bible, which, by a note at its end, is stated to have been written by S. Théodulf, Bishop of Orléans, in the ninth century, and sent by him, in accomplishment of a vow, to the shrine of Notre Dame du Puy. It is a quarto of 347 leaves of very fine vellum, some white with black letters, and others purple or violet with gold or silver letters. It contains the Old and New Testament, commentaries on the text, interpretations of Hebrew, Greek and Latin words, and some poems by Théodulf. The pages are interleaved with excessively delicate tissues of various colours and patterns, which appear to be of the same age as the book, and of Eastern manufacture. They are made of china crêpe, cotton, silk, linen, poil-de-chèvre, and camel's hair, of extreme fineness, and of various colours and patterns.[1] The

[1] M. Aymard. See footnote on preceding page.

binding is, however, later, and of red velvet on chamfered oak boards, with good simple metal knobs. There are also preserved here some wax candles, tapering considerably in their length, and stamped with a pattern made by a pointed instrument; and, finally, there is a tippet embroidered with a tree of Jesse, said to have been of Charlemagne's time. It is not so old as is said, but may possibly be (though I very much doubt it) of the twelfth or thirteenth century, but it has been much damaged by removal from its original ground and by partial re-working. The sacristy also contains a reliquary of very late sixteenth-century date, of which a photograph has been published by M. Aymard, but which was not shown to me; and an almost endless roll of vellum illuminated with a chronological tree of the history of the world.

How much has been lost may be guessed from some statistics which I have come upon as to the number of silversmiths and specimens of their work in Le Puy in the Middle Ages: in A.D. 1408 there were no less than forty resident in the city, whilst as to their work I find in A.D. 1444 there were in the sacristy 33 *châsses* and reliquaries, 26 chalices, 11 statues of the Blessed Virgin Mary, angels, and other figures, 10 candelabra, 9 crosses, 9 lamps, 9 mitres, crosses with their stems, episcopal rings, crowns for the Virgin, censers, paxes, basins, plates, books with covers adorned with chasings, pearls and precious stones, and many like things; and in A.D. 1475 I find that Louis XI. gave 30 silver marks for a canopy over the miracle-working figure of Notre Dame du Puy, which was made by François Gimbert, a silversmith of Le Puy. Other churches in the neighbourhood have been more fortunate in retaining some of their old plate, and a fair list might be made out, if I had time, of their possession, many of which have been photographed by M. Aymard.

The building of the greatest interest, after the cathedral, is the little church of S. Michel, which crowns the rock fitly called the Aiguille. It is reached by steps winding irregularly round the rock, to the shape of the summit of which it has been most ingeniously adapted. The oldest portion of the building is the square choir, covered with a dome, under which stands the principal altar. To the (ritual) east and north of this are apsidal projections, and to the south an archway, which as it agrees exactly in dimensions with the others, opened, no doubt, into a third apsidal chapel, like the others, whilst the entrance was at the west. This archway now leads into a chapel of very irregular form, part of which extends over the porch of entrance, in the arrangement of which one may trace a certain kind of analogy to that of the cathedral, though it is perhaps older. West of the choir is a nave, somewhat like a cone in plan, and surrounded by an aisle, from which it is divided by arches supported on slender shafts. The choir has a square domical vault, and the chapel over the porch a true dome, the pendentives under which are just like those of S. Fosca at Torcello. The apsidal chapels have semi-domes and the rest of the church has a waggon-vault of very irregular outline. An arcade against the walls of the side corresponds with that between the aisle and the nave. At the end of the nave is the tower, which was probably built at a slightly later date than the main building. The whole interior appears to have been

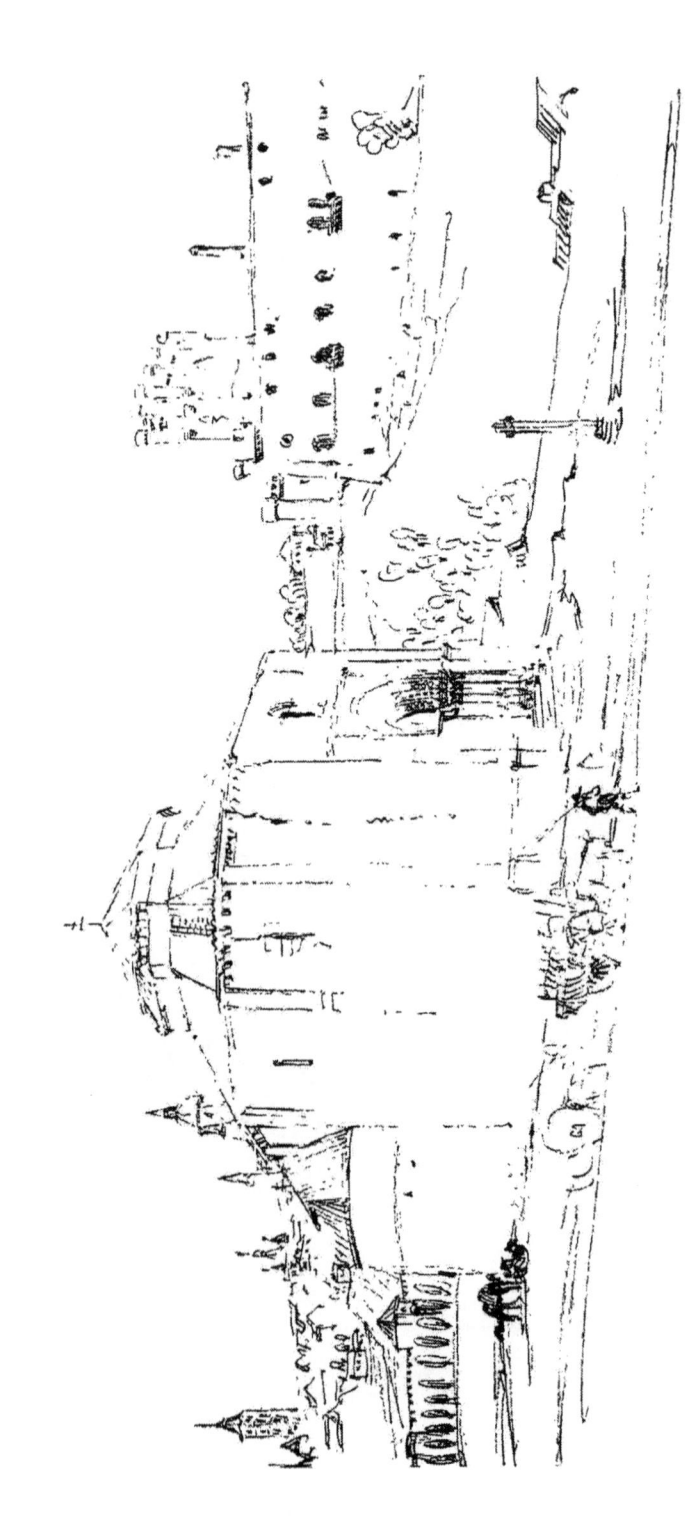

THE TEMPLARS' CHURCH AT SEGOVIA

richly painted, but faint indications only of this portion of the decoration remain. In the central dome there is a sitting figure of our Lord on the east side; emblems of the evangelists are at the angles, and angels and seraphim around our Lord. Below these is a line of single figures, six on each side — the four-and-twenty elders — and below this again are subjects, the whole combining together to make a very interesting example of the treatment of the Last Judgement. The dome of the chapel over the porch is also painted with our Lord, angels, and the evangelists.

The walls generally are built of lava, though a little white stone is used in the steeple and for the sculptured capitals.

The columns are very small, averaging eight inches in diameter, and decrease considerably in diameter from the base to the capital. The dimensions are exceedingly small, the central choir being only thirteen feet six inches in diameter, and the spaces between the principal columns in the nave varying from four feet to four feet nine inches. The effect is rather that of a crypt, but, in spite of its small size, it is solemn and religious.

The steeple suggests comparison, in some respects, with that of the cathedral; the arches are built with alternately light and dark voussoirs, and there is a peculiar spire-light rising out of the parapet, as to the antiquity of which I have my doubts.[1]

The only part in which any rich decoration has been introduced is the front of the porch. It has a semicircular arch, trefoiled above a horizontal lintel. The walls

[1] The spire-lights in the cathedral steeple are very similar, and the same form is seen in the steeple of the church of S. Marie des Chases, in Auvergne.

are richly inlaid, and there is also a good deal of sculpture. In the centre division of the trefoiled tympanum is an Agnus Dei, and there are figures kneeling and holding chalices within the cusps on either side. In the five divisions of the arcaded cornice are — in the centre our Lord, on His right S. Mary and S. John, and on His left S. Michael and S. Peter. The mosaic is executed with black tufa, red and white tiles, and a light yellow sandstone. I know no other example in this district of the use of tiles for inlaying, though M. Mallay mentions one at Merdogne in Auvergne, which he says is of the seventh century, though his dates are not always to be implicitly trusted; but at Lyon, in the extremely beautiful Romanesque domestic building called the Manécanterie, and at a slightly later date in the church of Ainay, in the same city, they are freely used and with admirable effect. Odo de Gissey, in his history of Le Puy, published in A.D. 1619, states that the first stone of S. Michel was laid in A.D. 965, and that the church was completed in A.D. 984, when Guy II. was bishop of Le Puy, "as one may learn from the ancient charter of its foundation, and from other manuscripts which I have read." Brother Théodore, in his *Histoire de l'Église Angélique de Notre Dame du Puy*, A.D. 1693, says that the first stone was laid in August, 962, and that his statements are "derived from the deed for the foundation of the church, and from the book of obits in the cathedral." These dates, if they refer to the existing building, can only do so to the central portion with its apses; the nave may have been added some time in the eleventh century, and the steeple, perhaps, in the course of the twelfth.

At the foot of the flight of steps which leads up to the picturesque entrance of this little chapel are the remains of a small detached building, probably a residence for a sacristan or priest.

Very near the Aiguille of S. Michel is a curious chapel. It is an octagon, with an apse projecting from the eastern face, the octagon covered with an octagonal domical vault, and the apse with a semi-dome. The walls are arcaded inside and out below the vault, the internal arches springing from engaged shafts in the angles. Some of the arches outside are cusped in the usual way, the cusping not starting from the cap with a quarter-circle, but with a half-circle, the same as all the rest. There are doors in the west and north sides, with tympana filled in with mosaic, and the wall in the spandrels between the arches outside is also inlaid. The exterior of the apse is not visible, but I found, on making my way into the cottage and barn built against it, that it is perfect and undamaged. The popular opinion at Le Puy is that the chapel is an ancient temple of Diana, a fiction which a minute's examination destroys. M. Didron maintains that it was a mortuary chapel, and he refers to the chapel of S. Croix, at Montmajour, as an example akin to this. M. Mérimée, on the other hand, says that the Templars had property in the Faubourg de l'Aiguille, and compares it to the similar oratory of the Templars at Metz, and he might have added the curious Templars' church at Laon as another case in point.[1]

This concludes my notice of early buildings in Le

[1] Also the octagonal church, surrounded by an octagonal cloister, of the Templars at Eunate in Navarre, and the church of Vera Cruz at Segovia.—G. G. K.

Puy, and I have no more than time to catalogue the church of S. Laurent, famous for the monument of the Constable Duguesclin, a large second-pointed building of poor character, and very Italian in its plan and design,[1] and with an enormous sham front; the gabled end of the hospital chapel, with its fifteenth-century bell-turret; a pretty little fountain, and a large number of picturesque houses of the fifteenth and sixteenth centuries; and a very scanty remnant of a gateway at the bottom of the town, called, I think, the Porte de Panessac, against the proposed destruction of which I find M. Aymard protesting only a few years back in the *Bulletin Monumental*.

About four miles to the north of Le Puy, close to the ruins of the magnificent castle of Polignac, is the Romanesque church of the village. This is parallel-triapsidal in plan, and the piers are planned, as are those in the cathedral, in the shape of a cross, with columns in the re-entering angles. The little church at Monistrol is a good example of the Le Puy style applied to a very small building; and the church at Le Monestier, which has many features of similarity to the cathedral at Le Puy, and is rich in early plate, ought not to be forgotten, but I am unable to speak of it from personal inspection.

I will now turn to the churches of Auvergne. Though numerous, they are so much alike in their character, details, and design, that a description of their peculiar-

[1] The elevation of one bay of the nave of this church is almost exactly the same as that of S. Petronio, Bologna, though of course on a very reduced scale. The plan is Italian also, the nave groining-compartments being square, whilst those of the aisles are very oblong; the contrary arrangement is, as I need hardly say, almost invariable in northern Gothic plans.

ities need not be so long as might be supposed. These churches all lie in a group together, Clermont-Ferrand being their geographical centre,[1] and to its north are Riom, Volvic, Menat, Mozat, and Ennezat; to the east Chauriat; to the west Royat and Orcival; and to the south S. Nectaire, S. Saturnin, and Issoire.

Beyond the bounds of the province, at Brioude, at Conques, at Toulouse, and in the church of S. Étienne at Nevers, there are, among many others, examples of precisely the same description of design and construction.[2]

It will be well to describe the general type of these churches, and then give a few notes as to particular examples. In plan they consist of a nave and aisles, western narthex and steeple, central dome and steeple, transepts with apsidal chapels on the east, and apsidal

[1] The cathedral of Clermont-Ferrand, a fine fourteenth-century church, is said to have been originally on the same plan as Notre-Dame-du-Port; excavations have proved this to have been the case. The present cathedral is almost precisely similar in plan to those of Narbonne and Limoges (see Viollet-le-Duc, *Dictionnaire*), and is said to have been commenced in A.D. 1248 by Bishop Hugues de la Tour.

[2] I give a list of some of the churches which either belong to or illustrate the Auvergnat type, with their dates, as nearly as I can ascertain them: — Conques, completed by A.D. 1060. S. Étienne, Nevers, commenced A.D. 1063, consecrated A.D. 1097. S. Eutrope, Saintes, consecrated in A.D. 1096. S. Genés, A.D. 1016–A.D. 1120. S. Front, Périgueux, A.D. 984 to A.D. 1047. Angoulême, A.D. 1109–1136. Fontevrault, A.D. 1100. S. Hilaire, Poitiers, A.D. 1049; Moustier-neuf, ditto, A.D. 1069–1096; S. Radegonde, ditto, A.D. 1099. Riom (S. Amable), A.D. 1077–1120. S. Sernin, Toulouse, *circa* A.D. 1150. Cluny, commenced A.D. 1089; consecrated A.D. 1131. Dorat (Hte. Vienne) and Bénévent (Creuse), *circa* A.D. 1150–1200. S. Germain-des-Prés, Paris, consecrated A.D. 1163. Le-Moûtier (suburb of Thiers), A.D. 1016. S. Saturnin, Volvic, Issoire, S. Nectaire, N.-D.-du-Port, Clermont, *circa* A.D. 1080–1160. Brioude, *circa* A.D. 1200. Orcival.

choirs with the aisles continued round them, and four or five apsidal chapels round the aisle. Under the choir is sometimes a crypt, in which, in addition to the columns under the columns of the apse, are four shafts which were intended for the support of the altar, and whose presence certainly seems to suggest that it must have been a baldachin and not merely an altar that they were designed to support.[1]

The naves are roofed with waggon-vaults, either with or without cross ribs below them. The aisles have quadripartite vaults without ribs, and the triforia above them are roofed with a continuous half barrel-vault, which resists the thrust of the vault of the nave, and is, in truth, a continuous flying-buttress. The triforia galleries are lighted with small windows, and this, the only light analogous to a clerestory, being entirely inadequate, the effect of the nave roof is generally very gloomy. The transepts are vaulted with barrel-vaults like the nave, and in one or two instances are divided in height by a sort of tribune level with the triforium. At Brioude, where this arrangement is seen, there is an original thirteenth-century open fireplace in the tribune, and M. Mérimée ingeniously suggests that the noble canons of Brioude, for they all had the rank of Count, were in the habit of hearing mass before a good fire; but it is fair to them to say that the fireplace is in the east wall, and that I saw no signs of an altar near it. The cross-

[1] St. Gregory of Tours (Hist. Francorum) says that in A.D. 440 a church was erected in Clermont by the Bishop Namacius, 150 feet in length, 60 feet wide, 50 feet high from the seat of the bishop to the vault; a circular gallery surrounded the choir, and on each side were two aisles elegantly constructed. The church was in the form of a cross, had 42 windows, 70 columns, and 8 doors. — *L'Auvergne au Moyen Age.*

ing under the tower is generally roofed either with an octagonal vault or with a circular dome with an opening in the centre. To resist the thrust of this dome on the north and south sides the upper vaults of the triforia are continued on between the transepts and the crossing, or else vaults of the same section are introduced at a higher level, where the central dome is raised (as it often is) higher than the barrel-roof of the nave. The western steeple, as well as the centre lantern, was sometimes domed; and that at Brioude is a most valuable example of the best type of dome in the district. The choirs are vaulted with waggon-vaults terminating with semi-domes, and the apsidal chapels are also each covered with a semi-dome. The columns are generally square, with half-columns engaged on three, and sometimes on four sides, the latter only when the main vault of the nave has transverse ribs below it. The columns round the apse are circular, and detached shafts against the apse walls carry the groining, and occasionally shafts are introduced inside and outside the window-jambs of the choir. In the nave and triforia, the windows are generally very plain with a label containing a billet-moulding, though the latter have sometimes, as at Notre-Dame-du-Port and Issoire, jamb-shafts. The capitals of the columns are carved with great richness, sometimes with foliage, but often with Scripture subjects. At S. Nectaire, for instance, perhaps the most elaborate of all these churches in this respect (M. Didron is my authority), the capitals round the apse have subjects from the New Testament, four on each capital. Frequently griffins and other animals are carved, and in one case, at Brioude, is a demon holding an open book on which is written the sculptor's name, which does not seem to be a very complimentary arrangement. It is in the earlier examples that sculpture of subjects and figures is commonly seen, and, as the style developed more towards Gothic, foliage took the place of subjects. The arcades are remarkable for their generally lofty proportions. They are of course not so lofty as pointed arcades, but they have seldom, if ever, the heavy and low proportion commonly found in the arcades of Romanesque buildings. The arches are generally semi-circular, and in the apses stilted.

The walls were probably covered with paintings of Scripture subjects. At Brioude there is some of this decoration remaining in a chapel dedicated to S. Michael in the gallery over the narthex. The semi-domes of the apsidal chapels in this church were also richly painted, and in one of them traces of colour exist all over the window-jambs. At Notre-Dame-du-Port, Clermont, in cleaning the nave, after removing seven or eight coats of whitewash, considerable traces were found of gilding on the capitals, and if this portion of the church was thus highly decorated, there can be no doubt that the colouring of the choir was at least equally sumptuous.

A stone seat is in some cases continued all round the walls of the apse and its chapels inside and out, and in one or two cases the iron grilles still remain. The only instance of the old pavement that I saw was at Brioude, where it is composed of black and white stone in chequers; but this is a mere fragment and of poor design.

The entrance to the crypts is by stairs from the transepts or crossing. The staircases to the upper portion of the building are variously placed. At Notre-Dame-du-Port they are in the middle of the north end of the aisles; at Brioude, in the transepts, and also at the west end; and in this church, an enormous wooden stair leads from the south door up to the chapel of S. Michael over the narthex.

On the exterior the designs are as much alike as in the interior. The aisle-walls are divided into bays by pilasters, above which arches are turned over the aisle windows, and then above are the windows lighting the triforia, which are generally more richly decorated than those below, and form part of an arcade with carved capitals and moulded bases. The walls are finished by a boldly-projecting cornice supported on large corbels. The transepts are buttressed at the angles, have a heavy engaged column in the centre, from which two arches spring, within which are pierced two windows; above these are other windows, either two or three lights, and the gable is either filled in with mosiac or pierced with more windows. It is on the exterior of the apse that the main effort at display is made, and the more ornate examples of the style, as Notre-Dame-du-Port, Issoire, and Brioude, are singularly rich in their effort. The two former examples are of very nearly the same date (about A.D. 1080 to A.D. 1130); the latter is considerably later (probably *circa* A.D. 1200). I will describe Notre-Dame-du-Port first. Here the transept-chapels are much lower than those of the chancel, and the latter (four in number) have cornices below the cornice of the aisle, and gable walls are raised on the aisle walls to receive their roofs, which would otherwise run back to the clerestory. There are windows between each of the chapels, and a great part of the beauty of the effect, both internally and externally, is to be attributed to this fact. I am not sure that the whole arrangement is not a modification of the original plan, for on close examination I found that the labels of the large windows between the chapels are returned and mitre with another label against which the chapels are built, and which might very well have formed part of an arcade pierced at intervals with windows. In the neighbourhood, about half-way between Clermont and Issoire, at S. Saturnin, there is a church precisely similar to what this would have been without its chapels, and the eccentric position of the chapels at Notre-Dame-du-Port, there being none opposite the centre,[1] would be just such as would have been rendered necessary if it had been desired to add them after the work had progressed somewhat towards completion. In any case, however, there could not have been any great interval of time between them, and probably the chapels and the clerestory are of exactly the same age. The whole of this apse is full of beautifully inlaid patterns, made with red and black scoriae and white stone. The enrichment is always confined to the walls above the springing of the windows, and does not generally extend quite to the cornice. The spaces between the corbels under the cornice are inlaid and the under side of the cornice is carved with a sunk pattern and in some cases appeared to me to have been coloured. Between the clerestory windows is precisely the same arrangement of shafts supporting a flat lintel under the cornice that I described in the first

[1] S. Hilaire at Poitiers and Angoulême cathedral have only four chapels.

portion of the clerestory of Le Puy, and here, as there, the recessed wall is all inlaid.

At Issoire the general scheme is precisely similar. Here, however, a square chapel juts out from the centre of the apse, and the question arises whether this is an original arrangement. The suggestion I should throw out here, as at Clermont, would be that this is the only original chapel, and that the others were added, just as those at that place may have been. In both these churches the buttresses are alternately rectangular and circular, and the latter are always finished with carved capitals.

S. Julien, at Brioude, is an example of a later date, but it adheres closely to the same type, save that there are five apsidal chapels; and though the windows are much more elaborate, having jamb-shafts and moulded arches, and being arranged in a regular arcade of triplets in the clerestory, there is much less positive effect of decoration owing to the comparatively small amount of inlaying.

The churches at Brioude and Issoire are both on a much larger scale and generally finer than Notre-Dame-du-Port.

Lastly, I come to the steeples of these churches. Of these there were generally one or two at the west end and one over the crossing. I believe that not one of those over the narthex now remains, though two or three have been recently rebuilt. Those at the crossing were treated in a singular manner. The eastern wall of the transept, carried up much above the height of the walls of the apse, forms an enormous mass for the support of the steeple, and is arched and pierced with windows, or inlaid. The steeples seem generally to have been octagonal, and to have consisted of two stages arcaded and sometimes shafted at the angles, and capped with stone spires sloping at an angle of about sixty degrees. The steeple at Issoire is quite modern, and I believe no authority existed for it. That of Notre-Dame-du-Port is also new, the finish having been a bulbous slated erection, with an open lantern at the top, only a few years ago. Ancient examples, more or less perfect, still exist at S. Saturnin, Ennezat, Orcival, and S. Nectaire, and all of these are octagonal. These churches tally with most other early churches in this feature of central steeples.

I have not yet mentioned the roofs. In those which I was able to examine, they are covered with slabs of stone, supported from the stone roofs without any use of timber whatever. The ridges are also of stone, elaborately carved, and the whole construction seems to be as imperishable in its scheme as anything I know of the kind.

The churches of the Auvergnat type present so little variety, and were built within so short a space of time, that a description of each of them in succession would be wearisome. Of course there are some variations. S. Amable at Riom, for instance, has the main arches pointed, whilst the triforium arcade is round-arched, and the vault of the nave is also pointed instead of round. The vault of the nave of Issoire is another example of a pointed vault. At S. Nectaire the usual piers in the nave have given way to columns. At Brioude, the style reached its perfection, and, indeed, I know few effects more striking in every way than that of the aisles round the choir; the roof, constructed as a regular barrel-vault and without any ribs, seems to be true in principle, and to carry the eye on even more agreeably than our ordinary Gothic vaulting of circular aisles, in which the eye is often distracted by numbers of conflicting lines of ribs. The wall arcades between the chapels recall the peculiar form of trefoil to which I have before had to refer, and it is again met in the triforium of the south side of Notre-Dame-du-Port.

The doorways appear to be of two kinds; one enriched with sculpture, the other with inlaid work. Of the former the south door of Notre-Dame-du-Port is a fine example. The opening is square, covered with a pediment-like lintel, on which are sculptured in low relief the Adoration of the Magi, the Presentation in the Temple, and the Baptism of our Lord. Above the lintel is a round arch, under which is a figure of our Lord, seated, with a seraph on either side. Against the wall, below the lintel on each side of the door, are figures of Isaiah and S. John the Baptist. In the much-altered church at Mozat,[1] near Riom, is a door of a somewhat similar kind, and both are very like the doorway in the north transept of Le Puy. At S. Nectaire is an example of a door with the tympanum filled in with mosaic.

The masonry is usually of wrought stones squared, but not very neatly put together. M. Mallay, the architect of Clermont, who has restored some of them, ascertained the curious fact that the stone-masons who wrought the stone for the arches, and wherever else

[1] At Mozat is a magnificent shrine of copper, enamelled, and at S. Nectaire a variety of precious relics, crosses, reliquaries, and the like, of which M. Mérimée has given a list.

superior work was required, marked their stones with the usual mason's mark, whilst those who wrought the stones for plain walling, jambs, and quoins, made no mark; and he found that precisely the same masons' marks occurred at Issoire and Notre-Dame-du-Port; whilst the details and plan of Orcival, a few miles southwest of Clermont, are again so identical with both of these, as to leave little room for doubt that it was executed by the same workmen; and I found another evidence of the way in which details were repeated, in some fine iron-work in the south door of Brioude, which occurs again at Orcival.

The arches are generally built with small stones of the same size and of even number, so as not to allow of a keystone. M. Mallay says that the mosaic work in the walls of these churches had wide joints of red mortar, projecting from the face of the wall. These mortar joints in the restored work appeared to me to be a bad modern device, and I think that the evidence in their favor ought to be very strong to be convincing.

The proportions of these churches are very similar. At Issoire, the width from centre of aisle wall to centre of nave column is one-fourth of the whole width, equal to the width from centre of nave columns, and to the diameter of the chapels in the apse, and one-half the height of the aisle, and one-fourth that of the nave. The height from floor to ridge is equal to the extreme width at base of walls. At Notre-Dame-du-Port the same kind of proportion exists, but from the outside of the buttress to the outside of the nave pier is one-fourth of the whole width.

I must now, before I conclude, say a few words as to

the date of these churches, for which M. Mallay[1] is inclined to claim rather too great an age. He dates most of them (conjecturally) in the tenth century, though he admits that buildings in which the pointed arch is introduced may be as late as the twelfth century; and he considers the date of Notre-Dame-du-Port, Clermont, as *circa* A.D. 863 to 868. He founds this belief on the fact that no lava was used in its construction, and that the mosaics in its walls were formed of scoriae found on the surface of the soil. He considers that lava was not used until the eleventh century, but he must also prove (which he has not done) that stone was never used in Auvergne after the lava had once been admitted. M. Mallay depends no doubt to some extent on the admitted date of the nave of S. Amable, at Riom, where the main arches are pointed, as A.D. 1077. But the presence of the pointed arch proves nothing as to date, for we see it long before this in S. Front, at Périgueux; and in every other respect there is no doubt that S. Amable presents every evidence of being older than Notre-Dame-du-Port, and others of these churches, in which none but round arches occur.

On either side of Auvergne there are other churches, of precisely the same character as to plan and mode of construction, the dates of which are pretty certain. One is S. Étienne, at Nevers, which was commenced in A.D. 1063, and completed and consecrated on the 13th December 1097. The plan of this church is similar in nearly every respect to that of the Auvergne churches. But, so far as one may judge of date from style, I should

[1] See M. Mallay's *Essai sur les Églises Romanes et Romano-Byzantines du département du Puy-de-Dôme*. Moulins, 1838.

have no hesitation in saying that this church must be older than either Issoire or Notre-Dame-du-Port. It is ruder in character, there is very little sculpture on the capitals, which are mostly a sort of rude imitation of Doric, and in the transepts there are not only round arches, but also some straight-sided.

At Conques, south of Auvergne, is another church on the same plan as S. Étienne, Nevers, in almost every respect, which there is little doubt was completed in the first half of the eleventh century, by the founder Abbot Odalric. Then again to the west there is the church of Moustier-neuf, Poitiers, commenced in A.D. 1069, and consecrated in A.D. 1096, which has a *chevet* evidently formed upon the same type as Conques; and at S. Hilaire, in the same city, consecrated in A.D. 1069, whilst the ground-plan of the chevet is just the same as that of Conques, the nave columns are analogous, there, to the half barrel-vaults of the triforium in Auvergne. Now none of these churches is earlier than the beginning of the eleventh century, and yet it is hardly credible that a province shut in as Auvergne was should have received a perfect and complete new style, or invented one and carried it to the degree of finish and perfection at which it had arrived when Notre-Dame-du-Port was erected, without our being able to trace, somewhere, the source from which it was developed. I believe, however, that its origin may be traced if we examine carefully the architecture of the church of S. Front at Périgueux, commenced in A.D. 984 and completed in A.D. 1047. This church, founded on the same type as, if not copied from St. Mark's, Venice,[1] exercised

[1] St. Mark's, Venice, was commenced in A.D. 977.

a vast direct influence on the architecture of the day. It is seen most clearly in churches which are, like itself, cruciform, without aisles, and covered with domes. The churches of Auvergne, and those other examples to which I have referred, seem to me to be clearly derived from S. Front, or from the Eastern models on which it too was founded. The east end of St. Mark's presents a circular wall, with a succession of semicircular recesses or apses in its thickness. S. Sophia contains the same feature, though differently treated. The Roman circular buildings which have so much in common with early Byzantine architecture have the same feature; and S. Vitale, Ravenna, whether it is Romanesque or Byzantine in its origin, is planned in a similar way. The architect of S. Front evidently copied his apses from these models, only converting the recesses of St. Mark's into chapels projecting from the walls.[1] The Auvergne architects attempted to combine the plan of the basilica, with its nave and aisles, with the features which were seen at S. Front. They retained its external wall and projecting chapels, therefore, but placed within them the cluster of columns round the apse forming an aisle between the chapels and the choir. By this simple and natural modification of the S. Front plan to meet the necessities of their triple-aisled churches they at once invented, one may almost say, the perfect French chevet. I know no other churches in France of the same age which appear to have suggested so much in this respect; and you will realize it if you compare their plans with, among others, those of

[1] Plans (to a uniform scale) of S. Mark's Venice, and of S. Front, Périgueux, are given in *Transactions*, Vol. IV. n.s. Illustn. xxviii., pp. 172-173.

Bourges cathedral, S. Pierre at Bourges, S. Martin at Étampes, Chartres cathedral, the destroyed church of S. Martin at Tours, and finally what is, I think, almost the best complete Gothic plan, that of Rouen cathedral. In every one of these we see the surrounding aisle lighted by windows between the chapels, and the chapels are distinct and well-separated on the exterior, precisely as in these older churches in Auvergne. These buildings, therefore, have great value, not only as illustrating a chapter of the history of our art, but because the chapter which they do illustrate is just one of the most interesting I can conceive; being that which explains how and by what steps Gothic architecture, of which, as our national style, we are so justly proud, was developed from the noble architecture of the old Romans and Greeks, an architecture to which we owe, among other things, this great debt of gratitude, that it naturally led up to, and rendered possible, a Westminster, a Chartres, an Amiens, and all the other glories of our Christian architecture.

You will have gathered that there are many similar features in the churches of the two provinces which I have been describing. They are shortly these: vaults and quasi-domes alike, and carried on the same kind of squinches or pendentives; the decoration with mosaics and its detail; the design and treatment of doors, either sculptured or inlaid; the form of trefoil cusping of arches, character of mouldings, sculpture, and decoration with painting, all of these are the same throughout both districts. The only marked difference, and it is important, is in the ground-plan, the cathedral of Le Puy having no chevet, but an east end derived from

Romanesque rather than Byzantine precedents; and the other churches in its neighbourhood are generally similar in their plan.

There are two important heads of my subject to be shortly discussed before I conclude. One of them refers to roofing; the other to coloured decoration. First, as to roofing. I have already explained how this was executed; let us now consider why the modes which we see were adopted. At S. Front the experiment was tried of covering a nave and transepts with a succession of domes resting on pendentives, and supported on pointed arches spanning the nave. These domes were the only covering of the church, and were visible on the outside as well as on the inside. At Conques, the architect, unable to carry domes on the comparatively delicate piers which were all that were required for the division of a nave from its aisles, contrived a barrel-vault for his nave, the thrust of which was resisted by the half barrel-vault of the triforium; a device not improbably obtained from Byzantine churches: for if we compare the section of S. Sophia with that of the crossing and central dome of Notre-Dame-du-Port, we shall find the semi-domes affording abutments for the great domes in the former, absolutely identical in their section with the half barrel-vault, which forms the abutment on the north and south sides of the central dome of the latter.[1] But it was impossible to obtain any light for a

[1] Mr. Fergusson gives a section of a church at Granson on the Lake of Neufchâtel, in which the aisles and nave are roofed in the same way as at Conques and in the Auvergne churches. He says that the date of this church is the end of the eighth or beginning of the ninth century, but I do not know what his authority for this very early date is.

clerestory roofed and supported in this fashion, and one is rather disposed to wonder how it was that so many churches should have been built on the same gloomy scheme. It was, no doubt, because in that part of France wooden roofs were thought to be undesirable, and no other economical way was seen of combining the nave and aisles with what was intended to be an indestructible stone roof. I need hardly say that at the same period, in the north of France, in Normandy, and in England, the nave was seldom, if ever, roofed with anything but timber, and the aisles only were vaulted in stone.

At Tournus, on the Saône, another device was adopted to serve the same end as the Auvergne roof, but admitting of a clerestory: this was the covering of the nave with a succession of barrel-vaults at right angles to the length of the church, and supported on bold transverse arches. But I doubt whether it was ever repeated on a nave, though there are several examples of aisles thus roofed;[1] and it was, no doubt, ugly and ungainly. The Le Puy architect devised yet another plan, which combined to some extent all the others, and this was, as I have explained, a succession of domical vaults, which, while it was much lighter and more practicable (owing in part to the difference of scale) than the S. Front plan of a series of genuine cupolas, achieved, nevertheless, much of the effect that was there gained. A very small portion only of the weight of the vault exerted a direct lateral thrust, and it was possible, therefore, to erect such a roof upon a clerestory; and though the

[1] The Abbaye-aux-Hommes, Caen, has its aisles roofed with transverse barrel-vaults.

transverse arches limit the height of the building in one respect, in another there is no question that the height is apparently much increased; for in looking down the interior it is impossible ever to see the apex of any of the domes, and the vault lost behind the transverse arches gains immensely in mystery and infinity, so as to produce the effect of a larger and loftier building than the reality. But, on the other hand, the disadvantages were great: the piers between the nave and its aisles were so large as to render the aisles nearly useless; and I can hardly wonder, therefore, that the example set here was not generally, if, indeed, at all followed.

It is doubtful where the kind of vault used at Le Puy was first devised. The central dome of S. Michel de l'Aiguille is, perhaps, the oldest of all, and this is, in fact, a square dome, if one may use the expression. The octagonal dome-vaults of the cathedral are probably a little later, but that over the crossing of the church of Ainay at Lyon may possibly be older. A comparison will make it evident that one is copied from the other; and if the Le Puy vault was derived from Lyon, it becomes possible to make the important inference that it was an Eastern influence travelling up the Rhone and distinct from that which is seen at Périgueux, to which we owe this kind of domed roof. Further evidence of this is found in the pendentives of the dome at Brioude,[1] which are identical in intention with the plan of the church of SS. Sergius

---

[1] I ought to mention that this dome and the western part of S. Julien at Brioude are much older than the choir, to which I have before referred in speaking of the date of the church.

and Bacchus, at Constantinople, and yet quite unlike the kind of pendentive common in churches of the S. Front type. They are, in fact, the Le Puy and Ainay pendentive reduced to the very simplest conditions. The invention of the flying-buttress adumbrated in, and possibly suggested by, the quadrant vaults of Auvergne, finally stopped these various endeavors after new forms of roofs, and set men to work to see how it might most readily be made to serve the boldest and most airy system of design and construction; and in the rage for these, that old system of roofing with domes, which had been, so far as is known,[1] first tried in France at Périgueux, and had afterward spread with such rapidity over a very large district, though with many modifications and variations, was entirely ignored or forgotten. Is it well that we too should ignore it? It is clear that the disciples of the Gothic school may claim it as their own with just as much truth as any other school can; and in some form or other it is often so attractive, so majestic on a large scale, so impressive even on a small scale, that few of us who have much work to do should altogether eschew all use of it, or treat it as though it were the exclusive property of the architects of Classic and Renaissance buildings. I do not feel, however, as most who write on the subject seem to do, that our domes must invari-

---

[1] This qualification is necessary, for the curious evidence which M. Verneilh has given of the existence in the tenth century of a Venetian colony at Limoges would be enough to make it probable that, though S. Front is the earliest complete example extant of a French domed church, others may have been built before it and that some of those which M. Verneilh supposes to have been derived from S. Front may really have been derived more directly from the East.

THE WESTERN PORCH, SAUMUR

ably be supported on what are called true pendentives. I think they are not beautiful, and I do not see that they are especially scientific. The S. Front pendentives are mere corbellings out of the wall, and in truth only imitations of pendentives. At S. Mark's they are formed with a succession of arches of brick work across the angle of the dome, though this construction is not visible, and these, I suppose, are all wrong; but they are very similar in their intention to the kind of pendentive which I have had to illustrate to-night, and which is in truth much more Gothic and picturesque in its character than the true pendentive, for it admits of any amount of decorative sculpture, and is really precisely similar in its object to the squinches under our own English spires.[1]

I will add but a few words as to the constructional polychromy which distinguishes the exterior of the churches throughout this volcanic district. So far as I have seen, it was never, save in Le Puy cathedral, admitted into the interior,[2] and this is much to be regretted, because it seems that the vaults of their naves, the domes of their crossings, and the semi-domes of their sanctuaries, would have afforded most admirable

[1] There is no end to the diversity of the countries in which they are found. In the cathedral at Worms there are squinches formed by semi-domes. In S. Nicodime at Athens they are identical with those of S. Étienne at Nevers, and the same form is repeated in the domical vault of the steeple at Auxerre cathedral. At Notre-Dame-du-Port, Clermont, the dome is circular, but the squinches below are octagonal in plan, and the circle (which is not, however, a true circle) is set upon the octagon.

[2] This statement must of course be made with caution, inasmuch as the invariable whitewashing of the interior makes it very difficult to say what was the exact nature of the decorations with which they were adorned.

fields for this kind of decoration. As I have stated, the walls were once covered with painting, and as long as this existed a mosaic of black and white and dull red would have been valueless; but now that the iconoclast, the whitewasher, and the restorer have done their worst, the want of some decoration on the otherwise bald surface of the vaults is painfully felt everywhere. Externally the coloured materials are used in two ways; sometimes the whole of the wall is built of the dark volcanic products, and patterns are obtained by the occasional use of white stone or by alternate courses of this and the darkest scoriae that can be found. Or else the walls generally are built of stone, and the patterns only formed with the dark material. Here, too, as is the case in all old examples of coloured constructions with which I have ever met, the colours follow the natural course of the construction. At Le Puy, for instance, the courses are alternately light and dark, producing bold horizontal bands of colour. The arch stones are continued generally in one line of colour all across an arch, even when it consists of several orders, and from the arch on into the wall. The bands of ornament are similarly arranged in horizontal stripes, generally placed where they will dignify and give value to some very prominent architectural member. They never occur below the line of the springing of an arcade, and are richest under cornices and between their corbels. And when we consider the date at which this inlaid work was executed, and compare it with what we know of our own art at the same period, or, indeed, with that of any other portion of the country which is now France, we cannot too highly extol its delicacy and grace and its carefulness of design and execution. I believe that we may regard the whole of the work in Velay and Auvergne as that of native artists. The detail of sculpture is, when compared with such work as is to be found in Provence, exceedingly rude. It is vigorous, indeed, but wanting in that extreme delicacy and refinement which marks the work of the early Provençal artists.

Were I to attempt to say anything about the buildings of a later date, it would be impossible to do more than give a catalogue, which would be as unintelligible as it would be tedious. I will only say, therefore, on this head, that Clermont cathedral well deserves careful study, and is rich in very fine glass; that at Montferrand may be seen as large a collection of mediaeval houses of all dates as in almost any small town that I know; that Riom possesses a fine S. Chapelle; and that in the abbey of La Chaise-Dieu is still preserved a very rare and complete series of tapestries of the sixteenth century. Besides these, a large number of articles of church-plate are to be found scattered up and down in the village churches, and all this goodly store of antiquities is set before you in a province whose physical features are so full of interest and beauty as in themselves to make a journey through Velay and Auvergne one which none will repent having undertaken.

APPENDIX

I. *S. Mary's, Stone*
II. *Churches in Northern Germany*

    I. *Lübeck*
    II. *Naumburg*
    III. *Erfurt and Marburg*
    IV. *Münster and Soest*
    V. *German Pointed Architecture*

I

SOME ACCOUNT OF THE CHURCH OF S. MARY, STONE, NEAR DARTFORD

(From the papers of the Kent Archæological Society, in Archæologia Cantiana, 1860)

HAVING given these preliminary notes, illustrative of the history of the church, it will be well now to give a detailed architectural description of the fabric, illustrated, as far as may be, by the discoveries which have been made in the course of its restoration.[1]

The church appears to have consisted at first of a chancel, nave with north and south aisles, western tower with the aisles prolonged on either side of it, and western porch. The only subsequent additions were, in the fourteenth century, a small vestry on the north side of the east bay of the chancel, and in the sixteenth century the Wilshyre chantry, in the space between the vestry and the east wall of the north aisle. In the fourteenth century (probably during the bishopric of Haymo de Hethe) the windows at the west end of the nave and aisles, and that in the west bay of the south wall, were inserted; and at the same time the tower-piers were altered. Probably they were, like the other piers throughout the church, exceedingly delicate, and were thought to be not sufficiently solid to carry the weight of the steeple; but at any rate it is clear that the piers, with their capitals, are not earlier than *circa* A.D. 1350, whilst the arches have earlier mouldings, and are of the same character as the rest of the church. It was at the same time that additional support was given to the eastern piers of the tower, by the addition of bold flying buttresses, spanning the aisles, and visible only on the inside of the church. The staircase to the tower, placed against the south-west angle, appears to me to have been added at the same time; whilst the upper part of the tower retains nothing

---

[1] The subject of this paper, the probable identity of the architect of S. Mary's with that of Westminster, interested Street greatly, and he refers to it often. The careful description of conscientious restoration has an interest for us as well. I have therefore reprinted the greater part of it without troubling the reader by indicating the trifling omissions.

but poor fifteenth-century work, and was probably entirely rebuilt at that time, if, indeed, it is not a work of the seventeenth century, undertaken after the fire which melted the bells, in A.D. 1638.

No other alteration was made in the church before the Reformation, and in 1638 the church suffered from the fire caused by lightning, mentioned by Hasted and in the Petitions to Parliament. The roofs throughout must have been burned, and, covered as they were with shingle,[1] it is not surprising that when once set on fire no part of them was saved. Traces of the fire are very evident, particularly on the stones of the tower arches, which are reddened by its action. We found also in the upper part of the aisle walls portions of molten lead, which had run into the interstices of the stone work at the time of the fire. The Petitions of the Parishioners of Stone give most exact information as to what happened before and after the fire; from them we learn (1) that before the fire the stone groined roof existed on the chancel, but was much dilapidated, and that the glass in the chancel-windows was in a sad state of decay: (2) "that the chauncell received little damage by the late fire," yet that a very large part of the brief-money, raised for the repair of the church, was "uncessantly wasted and bestowed on the same, soe that the church is like to remayne unfynished." This was in A.D. 1640, and I think we may gather from it the exact date of the alterations in the chancel. Its groined roof was taken down, its walls lowered some five feet, the tracery of the window in the north wall of the chancel partly destroyed in order to lower the walls, and the window then built up; the east window and probably one in the south wall destroyed, and imitations of perpendicular windows — poor in character, but nevertheless very good for their date — inserted in the place of the original windows in the north, east, and south walls of the chancel. The wall was rebuilt on either side of these windows with numerous fragments of the old groining ribs, thus affording the final proof that the windows were inserted and the groining taken down at the same time. This discovery was most grateful to me, inasmuch as it had been objected to the restoration of the original windows in the chancel, that those which we had to remove were fair examples of perpendicular work, and valuable in their way: in truth, they were examples of Gothic work in the years 1638–40, of no value at all in relation to the architecture of the rest of the church, though undoubtedly affording very interesting evidence of the undying love of Gothic architecture in this country, and of a not unsuccessful attempt at its revival.[2]

---

[1] Will of John Bokeland, p. 10.

[2] One of these windows is still left in the south wall of the chancel.

I have been unable to learn the exact date of the repair and re-roofing of the remainder of the church. The living was sequestered in A.D. 1650, and Mr. Chase must, I should think, in the ten years between the petitions and this date, have put his church into tenantable condition. The nave roof appears to be of about this date, and is framed with tie-beams, queen-posts, and purlines, with arched braces above the collars, and, though not very ornamental, has been re-opened, with the very best result on the general effect of the church. Subsequently to the erection of the new roofs, they had been churchwardenized, in the usual way, by the addition of plaster ceilings,[1] and in a less usual way, by the addition of a second roof over the other, and supported by it to the serious damage of the walls and piers.[2] The vestry seems never to have been repaired after the fire, and the Wilshyre chantry was roofed with a steep lean-to against the north wall of the chancel, and ceiled with a flat ceiling, for which I cannot be too grateful, as it made it impossible to insert a new window at this place in the A.D. 1640 restoration, and afforded me the only chance of discovering and restoring the original chancel windows. Knowing this before making my plans, I cut into the wall at this point, and was rewarded, even beyond my greatest expectations, by the discovery of the window-jamb, the monials, and a sufficient portion of the tracery to enable me to restore it exactly to its original design in every respect.

Having thus completed the notice of the alterations in the fabric, it is time to give a proper account of all its architectural peculiarities. The church is internally a rare example of a building as nearly as possible in the same state as when it was first built. For a village church its character is unusually sumptuous and ornate; and perhaps there is no example of any first-pointed building in England in which the grace and delicacy which characterize the style have been carried to greater perfection. It is impossible, indeed, to speak too highly of the workmanship or of the design of every part, and

---

[1] It appears from a note by Mr. Heathcote, a former Rector, in the parish book, that the church and chancel were ceiled in the year 1777. This is the only note in these books which refers to the building, if I except an entry in regard to the erection of a western gallery, which has been removed in the course of restoring the church. The old parish books are all destroyed, and no record exists earlier than the end of the last century.

[2] "Less usual," but not unique. The church at East Barnet afforded another example of the same mode of spending money in the palmy days of ample church-rates and irresponsible churchwardens.

close as is its similarity in many points to our glorious abbey at Westminster, it is a remarkable fact, that in care and beauty of workmanship the little village church is undoubtedly superior to the minster. This might well be, for with all its beauty, and with all its vigour, the mere execution of much of the work at Westminster is not first-rate, and hardly such as one might expect in so important a position.

The exterior of the church is exceedingly simple. There are doors at the west end and in the west bay of the north aisle. In front of the former there was a groined porch, of which a small portion of the springer for the groining on one side only remains; this was brought to light by the removal of a brick porch which had been erected in its place. The string-course above the door is of the thirteenth century, but the window above it of three lights, and three other windows of two lights in the western bays of the aisles, are of the fourteenth century, and the work, probably, of Bishop Haymo de Hethe. The north aisle door is remarkable for its rich detail and peculiar character. One of the orders is adorned with a chevron on one face and with dogteeth on the other, and the inner order is enriched with a rose. The dogteeth and the carving of the rose are quite consistent in character with the date of the church, and the chevron is no doubt a curious instance of imitation of earlier work, rather than evidence of the doorway itself being earlier than the rest of the church. The dogteeth are well developed, and the roses are similar in character to those in the internal jambs and arches of the transept doors at Westminster. The windows in the side walls of the aisles are all alike on the exterior, simply chamfered with labels over them, save the western window of the south aisle, where there is no label. Those at the east ends of the aisles are more important; that to the east of the north aisle being of four lights, and that to the east of the south aisle of two lights. The buttresses are very simple, of two stages in height, with plain weatherings. The north chancel aisle is the Wilshyre chantry, a late third-pointed work, with a battlemented parapet. The erection of this chapel involved the removal of one of the chancel buttresses, and in place of it a very bold flying buttress was erected, which spans the roof of the chapel, and adds much to the picturesque effect of this side of the church. Its erection in the fifteenth century was good proof, in the absence of any other, that at that time at any rate the groined roof of the chancel was standing, for otherwise its erection would never have been required. The removal of the high, tiled, lean-to roof of the Wilshyre chantry has exposed the flying buttress, the fine east window of the north aisle, and the still finer window in the north wall, restored, as I have said, in exact accordance with the window which I was so happy as to find there.

The vestry, which forms a continuation of the north chancel aisle, is lighted with two small windows, with ogee trefoiled heads. It was a roofless ruin, but now it has been re-roofed, and, as well as the chantry, is covered with a lead flat roof, which seems to have been the original covering, and has the advantage of not concealing any portion of the chancel. The east window is new, of three lights, corresponding in all respects with the restored north window, save in its dimensions, which are rather larger. So much of the east wall had been taken down and rebuilt, that it was impossible to decide exactly whether the east window was originally of three or four lights. I am rather inclined to believe that it was of four lights, for towards the end of the thirteenth century it is not at all unusual to find windows of an even number of lights in the east end; and the arcade below the window inside is of four divisions. Still, as there was no evidence whatever that this was the case, I thought it, on the whole, safer to repeat simply that in which I was certainly following the old architect, and the grandeur of the two restored windows is so remarkable that one need not wish them to be other than they are. In the south wall of the chancel one of the windows inserted *circa* A.D. 1640 still remains; it is of some value to the antiquary, and the contrast between it and the new windows, I hope, will amply justify the course I have adopted, in removing its two companions. The chancel buttresses are of great projection, but all their weatherings and finishings are modern, and for lack of funds remain for the present unaltered. The chancel is of two bays in length, and between its western buttress and the south wall of the nave is a space of six feet, through which, on the south, there appears to have been a doorway.[1] This would have opened into the western portion of the chancel, close to the chancel arch, and serves to prove that the chancel was not originally intended to be filled with wooden stalls.

Before the restoration of the church, the roof over the nave was steep, and flatter in its pitch over the aisles; and the chancel roof presented two gables towards the east, and had a gutter over the centre of the ceiling from end to end. All this is now altered. The nave roof has returned to its one uniform slope, simple and dignified in its effect; and the chancel walls, raised to their old height, so as to admit of the restoration of the groining, and surmounted by a high-pitched roof, finished with gable-copings and crosses, presents again the outline which no doubt it presented before the fire in A.D. 1638. The chancel roof is now much higher than that of the nave,

---

[1] John Bokeland, in his will, talks of the chancel door: I believe he means the door in the Rood-screen, from the nave into the chancel.

but I hope some day to remedy whatever defect there is in the external proportions of the building, by the removal of the poor modern battlements, and the erection of a wooden spire, shingled after the common Kentish fashion. The roof of the steeple was burnt in A.D. 1638, and the heat having been so great that the bells melted, it is fair to assume that the roof so burnt was rather a spire than a flat roof, and, indeed, Hasted's expression that the "steeple" was burnt, refers, it can hardly be doubted, to a timber spire.

I will now proceed to give a detailed description of the interior. The nave is entered by the west door, under the tower. The piers of the tower arches were re-cased in the fourteenth century, and the capitals, carved with poor stiff foliage at the same time, afford a marked contrast to the workmanship and design of the earlier capitals. The three arches under the north, south, and east walls of the tower are unaltered, of the same character as the arches in the nave, and evidently earlier than the piers which support them. The nave and aisles consist, in addition to the engaged western steeple, of three bays. The most remarkable feature in the design of this interior is the way in which the whole of the work gradually increases in richness of detail and in beauty from west to east. This will be seen immediately on an examination of the building itself. It is a very charming feature, and though one might have supposed that it would not be so very uncommon, suggested as it seems to be naturally by the respect which in almost all ages has been paid to the altar end of the church, I believe I may affirm that Stone church is unique in the studied way in which it has been done. At the risk of being very tedious, I give a detailed description of the interior, which will explain the variation of the design to which I have referred:

Western Bay (north side). — The window is of two lancets, with quatrefoil above: the inside arch chamfered, with a simple label returned, without any carving at bottom. The jambs are simply splayed: arches between nave and aisles moulded.

Middle Bay. — Windows of same shape, but the inside arch and the quatrefoil are richly moulded, and the internal jambs are finished with a moulding and stone shaft, with moulded base and carved capital. The label is enriched with dogteeth (it is the only label in the church in which they occur), and is terminated with heads of a queen on the right, and a king on the left, the latter much defaced.

The arches between the nave and aisles are moulded, but more richly than those in the western bay.

Eastern Bay. — Tracery of windows as before; the quatrefoil is not moulded. Jambs have two shafts (one stone and one marble) on each side, and a detached marble shaft in the centre. From these a richly-moulded rear-arch springs, with tracery of two lights corresponding with that of the windows. The whole composition of this window is of extreme beauty.

The arches between aisles and nave in this bay are richly moulded, and the centre of the soffit is enriched with a large dogtooth, making it much more ornate in character than the other arches.

The windows in the south wall correspond generally with those in the north, and exhibit the same graduation of enrichment. In the window in the eastern bay there are two circular bosses of foliage in the spandrels of the internal tracery;[1] in the opposite window these circles are plain sunk circles without any sculpture: and it appears that the architect, wishing to avoid the expense of sinking the whole surface of the stone, so as to leave the sculpture in advance of it, let in his bosses into a rebate in the stone work. This is a very rare mode of construction, but appears to be perfectly lawful.

The east window of the north aisle is richer than any of the others in the nave. It is of four lights, with two marble shafts in each jamb, and one in the centre monial. The tracery has quatrefoiled circles over the side-lights, under enclosing arches, and a large cusped circle in the head: the arch is extremely pointed. The mouldings throughout are more delicate than anywhere else in the church, and the large circle has a dogtooth enrichment. Externally this window is exceedingly simple: the rich mouldings of the interior being changed to a plain chamfer and broad flat tracery bars, very peculiar in their effect. This window was entirely blocked up, the cusping in the tracery concealed, and a four-centred brick arch under it connected the aisle with the Wilshyre chantry. We have taken away this brick arch, restored the old jambs and sill, and supported them on a flat stone arch. The flat roof of the chantry crosses the window just below the springing, and the portion above is to be glazed with stained glass, whilst that below is open through to the chantry. This was the best arrangement that could be made with the double object of preserving the old window in all its integrity and yet making the chantry available for use by the congregation.

The east window of the south aisle is much less magnificent than that last described: it is of two lights, with two marble shafts in each jamb, and an engaged stone shaft in the monial. Externally this window is remarkable for the curious freak by which the outer chamfer is gathered in with a curve some six inches on each side just at the springing.

The chancel arch is more richly moulded on the west face than

---

[1] The central shaft and part of the internal tracery of this window are destroyed, and we have been unable yet to restore them.

any of the others, and has a band of foliage enrichments of very magnificent character, very elaborate developments of the dogtooth; each being the general shape of a dogtooth, but filled up with intricate and beautiful foliage. Above the chancel arch on either side are two quatrefoils, within which are carved exquisite compositions of foliage, arranged in the form of a cross. Brilliant traces of red colour remain on these carvings. These quatrefoils were completely concealed by plaster before the restoration, and their re-opening has amazingly improved the effect of the wall above the chancel arch. The side walls of the nave are finished at the top with a moulded string-course, which is returned for about a foot on either side at the east, and was probably continued all round the church.[1]

The whole body of the church was covered with a coat of plaster. Most fortunately this had been put up by some pious plasterer, who, though he loved plaster well, loved the church better, and had no heart for hacking holes in its walls to afford a key for his plaster. The consequence was, that in an hour or two the whole of the walls were stripped of their covering, and displayed their old masonry fortunately intact. The walls above the arcades are faced with chalk, regularly squared and coursed on the side towards the nave, and built roughly on the sides toward the aisles, and are finished with a course of Gatton stone below the string-course at the top. The aisle walls are built of rough flint at their base; above this a course of squared chalk below the principal string-course, and on this there are traces of a thirteenth century pattern, painted in red. Above the string-course the walls are built entirely with coursed chalk, with quoins and dressings of Gatton stone.

The removal of the plaster between the two eastern windows in the south wall disclosed a portion of an arcade. This seems never to have been completed, for whilst the lower stone has the dogtooth enrichment of the arch finished, the upper stone has it simply blocked out in the square: we found a corresponding fragment of arcading built into the upper part of the chancel wall, and whilst that which exists in the south wall appears to have been always in the same place, it seems pretty clear that the other piece was never fixed near it. The conclusion at which I arrive is, therefore, that these are fragments of a work commenced but abandoned for another scheme at the very time the work was going on.

Before going to the chancel a note should be added here, as to the painted decorations which have been discovered. A portion of

---

[1] I see no evidence of the existence of a clerestory; and the columns are so delicate that I think it is impossible that it can ever have been intended to erect one.

these are architectural in their character, the rest pictorial. Among the former, is the running pattern forming a border under the string-course in the south aisle. This I hope to continue all along the wall, it being sufficiently clear in the one place where it occurs to warrant restoration; and I have no doubt of the importance attached by the old architect to decoration on a line so marked as that of the principal string-course. There is also a faint border round the chancel arch, painted in red, but rather later in its character than the string-course. The pictorial decorations are all on the north aisle wall. Between the first and second windows is a large sitting figure of the Blessed Virgin Mary nursing our Lord: S. Mary has a veil, and is not crowned, and has a red robe and a blue cloak. She is seated on a throne with shafts at the angles, and the canopy is a gabled trefoil with triple pinnacles on either side. As far as I can judge, this work appears to be very late thirteenth century or early fourteenth century work, and was evidently rich in colour. The painting between the two next windows is so damaged that I have been unable to decide what it represents. On the wall east of the eastern window is another figure of the Blessed Virgin Mary, also nursing our Lord, and seated under a trefoiled canopy. No other traces of painting remain, save the colour, already mentioned, on the sculptured crosses over the chancel arch, and some painted crosses on the east wall of the chancel.

From this description it will be seen how systematically all this portion of the work has been designed: subject to the carrying out of the general scheme there are, however, some small peculiarities which may point, either to the Gothic love of variety on the part of the architect, or (and as I think, more probably) to the fact that portions of the work may have been special offerings or donations from different persons. Certainly I see no other way of accounting for the repetition within a few years of two copies of the same painted subject on the north aisle wall.

It is to be noticed that there is no sign of a piscina in either of the aisles. I thought it possible at first that the arcade we discovered in the south aisle might have formed a portion of the sedilia for an altar in the aisle, but I hardly think now that this could have been the case.

The chancel consists of a western bay of seven feet in depth, from east to west, and east of this of two bays each 21 ft. 2 in. wide and 16 ft. 3 in. long, from centre to centre of the groining shafts. The west bay has no windows, but there is, as I have said, a trace of a doorway in the south wall. The other bays have each three divisions of wall arcading on marble shafts, and the east wall has four divisions of the same arcade. The spandrels of these arcades are filled in with sculptured foliage, so beautiful and delicate in its execution, and so nervous and vigorous in its design, that I believe it may safely be pronounced to be among the very best sculpture of the age that we have in this country. I shall have to enter again upon the subject of this portion of the work, in comparing it to the sculpture at Westminster. The work at Stone appears to me to be all by one man, and he seems to have been, if not the best of the Westminster sculptors, at any rate equal to the best.

There are in this chancel twenty-one of these spandrels, all different in design, but all nearly equal in merit. The aggregate amount of work bestowed here is as nothing compared with that which has been lavished in scores of cases on sculpture in our new churches: yet is there any one modern work which possesses a tithe of the value of this work? And would it not be far better to limit our nineteenth century carvers of foliage to work rather less in amount, and considerably more in merit, than that which they are wont to give us? The sculpture at Stone was no contract work: no exhibition of the greatest skill in covering the largest possible number of stones with the greatest possible quantity of carving: and it was executed with a delicacy of hand, a fineness of eye, a nervous sensibility so soft, that no perfunctory imitation can ever be in the least degree likely to rival its beauty. The small bosses of foliage which adorn the smaller spandrels in this arcade are very well carved; and it is worthy of remark that the same design is repeated several times. No. 1 is repeated four times, No. 2 six times, and No. 3 seven times; besides which the same design is used, simply reversed. It looks as though a model had been cut, and then copies made of it.

The walls of the chancel are only 2 ft. 3½ in. thick, but the great size of the buttresses amply compensated for this, and preserved them from suffering at all by the thrust of the groining. Before the restoration the state of the chancel was a sad falling off from its old state. The arcade at the base of the walls was perfect all round. The lower part of the groining-shafts remained, as also did the whole of a cluster of shafts on each side between the short western bay already mentioned and the next. The groining was all destroyed, but marks of it remained against the wall, and it was easy therefore to obtain its exact section. The treatment of the western bay was peculiar. It was clearly never covered, as the rest of the chancel was, with a quadripartite vault. The mark of a vault remained against the wall above the chancel arch, whilst the side walls showed that a barrel vault had sprung from them. The cluster of three shafts between this bay and the next remained to be explained. One of them only was the groining-shaft answering to the others; but upon a very close examination of a fragment of the wall above them and of the marks on the caps themselves, I was able to ascertain beyond doubt that the two other shafts had carried an arch moulded on the east face, the soffit of which, continued westward, formed the pointed barrel-vault over the western bay. This has now been all restored, and with so much certainty as to all its parts, that I trust it will not be opened to the criticisms to which too many restorations are liable, of being rather ingenious than true. I should mention that the new groining-ribs are of the same section as the old. The window in the north wall has been exactly restored after the old remains, some of which have indeed been incorporated with the new work. It is of three uncusped lights, with tracery composed of three cusped circles. The cusping was let into a groove, and a sufficient number of fragments remained to give the exact number of cusps, etc. On the exterior the jamb has two engaged shafts, with caps and bases, and on the inside the monials are well moulded and have each a detached marble shaft, whilst the jambs have two marble shafts and are richly moulded. Internally the arch and tracery mouldings are very delicate, whilst externally they consist of bold chamfers and hollows only. The detail of the sculpture of the capitals of the monials was managed with rare skill, as seen by a fragment found in the north wall. This window is now treated in the same way as that at the east end of the north aisle, being partly below the roof of the Wilshyre chantry. An old arch existed behind the arcade under it, and this has been replaced by one of stone, so that the chantry is now sufficiently open to the chancel for the purpose of use by the congregation.

On the south wall of the chancel is the old piscina, under one of the divisions of the arcading. The arcade is continued across the east wall of the chancel, in four divisions; and treated exactly in the same way as at the sides; it is pretty clear, therefore, that it can never have been intended to place the altar against the wall, and it was no doubt brought forward a few feet (with perhaps a low wall or reredos behind it) in the way so common in the case of apsidal chancels, and of which we have examples at Arundel and at Warfield in the case of square-ended chancels. In the two divisions of the arcade we found, on removing the whitewash and plaster, a painted cross pattee, enclosed within a circle: it was red on a white ground, and outlined with black. Whether this was a dedication cross, or only painted in connection with the altar, it is impossible to say.[1]

---

[1] I cannot express my vexation at finding that in spite of my earnest injunctions to the workmen to be careful, this painted cross was destroyed. It is often absolutely impossible for an architect to stop wilful destruction of this kind. I have sometimes thought that it might be a good plan to draw up a contract for church restorations, inflicting a heavy fine on the contractor for any such destruction of any old feature.

In the chancel floor are some ancient grave-stones, among which those of John Lumbarde, Rector, a fine brass cross of the fourteenth century, and the little brass of Sir John Dew, are well known, and of much value. They have been carefully relaid in connection with a new pavement round the altar. The altar-rail has also been brought forward; the altar set on a foot pace about three feet from the east wall, with a low stone perpeyn wall at its back, capped with marble, and showing the old arcade above it.

It remains to mention a few ancient fragments which have been discovered during the progress of the works.

They are:

1. A fragment of very richly cusped thirteenth-century tracery, very delicately moulded. This has not formed part of a window, and perhaps belonged to the reredos, if there was one.

2. A fine head of a monk (small).

3. A half-destroyed carved capital of a large shaft clustered of three: it looks like the capital of a groining-shaft, but agrees with nothing in the church.

4. One moulded marble capital, and two fragments of a marble monial, with engaged shaft inside and out. There is no existing marble monial in the church, and the only suggestion I can make is, that possibly the same increase of enrichment that I have noticed was carried on to the east end, and the east window executed with monials entirely of marble; but on the other hand, this monial, though of marble, is not so rich in detail and moulding as the stone monial, with its detached marble shaft in the north window of the chancel.

5. A portion of the lower part of a sitting figure of our Lord. This figure is that of a man about four feet six inches in height. The feet are naked and pierced with the wounds. There is no sign of any place from which such a figure could have been moved. Its date is about that of the church.

6. A spandrel of an arcade, sculptured with a portion of the resurrection of the dead. It very nearly fits the spandrel of the arcade discovered in the south wall of the south aisle, and, in order that it may be preserved, I have had it placed there. The treatment of the bodies coming out of the coffins is good, and the work is about the date of the church.

7. A large number of fragments of the groining-ribs of the chancel, of the windows, etc. etc., were also found. The bulk of all these were built into the upper part of the chancel walls, and into the gable wall above the chancel arch, and were no doubt placed there at the time of the alterations of the building, after the fire in the seventeenth century.

Of the works recently executed in the church, it will be sufficient to say, that the nave has been re-seated with open seats, and paved with the best red, black and buff tiles. The eastern part of the chancel floor has been repaved with marble and encaustic tiles, and want of the necessary funds alone has prevented the re-laying of the remainder of the chancel floor and the completion of the seats. The lectern for the Bible is of oak. The whole of the chancel has been groined in stone and chalk: the groining-ribs being of Caen stone, and the filling in of the vault of chalk. I have been unable, on account of the cost, to introduce any bosses at the intersection of the groining-ribs; we found no remains of any, but as they were used in the groining at Westminster Abbey, I should have preferred their introduction. On the same account the wall-ribs are chamfered, not moulded. The other ribs are exactly copied from the old fragments found in the chancel wall, and I was also able to obtain the exact height of the vault, and as nearly as possible the mouldings of the bold arch on the eastern face of the waggon-vault at the entrance of the chancel. The east and north windows of the chancel are both new, and copied from the old fragments found by me in the north wall. A pulpit of stone, alabaster and marble, carved by Mr. Earp, and the gift of the family of the late Archdeacon King, is placed in the north-east angle of the nave. The window in the east bay of the north aisle is filled with stained glass, and is to form one of a series, those in the north aisle illustrating the miracles of our Lord, and those in the south aisle the parables. This window is the gift of Mrs Cooper, and is executed (as are the others) by Mr. Wailes, of Newcastle. The east window of the north aisle is a memorial window to the late Archdeacon King, erected by his parishioners: and the subject is, our Lord in Majesty, with angels on either side. The east window of the chancel is also a memorial to the Archdeacon, and erected by his family; it contains a long series of subjects from the life of our Lord, in medallions, and is richly treated in Mr. Wailes's usual style; and it is only to be regretted that in brilliancy of colour and nervousness of drawing he does not yet by any means equal the old school of painters on glass. The altar-cloth is of red velvet, embroidered in the old manner by Mrs. G. Murray.

I referred, in the earlier part of this paper, to the similarity between the detail of the work at Stone and that of the earlier portions of Westminster Abbey; and before I conclude I will, as well as I can, explain the extent of this similarity. Few subjects are of more interest to me, and I suppose to all students of our ancient architecture, than this of the extent to which the work of the same artist may be traced in different buildings. I have been able, in a considerable number of cases, to prove pretty clearly what I now wish to prove about Stone and Westminster;[1] but I need hardly say that the evidence is always of a kind which it is extremely difficult to give in writing; though it is difficult to resist its force if the two works are examined one after the other, and their special peculiarities carefully noted. I will endeavour however to show the existence of something more than the ordinary likeness of all works of the same date and style, between Westminster Abbey and some portions of Stone church.

I. *The Arcades round the Chapels* of the choir at Westminster are almost identical in shape and design with that round the chancel at Stone. The proportions of their trefoil cusps are very peculiar, and as nearly as possible the same. The spandrels are filled with foliage carved exactly in the same spirit. The labels are terminated upon small corbels level with the capitals: a very unusual arrangement. The arcades rest upon a stone chamfered seat; and the arch-moulds, though not the same, are of the same character, and both of them undercut at the back.

II. *Window Tracery.* — The original window tracery at Westminster is the same as at Stone. The windows in the south triforium of the nave (four eastern bays) are of precisely the same character as the window discovered in the chancel at Stone. The latter are remarkable for the great width of the light (3 ft. 1 in. and 3 ft. 10 in. in the clear), and this is very characteristic of the Westminster windows. The Stone windows are remarkable also for very broad chamfered tracery-bars on the outside, corresponding with very rich mouldings on the inside. The triforium openings at Westminster are treated just in the same way on the side next the triforium, and a comparison of the triforium of the choir and north transept there with the east window of the north aisle at Stone would well illustrate the identity of character. The stone cusping in both is let into grooves in the way common in early tracery.

III. *The Sculpture of Foliage* is very similar in both churches. The spandrels of arcades are treated just in the same way: at Westminster sculptures of subjects are introduced here and there in place of foliage; at Stone all the spandrels are filled with sculpture of foliage; but we found in the thickness of the wall one spandrel sculptured with figures, which appears never to have been used.[2]

---

[1] See particularly papers by me on *Some Churches in Kent, Surrey, and Sussex,* in the *Ecclesiologist* of 1850, and *On the Middle-Pointed Churches of Cornwall,* in the *Transactions* of the Exeter Architectural Society, vol. iv.

[2] There are one or two points which appear to me to make it possible that the sculpture of foliage was not done at Stone, but wrought elsewhere and sent there to be fixed. The northernmost spandrel in the east wall should be examined with a view to this point.

The foliage of capitals is generally similar, and the very remarkable bosses of foliage in the chancel arch at Stone, arranged in something of the outline of an enormous dogtooth, are all but repetitions of the similar archivolt enrichments in the triforium of the north transept at Westminster. The roses round the archivolt of the south door at Stone are of the same kind as those round the inside arches of the north transept doorways at Westminster.

The foliage carved in the form of crosses in the quatrefoils over the chancel arch at Stone are repeated in a quatrefoil over the door in the cloister at Westminster, leading to the private apartments of the abbat. The crosses are, of course, not identical in their treatment; but the idea is the same, and one of rare occurrence.

IV. *The Materials* used in the Abbey and at Stone are as nearly as possible the same. The wrought stone work is executed in Caen stone and Gatton stone, and a great deal of chalk is used for wall-lining and groining, and all the shafts are of marble.

V. Finally, the same general system of proportion is observed in the minster and the village church. In both, the width from the aisle walls to the centre of the columns is equal to half the width of the nave. At Westminster the height is given by three equilateral triangles, whose base-line is the width across the nave from centre to centre of the columns; and two of these triangles give the height for the springing of the groining, and the third the height of the groining to its apex. At Stone, if we erect triangles on the same base-line, the first gives the top of the capitals of the nave arcade; the second, within very little, the height of the top of the wall; and the third may very well be supposed to have marked the height of the ridge of the timber roof. The width of the bays in the nave of Stone is equal to the diagonal of half the width of the nave; and the width of the bays in the chancel is equal to the diagonal from the centre of one column to the centre of the nave or aisle opposite the next column; whilst the height of the chancel is given by two triangles similar to those in the nave, whose base is the width from centre to centre of the groining-shafts.

I do not wish to lay too much stress on any one of these points of resemblance: it is not to be expected that two churches, built by the same architect, so unlike in size, in position, and in dignity, should show anything more than some general resemblance of character; but I cannot help thinking, that when I have pointed to such a general agreement in the proportions, the materials, the sculpture, and the details, as we find at Stone and Westminster, it would be almost enough to decide the question, even without the final and (as it appears to me) conclusive evidence afforded by the all but exact identity of the cusping and the general similarity of design in the wall-arcades in the two churches, which must either have been copied one from the other, or designed by the same architect.

II

CHURCHES IN NORTHERN GERMANY
(*From the Ecclesiologist, 1854–1857*)

I
THE CHURCHES OF LÜBECK

Three old cities far apart, across the whole breadth of a continent, enable us to form a fair judgement of what the whole of Europe may have been in the palmy days of the Middle Ages. They are Lübeck, Nuremberg, and Verona; each telling its own tale, each marked with the impress of national peculiarity, and each remarkable, among other things, the one as the city of brick work, the next as that of stone, and the last as that of marble. In Lübeck nothing but brick was ever seen; in Nuremberg, stone was used with an excellence seldom rivalled; whilst in Verona, though brick was most beautifully used, the great aim of its architects was ever to introduce the marbles in which the district around it is so rich. Each of these cities deserves a full and ample study, for each teaches its own lesson, and that a lesson scarcely to be learnt elsewhere; and if this evening I give you such notes as I was able to make in the course of a short sojourn last autumn in Lübeck, it is not because I do not value Nuremberg and Verona much more, but because it would seem that if one were to write of all three, this is the one with which one should commence, as nearest to and most connected with our own country and style of architecture, and because its features of interest are in some degree less remarkable than those of the others, and one would wish to reserve the best for the last.

In one respect, moreover, two of these cities may well teach us a lesson. Nuremberg and Lübeck were to the world in the Middle Ages what London, Liverpool, and Manchester are to the world in this age: the very centres of all commerce for all Europe; and we may surely not do amiss if we take to ourselves, and ponder well upon, the lesson which the singular difference between their earnestness in matters of religion and ours ought to teach us. There was in these two old cities such an appreciation of the value of religious ordinances, and evidently so very great a readiness to provide places

ROOD-SCREEN IN LÜBECK CATHEDRAL

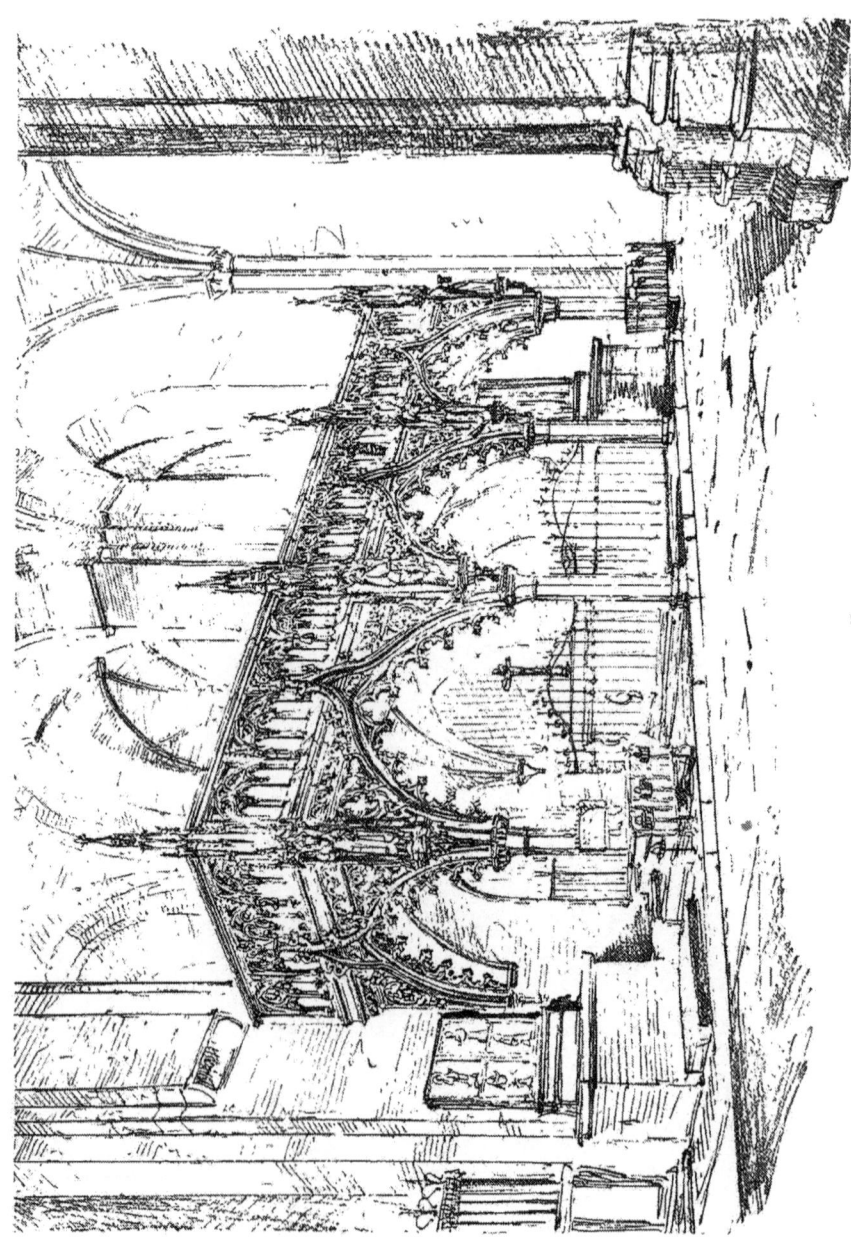

for their due celebration, that one cannot without a blush think upon the vast difference which such a city as Manchester displays, with its almost countless thousands of poor wretches uncared for and unthought of, and without any power of putting foot even in the sanctuaries of their God.

In the great Middle Age cities this never could have been the case, for apart from the fact that their churches stood with their doors ever open, while ours are ever jealously kept shut, they were so vast and spacious, and so crowded together, as it seems to us, that there never could have been a real difficulty in finding some home for the feet of the weary, how poor and how miserable soever they might be!

And Lübeck still shows this most grandly: you approach by a railway through an uninteresting country, passing one of those lakes which give much of its character to this dreary part of Germany, and suddenly dashing through a cutting, and under the shade of fine patriarchal trees which adorn on all sides the outskirts of the old city, you find yourself in such a presence of towers and spires as can scarce be seen elsewhere in Christendom. A succession of great churches standing up high and grand above the picturesque tall old houses which fringe the margin of the Trave, two of them presenting to us their immense west fronts of pure red brick, each finished with two great towers and spires, whilst others on either side rear their single spires and their turrets high against the sky, and here and there detached turrets mark where stands some other old building soon to be made acquaintance with; and all of these forming the background, as you first see it, to the most picturesque and grand old gateway — I am bold to say — in Europe, gives one a wonderful impression, vivid but dreamlike, and reminding one of those lovely cities with which Memling and his contemporary painters so often delight our eyes.

The plan of the city is simple enough. One great street runs the whole length of the peninsula on which it stands, from north to south, finished by the Burg-Thor, a fine old gateway, on the north, and by the cathedral and its close to the south. Right and left of this main street are a multitude of streets descending to the water which almost surrounds the whole town, and on the other side of the water are immense earth-works, rising really into respectable hills, and said to be the largest earth-works known; happily these great mounds — no longer useful for purposes of defence — are eminently so for ornament, and planted with great trees and laid out with walks and gardens form one of the most pleasant features of the place; on the outer side of those earth-works another line of water gives one certainly a very watery impression of the whole city.

The main features of interest to an architect are in the principal street. Beginning at the extreme south is the cathedral with its two towers and spires standing alone and forlorn in the most deserted part of the town, and even in the busiest days of Lübeck scarcely so near to the bulk of the people as a cathedral should ever be; then on either side we pass the churches of S. Giles and S. Peter, and going along under the walls of the picturesque old Rathhaus find ourselves close to the east end of the Marien-Kirche — a cathedral in dignity of proportions and outline, and here superior to the cathedral in its central position and in its greater height and general magnificence; next, the Katerinen-Kirche is left a few steps to the right, then S. James's is passed, another tall spire, and then the west front of the very interesting Heiligen Geist Hospital; and a hundred yards further on we are in front of the relics of the Burg-Kloster, and close to this find ourselves at the Burg-Thor, a picturesque gateway second only in effect to the Holsteiner gate which I have before mentioned as terminating one of the cross streets which lead to the railway. The Burg-Thor stands just at the neck of the peninsula, and beyond it is the Burg-Feld, a wood intersected with paths, and looking rather like the Thier-Garten outside the Brandenburg gate at Berlin.

And now to describe the architectural beauties of the town we must go back to the cathedral, and as in duty bound begin with what is at once the oldest and the chief in rank of the ecclesiastical buildings.

The tradition is that this church, dedicated in honour of SS. John Baptist and Nicolas, is built on the spot where Henry the Lion, when engaged in the chase, fell in with a stag having a cross growing between its horns and a collar of jewels round its neck, with the produce of which the church was first in part built. There is some account of a church older than this, and octangular in form, having existed near the cathedral about the middle of the seventeenth century; it cannot however have been older by many years than some parts of the cathedral, as the first foundation of the present city seems to have been laid in the middle of the eleventh century, and the cathedral was consecrated in A.D. 1170 by Henry, the third Bishop of Lübeck, having been founded by Henry the Lion, who in A.D. 1154 translated Gerold, Bishop of Oldenburg, and made him the first Bishop of Lübeck; possibly the destroyed octangular church may have been the baptistery of the cathedral, as at this date baptisteries of this shape are not unfrequently met (e. g. at Cremona and Pisa), and I know of but one case of a church of such a plan.

Of the present cathedral, the most ancient portions appear to be the lower part of the steeples and the main arcades throughout. These are all Romanesque, though under the original arches pointed arches have been since inserted. The piers are heavy and square, and the whole effect is poor and ungainly.

Next in date is a magnificent porch on the north side of the north transept, which is altogether about the best piece of architecture in Lübeck, and remarkable as showing much more freedom in the use of stone than is found elsewhere. The shafts are of marble, and the arches and groining-ribs are all of stone, and, on the exterior, stone capitals and shafts are also used, whilst the brick work is far superior to that in any of the later examples. I fear I must say that this one remnant of the art of the thirteenth century is by far the most beautiful thing now left in the city. The sculpture on the inner door is very masterly in its character, but unfortunately the whole porch is now most neglected and uncared for.

Besides this porch there is little to notice in the exterior, save that the brick work of the transept front over the porch savours of the Italian mode of treating gables with deep cornices and traceries, and that the two great brick steeples at the west end are fine examples of a kind of steeple of which the city possesses however others much finer. The spires are not ancient; the whole exterior is of red brick.

In the interior of the church the most interesting features are the choir-screen and loft, and the rood. The screen stands at the east side of the transept crossing, whilst the rood is supported on an elaborately carved beam, which spans the *western* arch of the crossing, and the effect is most singular and certainly very piquant; the whole being in a very late but good style, with figures remarkably well sculptured. Under the screen is an altar, and on either side still remains another. They are of stone supported on brick work, and there is no mark of piscina, or of lockers, or places for relics in them. The rood, and the figures of SS. Mary and John, are on a very large scale, so that altogether, with their supports, they reach nearly the whole height of the arch under which they stand.

There are also throughout the nave of the cathedral a number of very curious seats; they vary a good deal in detail, but their outline is similar, and their effect rather striking; I confess, however, that I was sorry to see examples of fixed seats of such a date in a cathedral church. In the nave there are some pendents for candles; one an angel holding a light, and strongly reminding one of those beautiful angels with candles above the stalls in the choir of S. Laurence at Nuremberg; and the other, a much more elaborate composition, and coloured richly in gold, red, and blue; it has two sitting figures of Bishops under canopies, and bears three very large candles. One of the great treasures of this church is the magnificent brass to Bishop Johann von Mull, and Bishop Burchard von Serken, who deceased in 1350 and 1317. I was unable to make so careful a rubbing of this magnificent brass as I could have wished, but I have done enough to show how grand it is, and how very similar in its details to the famous Flemish brasses which remain at Lynn, S. Albans, North Mymms, Wensley, and Newark. Like two of these, of which we fortunately possess rubbings, it is remarkable for being one great engraved plate, and not, as was the English custom, a plate cut out to the shape of the figure, and then inserted in an incised slab; and compared with the S. Albans brass, which hangs by its side, it will be seen that the detail is so exactly similar, that there can scarcely be a shadow of a doubt that they were both engraved by the same man. It is perhaps altogether the finest of the whole, and if so, perhaps the finest brass in Europe. It is appreciated by the sacristan, who demands a fee for lifting up a cover which he keeps on it, and whose temper was of so difficult a kind that I almost despaired being allowed to rub it. However, by persevering, I at last succeeded.

Lastly, there is in a chapel on the north side of the nave a most magnificent triptych by Memling, almost unequalled by any work of his I have ever seen. It has double shutters; on the outer, figures of SS. Blaise, Giles, John, and Jerome, and inside are painted the Crucifixion, and a number of subjects from the Passion of our Lord, all worked together into one grand picture in a manner favourite with painters of Memling's time, and not to be contemned because no longer the custom of our artists, inasmuch as Memling, Van Eyck, Giotto, and their contemporaries all did it, and what they did we may well believe not to have been done without good reason. The expression of all the faces is most careful, and the skill with which portraits are preserved throughout all the subjects, as e. g. of S. Peter, of Judas, and of our Lord, is very marvellous. They were obviously painted from actual faces, and not imagined. The colour of the whole is generally very rich and deep, the drawing very vigorous, and the whole forms one of the most magnificent specimens it is possible to imagine of the early German school.

I have forgotten to say that the font in the cathedral is of metal. It is a bowl arcaded and supported on four figures of angels; but it is not very good in its character; perhaps we might think much of it here, but in northern Germany, where I had just been seeing the wonderful fonts at Münster, Brunswick, and above all at Hildesheim, the metal fonts at Lübeck struck me as looking very poor.

I happened to come in for the end of a week-day sermon here, and was rather amused, after it was finished, to find the *Prediger* descending from the pulpit, and directing his steps towards me, whilst the people went on singing: however, he turned into a great sort of glazed pew in the choir-aisle, and there, having shut himself in, he enthroned himself in a comfortable chair, waited for about ten minutes until the sound of singing and music had died away, and then stole back and out of the church at the west. It is curious, in northern Germany, to observe how entirely, in public ministrations, the Lutheran ministers seem to consider preaching their only work; going in after the preparatory hymn is sung, and going away as soon as their sermon is finished, without regard to the hymn which always winds up their functions. In Lübeck there was a curious madness about preaching: every morning, between eight and nine, there seemed to be sermons going on; and as the congregations are infinitesimal, they do all they can to keep a stray listener, when they can have him within their walls, by locking the doors. Happily, I escaped, by judicious management, the sad fate of listening to a sermon from any of these divines in black cloaks and immense white frills, who look like so many repetitions of their great prototype, Luther.

And now I must leave the cathedral, and getting over the difficulties of the horrible pavement which distinguishes this end of the city as well as may be, take you to the Marien-Kirche; the church which, in one's first view of Lübeck, one naturally takes for the cathedral, from its central position and general grandeur. The whole church is built of red brick, though unfortunately, internally, it has been daubed all over with a succession of coats of whitewash. I was able to measure the ground-plan, which may be taken as a type of the ground-plan most in favour in Lübeck, and indeed generally in this part of Germany. All the columns, arches, groining-ribs, and even the window tracery, are built of moulded bricks; and, as will be seen from the detail, the piers and arches are particularly well moulded and good. Not so the window tracery, which is very plain, and like all brick window tracery, most unsatisfactory, consisting as it does of three arched heads within the window arch, without cusping or ornament of any kind to relieve its baldness. The transepts hardly show on the ground-plan, and externally they are finished with two gables instead of one, and are so insignificant, consequently, as hardly to deserve notice. Between the buttresses all round is a row of chapels, their external walls being flush with the face of the buttresses. Among other good features in this church are the Lady-chapel to the east of the main apse, and the late turret over the intersection of nave and choir; and lastly, the two grand steeples at the west end. This kind of steeple was not an invention peculiar to Lübeck, but is a kind of which one finds many examples throughout northern Germany. The earliest with which I am acquainted are at Soest and Paderborn cathedrals, both of them very fine, and much earlier in date than the Lübeck examples; and these clearly have some affinity to the Lombard churches on the Rhine, save that the continual repetition of stage above stage, exactly alike, is a feature of their own, and one which the builders of the great brick steeples in the fourteenth century always had before them. Certainly, the two western steeples of the Marien-Kirche are very noble, and make one admire immensely this kind of spire, which, as you will see, rises from the angles of the tower and the points of the gables, which are so great a feature as a finish to each face of the tower. These great gables are generally filled in with tracery, without much regard to uniformity or symmetry, but sometimes, as in the noble steeple of S. John, Lüneburg, most effective: the spires in this case, and indeed almost always, are of timber covered with copper.

It will be seen from the plan that the dimensions of this church are very grand. The length is 280 English feet; height to vault, 108 ft.; height of aisles, 59 ft.; the spires, 344 ft.

The church was founded circa A.D. 1276, the north-west tower in 1304, and the south-west in 1310; and the whole may, I think, from its mouldings, etc., be taken as an example of Lübeck middle-pointed.

In the interior arrangement there is no very distinct triforium, though the clerestory windows have their inside arches lengthened down to a string-course above the main arcade, and in the choir there is a pierced parapet above this string.

The east window of the main apse, and the east windows of the eastern chapel, are filled with exceedingly brilliant stained glass, said to be the work of an Italian; it was brought in 1818 from the Burg-Kloster church, which was destroyed at that time, and which, judging from what still remains, and from the relics of its art treasures, preserved here and elsewhere, must have been one of the most interesting churches in the city. The three windows contain the legend of S. Jerome, the legend of the finding of the Cross, and the legend of S. Peter. They are said to have been done by the son of Dominic Livi, of Ghambasso, near Florence, who, after he had learnt his art and long practised it in Lübeck, went back in 1436 to Florence, where he executed the celebrated windows in the Duomo. I have never seen these Florentine windows, but, judging from my knowledge of the very mediocre character of Italian glass generally, I should say that there could be no improbability on the face of a story which would account for really beautiful glass being done at Florence. Certainly, this Lübeck glass is very good and brilliant, and valuable, as being, with a little still preserved in one of the windows of the Katerinen-Kirche, the only old glass preserved in any of the churches in Lübeck.

The nave of S. Mary is pewed throughout, and encumbered at the west end with a prodigious organ; but the choir is fairly perfect. It is screened in on all sides; to the west by means of a rood-screen, similar in plan to that at the cathedral, but of earlier date, and at the sides with screens mainly composed of brass. These screens are very common in all the churches here, but these are the best I have seen: they are very late in date, not at all satisfactory in their design, and in all cases the cornices and the lower part of the screens are of oak, the brass-work being confined to the uprights and the tracery, if tracery it can be called.

In the choir there is a magnificent metal *Sakraments-Haus*, very elaborate, and full of most delicate work; it has been shamefully damaged, but enough remains to make one class it with the best of these often beautiful pieces of church furniture. About twenty feet in height, it stands on lions' backs, and finishes at the top with the Crucifixion.

One of the relics still preserved in this church is a Dance of Death, in a series of twenty-five paintings round the walls of a chapel which forms part of the north transept; it is a very complete painting, and its date, which is said to be A.D. 1463, makes it one of the earliest paintings of this very curious subject. Mr. Douce, in his treatise on the Dance of Death, mentions older examples at Minden, in the churchyard of the Innocents at Paris, in the cloister of the S. Chapelle at Dijon, and that at Basle, which is the most famous of all. Most, if not all of these, are, however, now destroyed, and the interest of this painting becomes therefore the greater. It is certainly very valuable; if for no other reason, for the variety of costume, of every rank and order of men, which it contains, beginning with the pope, the emperor, empress, cardinal, king, bishop, duke, abbat, and so on to the young woman and the little child.

Besides these paintings are two by Overbeck: one in the Lady-chapel, finished in 1824, of our Lord's entry into Jerusalem, is certainly very beautiful, in its calm simplicity and purity of colour, reminding one much of Raffaelle's early style, or of some work of that great Christian artist, Perugino; and therefore most grateful to me, and far more pleasing than the other, which is a Pietà, painted in 1847, and in a thoroughly different and much more naturalistic style. In the first painting the Lübeck people recognise and point out, with no little pride, Overbeck's father, mother, and sisters, all of them — as also the great artist himself — natives of Lübeck, and perhaps fairly enough introduced in this his offering to his native town. A lion of the Marien-Kirche is the clock — one of those clumsy pieces of ingenuity which so often annoy one on the Continent. There is also a metal font, said to have been made in 1337 by one Hans Apengeter; but like that at the cathedral, not very satisfactory.

After these two great churches, certainly by far the most interesting church is that of the Minorite convent, S. Katharine, which is in many ways so remarkable, as to leave perhaps a stronger impression on one's mind than anything else in the city. It is a desecrated church, but desecrated happily in a quiet way; unused, and not much cared for, but as yet not destroyed, and serving now only as a kind of museum of old church furniture, great store of which, from the Burg-Kloster church and elsewhere, is accumulated in its choir.

The date of the foundation of this church is given on an inscription near the door as A.D. 1335, and its founder Bishop Henry Bockholt; but an old chronicler, Reimar Cock, says that the guardian of the church, Brother Emeke, pulled down the church in 1351, and rebuilt it in three years more beautifully than before, with the alms which, during the time of the plague, were given to the monks.

I have drawn out the plan of this church, and, with the help of my sketches, this may, I trust, explain its extraordinary arrangement. This consists in the elevation of the choir, with a kind of crypt below it, above the floor of the rest of the church; the floor of the crypt being level with that of the nave, and divided into three widths with slender shafts, the whole groined, and when seen from the nave, presenting certainly one of the most striking and curious interiors I have ever met with. The west end of the under church opens to the nave with three arches, looking just like the ordinary arrangement of rood-screens in Lübeck; and this is just what it is: the whole choir is simply a prolongation eastwards of the rood-loft, and at the west end there is a raised screen surmounting the three arches, out of which rises a most magnificent and perfect rood, with SS. Mary and John on either side. The entire absence of seats in the nave, the great height of the church, the darkness of the long vista of arch and column under the choir, and the magnificence of the rood, make this interior one of the most satisfactory and least altered things I know; and if its arrangement is not absolutely unique, it is certainly not far from being so. In England I know nothing at all like it, unless such an example as the little church at Compton, near Guildford, be taken, in which there are indeed some points of similarity — the low sanctuary, with its groined roof, and the chapel above opening to the church, and fenced in with its low Romanesque screen-work; all this, though on a far smaller scale, certainly tallies curiously with this Minorite church at Lübeck.[1]

---

[1] I need not say, to those who know the north of Germany, that the arrangement of this church is, after all, only an exaggeration of a not uncommon plan. The cathedrals at Hildesheim and Naumburg, the Liebfrauen-Kirche at Halberstadt, and many others, have crypts, whose floor is but little lower than the floor of the church, whilst the floors of their choirs are raised immensely, and so shut in

An iron grill shuts off the chapels at the east end of the under church, and in the centre of these is a fine brass, of which I obtained a rubbing. It is to a member of the Lüneburg family, and contains the figure of the burgomaster John Lüneburg, who died in the last quarter of the fifteenth century. The inscriptions are curious, the name, etc., all in Latin, ending with "Bidde God vor em"; and another ending "Orate: ah werlt du hest mi bedragen!" It will be seen from the drawing of the interior that the whole detail is of a very severe kind, — all brick, and alas! all whitewashed. The access to the choir is by a staircase in the south aisle, which did not appear to me to be old. There is a space of some ten or twelve feet between the west side of the rood-loft and the choir-stalls, which are returned; and into this space the staircase leads. The stalls are old, and very good; and the whole pavement of the upper choir is of tiles, of a peculiar and interesting kind, if only for its novelty. The only pattern tiles are in the borders, the remainder are green, black, red, and light red, made in various shapes, and very good in their effect. One of the chapels in the Marien-Kirche is similarly paved, but not on so grand a scale, or with so many patterns. The only pavements at all approaching to the same kind which at the present moment I can call to mind, are that which has been so strangely — as it were providentially — preserved in the footpace on which once stood the high altar at Fountains Abbey, perfect and untouched, where all else is ruin and desolation; — and in those most lovely marble pavements in S. Anastasia, at Verona. Some of the arrangements of the patterns approach very near to these, but how much more beautiful the marble of Verona is than the tiles of Lübeck one can hardly say.

And with this ends all that one knows as positively belonging to S. Katharine; for in this unused choir is now a store of triptychs of that kind which, after some acquaintance with German churches, one learns to tire of, covered with carving, quaint, and richly coloured, or painted in Scripture story or strange legend, well enough in their proper place, and giving once doubtless great dignity to the altars they adorned, but here — collected and set out for view as a gallery of paintings — if not worthless, at best very unsatisfactory. But besides all these triptychs, there is a large aumbrye, with its old iron gates and locks still perfect, in which is a large collection of portions of monstrances, chalices, crosses, and the like: many of

---

with solid stone screens and parcloses, that little can be seen of them from the naves. The crypt at Wimborne Minster is a rare instance of the same kind of thing in England; but this is a middle-pointed contrivance for *crealing* a crypt in a first-pointed church, which was never intended to have anything of the kind.

them very beautiful, but all damaged and in fragments. Among other things I saw a curious leather bag for carrying books, with an ingenious pocket for money contrived in its folds and very securely fastened.

But what is most rare and curious is a collection of ancient linen altar-cloths, which I had great trouble in getting a sight of, and which I could not draw, as the curator of the museum insisted on showing them himself, and when I wished to draw them, told me that he had already himself drawn them: this, as may be imagined, was a very poor source of comfort to me.

There was a corporal about 2 feet square, and fringed; along the edge of which was worked an arcade with figures of saints, the dresses stitched in a regular pattern all over, and the folds left plain: the date of this was about A.D. 1280. There was another embroidered corporal which I managed to get a drawing of: this was 2 feet square, with a large cross in the centre and four smaller crosses in the corners; the whole worked in a cross-stitch with blue and red on the white linen. Date, I think, about 1450.

Then there were two linen cloths for the altar: one, 14 ft. long by 3 ft. 10 in. wide, with a great number of figures of prophets surrounded with branching foliage; from the character of the figures, I date this at about A.D. 1400. All the outlines of the figures, leaves, etc. were marked with coloured ink borders on the linen before the work was done: the hair and points of the dresses here and there were marked with bright colour, but generally the work was all in white thread, — the stitches rather long, and arranged in regular patterns and diapers.

Another linen cloth of the same size has the whole history of Reynard the Fox: a curious subject, it may be thought, for an altar-cloth; but I may remark that I found the same subject in the bosses of the under church.

Besides this there was a magnificent linen dalmatic with apparels beautifully worked and fringed with white, red, white, blue, alternately. The orphreys had been taken off. The apparels of the sleeves were a succession of medallions, six to each sleeve, containing the Twelve Apostles, and the apparel at the bottom of the dalmatic had in front our Lord and two saints, and at the back S. Mary the Virgin, SS. Peter and Paul. The work was most beautiful, and, I have no doubt of the end of the thirteenth century.

I believe there were other things of the same kind, but I fear my curiosity rather disgusted the curator, who was not very anxious to let me see very much of these precious and invaluable relics.

The exterior of S. Katharine will be best understood by my sketches. The most noticeable fact is that some of the tracery in the eastern part is of stone enclosed within a brick arch, and exceedingly good in its effect; proving satisfactorily that this is the real way to use brick and stone together. There is no comparison between these windows and all the other windows in Lübeck. The rest are all ugly: these quite beautiful.

The transept has a double gable, as in the Marien-Kirche, and internally is arranged like an aisle rather than a transept. The west front is curious and indescribable: an irregular assemblage of arcades and windows without order or definiteness, but withal very effective. And as will be seen from the ground-plan, the north aisle being much narrower than the south produces of necessity a great irregularity in the whole elevation, and this irregularity is so carefully managed as really completely to conceal the awkwardness which would otherwise be very apparent. There is no tower, only a turret on the roof, at the intersection of nave, choir, and transept roofs.

In buildings connected with the church is a large library, some cartoons of Overbeck's, and some work of Godfrey Kneller's, he, as well as Overbeck, having been born here.

The other churches are not very remarkable. S. Peter's has a good steeple with metal turrets at the base of the spire, and I believe there is a fine brass there, but I failed to see it.

S. James has a very plain brick tower, and a good triapsidal east end, very much like that of S. Katharine. The steeple is crowned with a modern spire: inside there is a late metal font, of the kind popular in Lübeck — a large vat-like vessel standing on the backs of four kneeling angels, and covered with small and ineffective arcading with figures and subjects. There is a large organ of rather early date, and two curious standard lanterns for carrying lights in procession: they are of very late date, but still so rare as to be worth notice.

S. Giles has no one feature of interest, save its very fine tower and spire.

Of the hospitals the most curious is the Heiligen-Geist-Spital: the ground-plan and general arrangement of which are most remarkable. The chapel is the oblong building at the west end, only two bays in length, but of great width: against its east wall is a rood-screen and loft, under which is the altar, and, on either side of the altar, doors which admit every one under the loft into the hospital. This, like many of our old hospitals (S. Mary's, Chichester, and Higham Ferrers, are cases in point) is one immense hall, 250 ft. long by 40 ft. wide, and has down its length two passages, and four rows of cubicles for the inmates, and accommodates no less than 150 poor people: truly a most royal provision for the poor. There is an entrance at the sides, but the main entrance is through the chapel, through which there is a constant passing, and it is therefore more like a great hall than a chapel. How much better is the ordinary English arrangement (of which I saw a grand example at Lüneburg), in which the chapel is at the east end of the hall. There the chapel sanctifies the whole, instead of being itself profaned, as is the case at Lübeck.

The hospital was founded by one Bertram Mornewech, in A.D. 1286, and is similar in plan, I believe, to the great Gothic Hospital della Scala at Siena.

In the chapel are some brass screens like those in the Marien-Kirche, but inferior to them. The west front is remarkable and certainly very picturesque, with its three gables and its multitude of turrets.

The most interesting building left to be described is the ruin of the Burg-Kloster. This was a Dominican convent, and at the Reformation was converted into a hospital for the poor. In 1818, a portion of the vaulting of the church fell in, and then they pulled down the rest of the church, sending their stained glass and the organ to the Marien-Kirche, and their triptychs and altar furniture to the Katerinen-Kirche. The north wall only of the church now remains, but this shows traces of stone windows enclosed within brick arches, like those in the apse of S. Katharine, and its destruction is therefore specially to be deplored. The foundation dates from A.D. 1229. The rest of the conventual buildings still in great part remain, but so mixed up with other and modern erections, that it is rather difficult to understand them.

There is, however, a fair cloister on the north side of the church, groined throughout and tolerably perfect: out of this, on one side, is a kind of open groined stall, which looks something like the ambulatories which are so beautiful a feature of our own abbeys; and out of this ambulatory, one enters a large hall once apparently divided by a row of columns down the centre. North of these buildings is a room which seems to have been part of the refectory, remarkable for an exquisite pavement of small tiles — red, black, and white — arranged in an ingenious and intricate pattern, of which I made a careful drawing. My drawing shows the entire remaining portion of this pavement which, it will be seen, continued on beyond the present partition-wall. A central shaft is still left, with an old oak sideboard framed round its base in a most effective manner. In another part of the Burg-Kloster there is a small fragment of similar pavement, which looks as if it had been the hearth under a fire.

Near S. Giles's church there is another ruined conventual building, S. Anne's Kloster. This was originally a nunnery of "Clarissernonnen" (I suppose these were nuns of S. Clare, an order who had a few houses in England), but has been converted into a workhouse. Unfortunately a great fire in 1843 consumed the church, and left nothing but the outer walls standing, and when I was there it was used as a place for the workhouse men to break stones or the roads. The church is said to have been designed and built by one Synsingus Hesse of Brunswick, who came to Lübeck in 1502 with five assistants, and completed the work in 1510. With this date the work tallies very well, though I confess there is no mark of the peculiarities of a Brunswick architect, which, as must be known to any who have ever seen that very remarkable city, are decided enough. Part of the west front of the church of S. Anne was built with courses of stone and brick, a most unusual arrangement in Germany, though common enough in Italian pointed, and always very striking in its effect; the domestic buildings retain a good many groined rooms, and a simple cloister in very perfect condition.

We come now to the Rathhaus, whose long line of picturesque front is so great a feature in the principal street of the city. Its history is so confusing and its style so peculiar, that it is very difficult indeed to affix any certain date to its various portions. It was burnt down in A.D. 1276, and there was another fire in A.D. 1358. In A.D. 1389 there were considerable works executed, including the famous cellars, whose still more famous wine was all cleared out by the French, when they sacked the good city in A.D. 1806. The portion of the Rathhaus to the south of the market-place seems to have been built in 1442-44, and the alterations of the Börse towards the street in 1570 and 1673; so that we may well expect a confusing and picturesque mixture of works of various dates. The earliest external portion appears to me to be the screen on the north side in front of the two gabled roofs; and this and the other great screens or parapets towards the market-place and towards the street are the most picturesque portions of the building. They are entirely executed in red and black brick, the cusping being all done in moulded brick. As a rich piece of colour this work is very valuable, but architecturally its sole merit is a kind of picturesqueness, which it certainly has in great force.

The fact is that in northern Germany all the domestic architecture was very full of faults; the fronts of the buildings were very seldom at all ruled by the roof line, and their stepped gables, traceried, mullioned, and pinnacled, had no reference to anything save a desire to look well; and so here some of the most striking portions of the old Rathhaus are done without any regard to constructional wants, and simply as masks of the construction; the fronts are built up to conceal the roofs, arcaded and pinnacled without meaning, and in a style very elaborate as compared with the other brickwork throughout the city.

A sketch of perhaps the most magnificent example remaining of north German domestic architecture — the Rathhaus at Münster — will show you how, even with the most beautiful detail and the best possible sculpture, this faulty mode of designing was always persisted in; from Münster in the fourteenth century one may trace it going into the brick districts to the north and — as at Lüneburg — filling entire towns with its extravagancies, and then settling down, as we find it at Lübeck, into a regular system of stepped gables and panelled façades, beyond which the dream of house-builders never went. I confess to having been sorely disappointed in the street architecture of Lübeck. In the first place everything except the churches, hospitals, Rathhaus, and gateways, is painted white, or whitewashed in the most ruthless manner, and the architectural merit of the houses before they were whitewashed must have been very small. The houses at the side of the Heiligen-Geist-Spital are the best specimens of the kind of elevation most in favour, and will, I think, quite justify my strictures, though they are less objectionable than most, in that the gables follow the roof line instead of being sham.

I have left until the last the town gateways, which are certainly two of the most effective I have ever seen. The Holsteiner-Thor has two spire-like roofs at its extremities, which are very effective, and its front towards the town is really a magnificent specimen of the good effect of a great quantity of arcading. The outer front of the gate is much less ornamental. In the string-courses there is a great deal of inlaid terra-cotta ornament. The date of this gateway is about A.D. 1477. The Burg-Thor and the buildings on the town side form about as picturesque a group as can well be imagined. It has all been lately restored, and, I fear, *painted:* the colour of the red and black bricks savouring to my eye uncommonly of artificial colour; but one can scarce imagine anything more strikingly picturesque than the whole group. The other side of the gate is almost exactly the same; but standing by itself, without the picturesque buildings on either side, is not nearly so effective.

All that I had heard of Lübeck made me promise myself a great treat in the study of the old brick buildings and the old treatment of brick. I must confess, however, that this was not so good or so satisfactory as I had expected, and that it is certainly very inferior to the Italian brick work. It is generally coarsely done, and there is but little attempted in the way of tracery, and that little is never very effective. I saw nothing, for instance, at all comparable to such brick work as one sees at Verona, Mantua, and Cremona; and I doubt much whether Germany produces any which can be compared to it. Except in one instance, and then only to a very slight extent, there is no attempt at all at mixing stone with brick, save at the quoins of the towers, where there are always immense blocks of stone, intended for strength, but contributing, I suspect, to the weakness which is quite a characteristic of all the churches in Lübeck, Hamburg, Lüneburg, and generally throughout this brick district. The brick churches of Italy are remarkable in that they owe much of their beautiful effect either to the mixture of stone with brick, or to the exquisite moulding of the brick, and the care and delicacy with which it was built; and one observes that whilst in Italy all the buildings have an air of refinement, in northern Germany they have an air of great coarseness, to which, perhaps, the entire absence of what can fairly be called window tracery in a great degree conduces.

Something may, however, be learnt even from the failure of other men, and so some points may well be attended to in this German brick work. And first it teaches us, distinctly and unmistakably, that brick is no material for window traceries; the necessity of using it ends either in the repetition of very simple and ugly windows, such as are almost universal in Lübeck; or, as in the Stadt-Haus, and again in the very remarkable church of S. Katharine, at Brandenburg, in the eternal repetition of the same small piece of moulded tracery, which, of necessity not very good in itself, becomes, by much repetition, quite hateful. And the effect is painful in the extreme upon the whole practice of art: in all cases, without any exception, I believe, where men have condescended to attempt to execute traceries or carvings in brick moulded in this way, the tendency has been, naturally enough, to repeat for ever things which by repetition become cheap. *One* moulded piece of brick tracery would be dearer than one like it in stone; but multiply it a hundred or a thousand times, and it becomes infinitely cheaper, but who can say by how much more infinitely tedious and unartistic! So at Brandenburg, crockets, crocketed gablets, component parts of tracery, and the like, are repeated over and over again, in a manner which is really marvellous; and because it was necessary to do this, immense sham fronts, sham parapets, and the like, must be raised, in order to display all the resources which were at their command. Now this is very poor architecture, very vile art; and it requires no argument to prove that it is only the natural and certain result of the attempt to use materials out of their proper place, and in a way in which it was never intended they should be used. Far worse would be an attempt to mould clay, so that it should counterfeit the work of nature; and so, in addition to the destruction of all art by its endless repetitions, insult God's handiwork by counterfeiting stone quarried from the bowels of the earth.

The Lübeck churches show us, however, in other respects, what great things may really be done, and done well and naturally, in brick. You may form mouldings to any extent, because each moulded brick tells its own tale, does its own work; and mouldings, so far from not bearing repetition, gain by it. All the windows in a noble church require varied traceries, but it were as well that no two of them should vary in their mouldings. Here, therefore, the reproductive power of the moulder is most valuable; so, too, is it in all forms of ornament (as, e. g., the billet, chevron, and the like) which become ornamental only by repetition, and not in any way by reason of art or skill in the man who works them. These are absolutely better in brick than in stone, because, as no thought and no taste are necessary in the man who carves them, it were better the human intellect should be as little as possible deadened by working upon them. The windows of S. Katharine, Lübeck, show how these moulded bricks may be used in conjunction with stone traceries, and with admirable effect, when compared with the attempts at tracery in brick which this and other churches here exhibit.

But one of the most important facts which we can learn here is, that brick is not only good outside, but just as much inside a church. All the Lübeck churches are built, inside and out, with red brick; most unfortunately, this has all been whitewashed, but I think we may have faith enough in the men who built them to be sure that they would not have been built with brick had not the effect been good. For myself, I am persuaded that they were right in so doing; because I have seen in Italy the wonderfully solemn effect produced in this way, and have since tested it myself. In truth, no red brick building should ever be plastered inside, save where it is intended to introduce paintings of some kind more brilliant than the colour of the bricks.

On the whole, therefore, though the brick work of Lübeck is far inferior, in delicacy and beauty, to that which I have seen in Italy, there is much to be learnt from it, and much proof to be obtained, if proof be needed, that brick is really a most noble and serviceable material, and one which, wherever it is the material of the district, ought invariably and unhesitatingly to be used.

But I feel that, in criticising its brick work, I have been led into abusing old Lübeck almost too much. Perhaps I ought only to express my grateful recollection of all the treasures which she still possesses, — of her screens, her church furniture, her spacious interiors, and her many picturesque features of antiquarian and ecclesiological interest, her triptychs, her brasses, and her gateways, — rather than attempt to draw a parallel between her and Italy; between the stern ruggedness of the north, and the sunny softness and delicacy of the south; between, moreover, a city built as it were in a day, — for Lübeck's rise was sudden almost beyond all precedent, without a history, and without older days to teach and to correct her, — and a land whose memories of the past and associations with old art were, even in the Middle Ages, well nigh as great, and as valuable in their influence on the mind of her people, as they can be even at the present day. More just it is, perhaps, only to be thankful for all the pleasures with which my three days' sojourn in this noble old city was full even to overflowing; and (forgetful of the faults of her architects) to dwell more upon the lessons which their works cannot fail to teach us, if we will only lovingly and patiently study and examine them.

II

NAUMBURG CATHEDRAL

I reached Naumburg late at night in a tremendous storm; but the sun rose cheeringly, and I started early for the cathedral fearful of disappointment, as I had spent half the previous day in a mistaken attempt to find something interesting at Merseburg, — a place against which it is only right to warn all ecclesiologists. At Naumburg my fate was happier. The first view of the exterior is not very striking. A fair apsidal choir with a tower rising on either side, Romanesque at the base, and finished in late third-pointed, does not rise above the picturesque, and gives but small promise of the excessive interest of the interior. The plan is curious. A late Romanesque, or very early-pointed nave finished with eastern and western apsidal choirs, and separated from both of them by rood-screens; that to the eastern choir Romanesque, that to the western of most exquisite early pointed, and both of them coeval with the portions of the main fabric to which they belong. The eastern choir extends across the transepts, and is raised considerably above them, with solid stone parcloses, arcaded on the faces towards the transepts with semicircular arches, a kind of parclose not uncommon in the churches in this part of Germany.

Under the whole of the choir is a crypt entered from the transept, and in the angles between the transepts and the choir are towers, the lower stages of which are open to the transepts and form chapels, whose altars stand in small apsidal projections on the east face of the tower. A door on either side of the sanctuary leads by a staircase in the thickness of the wall to rooms above the chapels in the tower. The entrance to the choir is through the old rood-screen by doors on either side of the altar, and by doors in the parcloses, reached by long flights of steps in the transepts. The nave is divided into three groining bays, each bay subdivided and having two arches into the aisles. The western choir has one bay and a five-sided apse. On either side of it is a narrow passage leading to staircases which lead to rooms above some chapels, which have now to be mentioned.

They form the base of towers at the west end of the aisles, but project considerably beyond them: only one of these towers has been built; the other is carried up and finished externally as though it was a transept, and produces at first some confusion when seen from the exterior. These tower chapels are very curious. That on the south side has a circular central shaft, decreasing in size to the capital, and the vaulting has four ribs springing from corbels in the angles of the chapel in a semicircular arch to the cap of the column, and there are no other ribs. In the *east* wall is a small semicircular recess, in which still stands the original altar with a double footpace. The north tower chapel is almost exactly like the other, save that it has a polygonal central shaft, and the recess for the altar is rectangular. Both chapels are lighted with small round-headed windows in their western faces. From this description it will be seen that the ground-plan of this church is so curiously alike at its eastern and western ends, as to be somewhat confusing at first.

And now to describe this most interesting church in detail. The eastern choir-screen is most remarkable. It has admirably carved capitals, and its three western arches (which are semicircular) rest on delicate clusters of shafts. The original doorways still remain, and in front of them steps, arranged in semicircles radiating from the centre of the door, which lead up into the choir. No doubt an altar once stood under this screen, but this has been destroyed in order to convert it into a pew! The front of the screen too is so much obscured by a modern gallery, and by the reredos of the Lutheran altar, that it is impossible to say how it was finished: there seemed to be traces of a vesica with sculpture just over the centre arch. Entering the choir by this screen, one finds all the old arrangements undisturbed. Between the two western doors there are three stalls with canopies, and on either side against the stone parcloses eleven stalls and ten subsellae. In the midst stand three ancient, heavy square desks for office books, and upon these five most magnificent books, well bound and of astonishing size, still maintain their old place. They are all manuscript on vellum, and two of them have very large illuminations of subjects, and foliage of very admirable and bold character. I never saw such magnificent books on their own proper desks, — never, I think any of such grand size anywhere. The stalls are not particularly good, and are of late date, with immense finials, of a kind I had met before at Halberstadt. A rise of several steps divides the choir from the first bay of the sanctuary, which is long and without furniture, save some late stalls, which do not seem to have any business where they are placed. This bay of the choir terminates the transitional work, which is carried throughout the whole church, with the exception of the eastern apse and the western choir. It is of the earliest pointed, very simple and bold in all its details; the piers looking rather like Romanesque in their section and capitals, carved in the most admirable manner. The foliage is all disposed in circles, being regular and geometrical and invariably kept severely and carefully to a regular outline; it is an example of the very perfection of that kind of conventional foliage, of which some of the early capitals at Venice are such admirable specimens, and I think in no way inferior to them. The groining throughout is very simple, with diagonal and transverse ribs. The eastern apse is an addition in most admirable middle-pointed, and (save the upper stages of the towers) the latest work in the whole fabric. The section of the groining shafts is particularly elaborate and good; corbels of foliage inferior to the rest of the carving throughout the church supported figures under canopies at a height of about eight feet from the floor, but the figures are all gone. A very bold string runs round the apse at this point under a passage-way in the wall, which is reached by a staircase between the choir and the tower-chapel apses. The windows are of three lights, and have good geometrical tracery, and the apse is well groined with boldly moulded ribs, the boss in the centre being four ivy leaves. In the sanctuary stand four oak sedilia of the thirteenth century, with open arcaded backs and carved ends, the carving peculiar, but the whole a very remarkable work and very perfect. The chapels in the towers on either side of the choir are not in the old state, one being used for rubbish, and the other as a vestry: above the former a room in the tower is used as a receptacle for hardware! Perhaps the *Prediger* deals in it! The crypt under the choir is very perfect and fine. We had an illumination of it, and consequently a careful examination. The capitals are all carved, and the arches all semicircular. It is divided by shafts, some of which are clustered, into three spaces in width, and in the length there are two bays under the choir, then a solid wall with a doorway, and then five bays, and an apse of three bays. The old altar still remains.

In the transepts there is little to notice, save that there is an old altar in each. The well-like effect of these German transepts, in which the choir is continued across with heavy stone parcloses of great height, is most unpleasant. In this case the parcloses are no less than 16 feet high from the floor of the transept; and, owing to the great elevation of the choir, the floor of the crypt is only 4 ft. 6 in. lower than the transept floor.

No one, going into the nave of the church as now arranged, would believe that he was in a church of more than very mediocre interest. Between all the columns are small tenements, painted white, carefully roofed in and glazed, and papered with whatever paper the fancy and good taste of their several proprietors suggest.

In front of these are rows of pews, arranged longitudinally, and all painted white; and as the aisles are by this arrangement practically lost to the church, galleries are built in them, to supply the created want.[1] A white wooden screen behind the Lutheran altar conceals the eastern rood-screen; whilst another white wooden partition, out of the centre of which projects the pulpit, serves also to conceal the rood-screen of the western choir. The whole arrangement is, in short, just the most judicious that could possibly be imagined for the entire annihilation of the architectural effect of the interior.

This western choir-screen is certainly the most striking I have ever seen even in this land of screens. No description can, however, do justice to its exquisite beauty, dependent as this is, to a great extent, on the exceeding originality and beauty of the foliage, which is all varied, and all executed from natural models. The doorway is double, and rather narrow; the doors of iron, cross-framed; and they form the only openings in the screen, the rest being quite solid, arcaded on the eastern side, and on the western (that is, on the inside, or choir side), remarkable chiefly for the exquisite open staircases on each side of the door leading to the loft. On the eastern side, against the doorway, are a Crucifix and SS. Mary and John; but these seemed to be of later date than the door. The figure of our Lord seated in the tympanum above is no doubt original; it is very curious, being partly painted, partly carved, and reminded me of an early picture, managed in the same way, which I saw in the gallery at Berlin. Above the arcading, on either side of the doorway, are a series of subjects, the execution of which (with the exception of the two last, which are not original) is marvellously good. They are, beginning at the south — the Last Supper, the Betrayal, ditto (S. Peter smiting Malchus), the Denial of S. Peter, our Lord before Pilate, the Scourging, Bearing the Cross. The open staircases on the western side of the screen are remarkable for the beauty of the succession of detached shafts, with finely carved capitals, which support them.

There are no fittings in this western choir save the altar, the mensa of which is 8 ft. 5 in. long, by 5 ft. 11 in. wide, and 3 ft. 8 in. high; and this faces west, as all the altars throughout the church do: so showing its back (in the centre of which is the usual closet) to any one entering through the door of the screen from the nave. It has a double footpace. The detail of this choir is earlier and bolder than that of the eastern choir; the windows of two lights,

---

[1] It is owing to this arrangement of the nave, and the consequent uselessness of the aisles, that several of the old altars still remain, one in each bay, against the north aisle wall, and one or two against the south aisle wall.

with very bold monials, and circles sexfoiled, with soffit cusping in the head. The groining-shafts are good; and, as in the other choir, there is a very bold string under a passage-way in front of the windows, at about 8 feet from the floor. The windows do not fill up the whole width of the bays, and on each side have small open arches, which add very much to the richness of the whole effect. Against the groining-shafts are figures, very well sculptured, and standing under canopies of very varied design, finished at the top with what seem like models of churches. Some of the windows retain some exquisite stained glass. The mouldings throughout this apse are exactly like those of the screen, and the foliage was evidently carved by the same hand, — that of as great a master in his day as was the artist who carved the early capitals in the nave. I think I have now described the whole of the interior.

On the exterior there is a large cloister (partly ruined) on the south of the nave; half of this is pointed, the other half late Romanesque. It opens into the church with a small round-arched door, in the third bay from the west; and on its east side into a large kind of porch or narthex, south of the south transept, from which there is a particularly grand doorway, with five shafts in each jamb, into the transept. This porch is groined in two bays, and communicates with other buildings to the south, one of which seems, by its apse and pointed windows, to have been a chapel. These old buildings group picturesquely with the east end of the church. The southern was not, however, the only cloister; the good men of Naumburg seem to have been specially fond of duplicates, and as they had two choirs, two rood-screens, and two towers at each end, so they thought right to have two cloisters. The northern cloister seems to have tallied in size with the southern; but all that now remains of it are the groining-ribs against the north wall, and the springers of the groining throughout. The base-mould of the western tower is continued all along this north wall, and the groining springs from corbels; all which makes it look as though it were a subsequent addition: but its arches are nevertheless round, whilst, as we have seen, pointed arches are used throughout the main arcade. There are two doors from this destroyed cloister into the church — one into the north aisle, the other into the north transept.

The western apse is remarkable, on the exterior, for the excessively beautiful carving of its cornices; these are varied in every bay, and, I think, the best I have ever seen. They are of that exquisite imitation of natural foliage, springing upwards, and filling a large hollow with its ramifications, which commends itself to my mind as the most perfect type of cornice foliage. There is a somewhat similar carved string under the windows, equally good, but much more simple. The buttresses finish at the top with delicate pinnacles.

At the east end the detail is also good, the windows being well moulded, and the buttresses finished with good simple niches and figures. The apsidal projections on the eastern face of the towers finish with pyramidal stone roofs against the towers, at a low elevation.

The north-west tower is late, and has open turrets at its angles, beginning at the second stage; it is picturesque, but not very good. The upper stages of the eastern towers are also octangular, but without pinnacles; and what ornament they have is of a very late kind, and not effective.

Such is the cathedral of Naumburg — little known to, and scarce ever visited by, English tourists; and yet undoubtedly one of the most interesting and least altered churches in Germany: its two rood-screens would be alone sufficient to give it high claims upon our admiration, since they are, so far as I know, the two earliest examples remaining, and certainly older than any quoted by Mr. Pugin in his work on Screens. Besides this, the architectural value of some parts of the building is so pre-eminent, as in itself to repay a long journey.

III

ERFURT AND MARBURG

At Naumburg there was little, save the cathedral, to detain an ecclesiologist. The Stadt-Kirche deserved little more than a hurried visit, though the singularity of its plan deserves a note. It has an immense apsidal west end, a vast semicircle on the plan, embracing both nave and aisles, and its choir is also terminated with an apse. Beyond this the only remarkable features are the large multifoiled arches which occupy the space between the windows and the plinth in each bay of the eastern apse.

From the railway station one obtains a good view of the cathedral steeples over the vine-clad hills on which Naumburg stands — refreshing sight after the dreariness of the country generally in which I had been journeying. From Naumburg to Erfurt the railway runs through a really pretty, often very picturesque, country, with hills and rocks by the river-side, ever and anon capped by those feudal keeps in which all German rivers seem to be so rich; as picturesque now as they were formerly advantageous to their predatory chiefs. I had but two or three hours at Erfurt, but this was enough to show me that much was to be seen. The Barfüsser-Kirche was the first that I saw — one of those immensely long churches of which Germans were rather fond; a nave and aisles, and an apsidal choir, all groined at the same height, with windows of the same size and character throughout, and the whole "restored" in that peculiarly chilling fashion, which Lutherans are so singularly successful in achieving, which makes one's recollection of such a church not very grateful. There is, however, some old glass in the choir windows, and a most prodigious carved and painted reredos behind the altar, which, though apparently to some extent modern, is nevertheless striking in its effect. The entrance to this church is by double doors on the south side which run up into and form part of the windows, the same jamb mould being continued all round.

I had some difficulty in finding my way to the cathedral — strangely enough too, for when at last I reached the Dom-Platz, there, rising high into the air, and approached by an almost endless flight of steps, stood the magnificent choir of the cathedral, surmounted by its singular triple arrangement of central steeples, and by its side, and on the same high plateau, the church of S. Severus emulating, I should almost say, aping, the cathedral both in height and design very curiously. The east end of the cathedral, built on the precipitous edge of a rock, has been under-built with a terrace supported upon arches, which, concealing the natural rock, gives it an effect of extraordinary height. These arches have been all modernized, but there are traces here and there which prove the arrangement to be original.

Let us mount the flight of steps which lead by the entire length of the north side of the choir to the porch, and we shall see reason to class one at least of the architects of Erfurt, with the greatest of his race. No position can be conceived which would present more difficulty to one who wished to show the doors of his church to the people who might gather in crowds in the Dom-Platz, and seeing nothing but the tall east end of their church and the sharp perspective of its side, shrink from the attempt to find a door at the end of the long flight of steps before them. Every one must have felt how those great foreign doorways call upon all to enter; they are always open, guarded on either side by kings, and saints, and martyrs, and revealing glimpses, precious because vague, of glorious interiors and worshippers within on their knees. They call upon all to enter, and who can refuse? At Erfurt, however, one might have deemed it impossible that people should be made to feel this, but yet it has been done, and done nobly and magnificently. There are no transepts, and so against the eastern bay of the north aisle of the nave is set a triangular porch of grand size and lovely design and detail. Its base rests against the church, and its two sides, jutting out at angles of sixty degrees from the wall, show both from the west and from the east the whole width of its two glorious doorways. So, as one gazes up from the Dom-Platz, and wonders at the singularity of the position of the church and the beauty of the choir, one's eye follows up the track of those who ascend the toilsome flight of steps till it rests upon the doorway at their summit, and one is led at once to find one's way through its great opening into the nave of the church. Sad to say, wanton havoc has destroyed much of the more delicate ornaments of this most noble piece of early fourteenth century architecture. Of the nave little can be said, save that it is entirely unworthy and unsatisfactory; between it and the choir is a great mass of wall, pierced only by a narrow arch opening into the choir, and supporting a curious combination of towers — a central tower rising from between one on either side — in a singular and rather picturesque fashion of which I recollect no other examples than the imitation of it here in S. Severus, and the cathedral at Constance. The interior of the choir is very noble; its elevation very great, and its windows of rather late middle-pointed, full without exception of brilliant though late glass; too rich in colour however for the traceries, which it quite conceals, giving a useful warning to architects in dealing with stained glass.

The only piece of old furniture in this choir of which I made a note, is a curious figure in brass, supporting three branches for lights, one in either hand, and one growing out of his back. The effect of this is not at all satisfactory.

This cathedral is Catholic, as also is S. Severus and some of the other churches, the Lutherans holding about an equal number.

S. Severus imitates the cathedral very curiously; it is within some thirty or forty feet of its northern side, and has in the same transeptal position a great mass of tower, the outer flanks of which are crowned with tall spires, whilst from the intermediate wall, and raised above the others, rises the central spire; the mass of tower is smaller, but nevertheless by dint of its slated spires, S. Severus manages to rise higher than the cathedral. As may be imagined, the whole group is one of most picturesque character. S. Severus has some very good middle-pointed detail, especially in its window traceries.

It was late in the evening when I left the Dom-Platz, but I saw hurriedly the exteriors of some eight or ten pointed churches. They were mostly of the same date, *circa* 1320 to 1400, and of very various degrees of merit. One — the Prediger-Kirche is the not pleasant dedication by which it is now known — is of enormous length as compared to its width and height: fifteen bays to a church consisting of a not very lofty nave with narrow aisles is an excess of this proportion; its length cannot be less than about 225 feet. Near it, but apparently having no connection with it, is a detached campanile.

In one of Erfurt's many squares or market-places, is a good pointed house, with a large bay window, and three traceried windows, one on either side, and one above it in its gable end.

In another Platz is a church with two western steeples, one with a spire rising from the gabled sides of the tower. Another church occupies a triangular piece of ground, the tower being at the western angle, between two streets. It is desecrated, and I could not get into it, but its internal arrangement must be most singular.

These hurried notes are all that I could make. I was homeward bound, and obliged to travel all night to Marburg. So I did what a pilgrim to the shrine of S. Elizabeth of Hungary ought, I suppose, not to have done — I slept as the train passed Eisenach, and neglected therefore, even to get a glance through the starlight of the castle on the Wartburg, her residence and the scene of most of the beautiful story of her life.

It was early morning when Marburg was reached. Under high hills, covered with vine and picturesque in their outline, stands the noble church, conspicuous as one first sees it by its two completed and nearly similar towers and spires rising in all the beauty of their deep-coloured stonework against the green hillside which rises so precipitously close behind them. On the summit of the hill are the tall walls of the fine old castle, and to the left of the church and below the castle the town covers the hillside with the ramifications of its old steep and narrow streets. The church is perhaps rather too much outside the town for the use of the townspeople; but then it was not built for them, and in the general view it certainly gains much by being placed where it is.

And now, before I say anything about the church, two or three dates, which seem to be settled beyond dispute, may as well be mentioned.

S. Elizabeth of Hungary was born, then, in the year 1207, was married when but fifteen years old, and ere she was twenty left a widow, her husband having laid down his life in the third Crusade: three years and a half of widowed life were all she saw before an early grave received her; and from thence forward year after year saw fresh fervour excited by the contemplation of her virtues, and fresh enthusiasm awakened about the old city of Marburg, in which the last years of her life had been spent in the practice of austerity and self-denial such as the world has seldom seen. She was canonized in A.D. 1235; and in the same year the church as we now see it was commenced, and completed by about A.D. 1283.

More I need not say; for the life of her whose memory gave rise to this grand architectural effort is foreign to my present purpose, and moreover is too well known to need repetition.

Judging by the evidence of style — which is not however very strong, as the whole work has been completed carefully upon a uniform plan — I should say that the work commenced at the east, and was continued on westward, so that the west front, with its two towers and spires, was the latest portion of the work. I am inclined to think, too, that the sacristy, a large building of two stories in height, filling the angle between the north transept and the northern side of the choir, is an addition to the original fabric, but probably earlier than the steeples.

The plan shows a very regular cruciform church, the choir and transepts all having apsidal ends, a large sacristy, and two western steeples; the whole very regular and similar in character throughout.

The exterior of the church is perhaps, with the exception of its west front, more curious than really beautiful. Throughout its whole extent every bay is similar, and consists of two stages, the upper an exact repetition of the one below, each lighted with a simple two-light window with a circle in the head, and divided by a great projecting cornice, the top of which is on a level with the bottom of the upper windows. The nave and aisles are all groined at one height without triforium or clerestory; and the outer walls are, therefore, the full height of the groining of the nave. Now this endless repetition of the same windows in a manner so apparently unnecessary was at first most perplexing to me, inconsistent as it seemed with the delicate taste exhibited elsewhere by the architect; but I was not long perplexed. The cornice between the windows was, in fact, a passage-way extending all round the church in front of the windows and, by openings, through all the buttresses: whilst in front of the lower windows a similar passage, not corbelled out, but formed by a thinning of the wall from this point upwards, again encircles the church. The sacristy is the only portion of the building not so treated. The church has not and never had cloister, chapter-house, or any of the ordinary domestic buildings of a religious house, attached to it; it stood on a new piece of ground, away from houses, and with an open thoroughfare all round, and all this helps in the solution of its singular arrangements. We have but to recall to mind that the relics of S. Elizabeth were visited by more pilgrims for some two or three centuries than any other shrine almost all Europe could boast of, to see the difficulty accounted for. It was built from the first to be a pilgrimage church, and carefully planned with an especial view to this. No doubt it was a great shrine, round which thousands of pilgrims congregated in the open air, to watch as processions passed with the relics they came from so far to see, passing by these ingeniously contrived passages round the entire church again and again, seen by all, but unencumbered by the pressure of the multitude.

The whole arrangement is so curious that I have dwelt at some length upon it, feeling that it certainly shows well how boldly a thirteenth century architect ventured to depart from precedent when he found a new want to be provided for, and when a before unthought of necessity had arisen. I need hardly say, that the effect of the corbelled-out passage is to divide the height distinctly into two parts, a division perhaps more difficult of satisfactory treatment than any other that one can imagine. The only variety in the tracery of the windows throughout the body of the church is, that the centre window of each apse has a sexfoil in the circle in its head, none of the other windows having any cusping whatever. The moulding of the windows is very simple, — a very bold roll and chamfer; and it is noticeable that in the tracery the roll-moulding does not mitre with the same moulding in the arch, but is just separated from it, an ungraceful peculiarity; the roll-moulding of the tracery is treated as a shaft in the monial and jambs, and has corbelled bases, the effect of which is not at all good. The buttresses run up to the eaves, but finish abruptly without pinnacles, nor is there any parapet. It seems probable that something must have been intended, but possibly never done; and I confess I should shrink from venturing now upon the introduction of either pinnacles or parapet, and I cannot but trust that in the extensive repairs now in progress, restorations of this conjectural kind will not be attempted. Better, in such a case, let well alone, rather than run the risk of destroying everything by some monstrous mistakes!

The west front is quite a thing to be considered apart from the rest of the church, later in character, and the work, I am inclined to think, of another man, who did not only this but all, or nearly all, the magnificent fittings of the interior. The first man worked under the trammels of a transitional style, endeavouring after yet not achieving the beauties which the second man was able, in all that he did at a more advanced day, so completely to realize.

The west door at once fixes one's attention. It is very lovely: the jamb perhaps too plain, and lacking mouldings between its shafts, but the arch absolutely perfect; it has two rows of the freshest and brightest stone foliage ever seen, and the tympanum — diapered over one half with a trailing rose, and on the other with a vine, both creeping naturally upwards with exquisite curve and undulation, regular in their irregularity, — is certainly of a degree of exquisite and simple beauty such as I have never seen surpassed. In the midst of this bower stands a fine figure of S. Mary with our Lord in her arms, and on either side an angel censing. As one looks at the carving, one thinks of the prettiest perhaps of all the legends of S. Elizabeth, and it may be that the sculptor, as he struck out the bold and beautiful work, which even now surprises by its beauty and its sharpness, thought of those roses of paradise with which S. Elizabeth in the legend surprised her doubting husband.

Above this doorway a pierced parapet carries a passage in front of the fine and thoroughly geometrical west window of six lights.

Another parapet, and then a row of traceries and canopies which mask the roof gable. On either side the great buttresses of the steeples give an air of solidity and plainness to the whole elevation, which I think very satisfactory. A two-light window on the same level as the great west window, and very long narrow belfry windows, also of two lights, are the only openings in the towers. The buttresses finish with pinnacles, and the towers with pierced parapets, above which, on the cardinal sides, are gables with windows, and at their summit an octangular open parapet, from which the spires then rise without further break or ornament. The composition is unusual and very good.

Besides these western steeples there is a turret of poor and modern character over the intersection of the transept and other roofs.

And now let us enter, and we shall find ourselves in what seems like a very lantern; windows everywhere, tier above tier, and admitting a flood of light which is bearable only when — as happily still in the choir — all the windows are filled with the richest stained glass.

The architectural peculiarities of the exterior are as marked but not as intelligible in the interior; and one cannot cease to regret the effect of the reiteration of the same window everywhere: otherwise, however, the interior is full of beauty; the nave piers very simple — large circles with four engaged shafts — very lofty and with finely carved capitals. The transept piers are clustered, and the groining throughout is very simple, but of exquisite proportions.

And now I must go on to describe the fittings and arrangements of this interior, which are so perfect as to make it, perhaps, the most interesting and complete church in Germany.

The choir extends to the western side of the transepts, and is finished towards the nave with a high stone screen, against the western side of which is a large people's altar. The screen is traceried and panelled over its whole western surface, and surmounted by a delicate open arcade finished with pinnacles and gablets; the portion over the altar being elaborated so as to form a reredos rather than a screen. The only openings in this screen are a row of small windows (as one may almost call them), opening just above the backs of the stalls, which in the choir are continued not only on the north and south sides, but quite across the west side also. The only entrance to the choir, therefore, is on either side from the transepts to the east of the stalls. On the eastern face of the screen, a kind of large ambon is corbelled forward in the centre, just the width of the people's altar; and above this rose — I say "rose," for when I was there, it was lying on the floor, as a first step to "restoration," which may not, I trust, mean "destruction,"

— a grand trefoiled arch of timber, covered with very boldly carved natural foliage, and flanked by two massive pinnacles. All trace of the figures is gone, but there can be no doubt that this arch and the pinnacles bore on their summits the Crucifix with the figures of S. Mary and S. John; and, indeed, the marks of their having once been affixed still remain.

In the choir there is a double row of stalls round three sides, the subsellae having low original desks in front of them. These are perfect all round, and, as I need hardly say, valuable for their rarity. The stalls are finely treated, and the upper row is well raised. The effect of the whole is most singular and very new to an English eye, for though, as I had occasion to show at Naumburg, and as I saw elsewhere in the same part of Germany, stalls against the centre of the eastern side of a screen are not uncommon, I have nowhere else seen such a complete shutting-off of the choir from the church as has from the very first existed here. There is a space between the back of the stalls and the rood-screen, in which probably an entrance was originally contrived to the ambo under the rood, though of this no trace now remains.

There are no parcloses between the choir and the transepts, whilst between the latter and the aisles of the nave there are only rude and modern screens, without any trace of the original arrangement.

And now that we are in the choir, the most noticeable feature is the altar with its reredos, and its great standard candles on either side.[1] The reredos is elaborately decorated with colour, and consists of three very fine trefoiled arches with crocketed gables above, and elaborate and lofty pinnacles between them. The spaces within the three arches are much recessed, and ornamented at the back with sculpture of figures in niches, and tracery; the whole very full of delicate taste in its execution. The altar is perfectly plain and solid, with a moulded mensa, and footpace of three steps in front and at the ends. It stands, of course, on the chord of the apse. The arrangement at the back of the reredos is most singular: there are two lockers on either side, and in the centre a doorway, which when opened discloses steps leading down to the space under, and enclosed by, the altar. In this space there are five square recesses below the level of the floor: three on the west side, and one at each end; the dimensions of this chamber are 8 ft. by 3 ft. 6 in., and 7 ft. 3 in. to the under side of the mensa of the altar; the recesses in it are 1 ft. 8¾ in. wide by 1 ft. 7 in. deep. But one of the most singular

---

[1] I have given a drawing of these candlesticks for the *Instrumenta Ecclesiastica*. They are not movable candlesticks, but regular fixtures to the pavement, and made in some kind of white metal.

features in it is, that there were evidently originally sliding shutters in front of each of the three recessed niches which form the front of the reredos. These are all gone, but the grooves remain both above and below, and leave not a shadow of doubt as to their former existence. There are two grooves in front of each division, and of course there are corresponding openings in the mensa of the altar. The arrangement is so new to me, that it is difficult to say exactly for what specific purpose it may have been made; but it seems obvious that it might allow of great variety of decoration or illustration of subjects suited to the varying seasons of the Christian year, supposing the sliding shutters to have been decorated with paintings.

To the south of the altar are oak sedilia — a long seat undivided, but with five canopies above: the work all good, but defective in not having its divisions marked through the whole height.

The windows in the choir are, as I have before observed, full of fine stained glass, some of which is of very early character. The lower tier of windows is filled with subjects in medallions, the upper with two rows of figures and canopies — a satisfactory and common arrangement in old work.

Some old lockers in the walls, and banners suspended round the apse, serve to complete a most striking and long-to-be-remembered *tout ensemble.*

Unfortunately there are no signs of any ancient pavement, unless we take for old the wretched gravestones of the Landgraves of Hesse and their family, which almost cover the floor. They are effigies of recumbent figures in not very low relief, but partly sunk below the proper level of the floor and partly raised. One stumbles over these wretched man-traps at every step, and wishes heartily that such a device for damaging ankles had never been invented. In the south transept there are a number of high tombs with recumbent effigies, beginning with one of early date and fine character.

The north transept, however, contains something better than these monuments, and one of the greatest curiosities of the church — the chapel, as they call it, of S. Elizabeth. It never had an altar, and was not a chapel, but simply a very beautiful kind of tabernacle, within which was deposited the marvellously beautiful shrine in which were preserved the relics of the saint, and which — now removed to the sacristy — is still the great treasure of the church. The relics were all dispersed, I believe, at the time of the Reformation, though the church is still held by the Catholics. This tabernacle, if I may so call it, is a rectangular erection, narrow at the east and west, and with its principal front towards the south. A trefoiled arch on each face, supported upon clusters of shafts at the four angles, forms the design, the arches inclosed within a square projecting moulding, with their spandrels not carved but bearing marks of painting. The great beauty of the work is the exquisite foliage which is carved in such masses all round the arches and elsewhere as quite to take the place of mouldings. All this foliage is natural, much varied, and undercut with such boldness as to stand out in very great relief. I would that every carver in England could have the opportunity to study this exquisite work, and still more, the sense to profit by it. All the openings are filled in with iron grilles; and the whole is just large enough to contain and protect the shrine. It stands upon double steps, which are prolonged to form a footpace for an altar which has been built against its west side, and which, on the south, are worn into hollows by the knees of pilgrims.

Above the stone work is an open wooden railing, apparently of the same date; and this incloses a space which is reached by a staircase from behind. In the reredos of the altar erected against the shrine are some sculptures from the life of the saint, her death, her burial, and the exaltation of her relics after canonization, etc., whilst on the shutters are paintings representing some of the more remarkable subjects in her story.

The shrine has been removed for safety to the sacristy, and is carefully guarded and fenced about with iron-work, as well it may be. It is an exquisite work of the best period — *circa* 1280-1300 — covered with the most delicate work in silver-gilt and adorned profusely with jewels and enamels, and on the whole I think the finest shrine I have ever seen.

The doors in the sacristy and elsewhere throughout the church are of deal, and were originally covered with linen or leather, which as far as I could make out was always coloured a bright red; it is a most curious evidence of the extent to which colour was introduced everywhere, and must have been most effective. It is not, however, the only instance with which I have met; and I may mention the magnificent north transept doors of the cathedral at Halberstadt as examples of the same thing.

Between the north transept and the sacristy is a passage, which leads to the external passages which I have already described as surrounding the whole exterior of the church.

My notice of Marburg has already extended far beyond what I purposed, though not beyond its deserts; and yet I cannot conclude without saying a few words about the castle, which so grandly towers over the old tower and church.

The climb up to it is really a serious business; and when I reached the summit I had to exhibit no little adroitness in passing a sentinel who obstinately wanted to send me back, in order that I might ascend by some more tortuous and more legal path than I had chosen.

I went first into the chapel. This is raised to a considerable height upon other buildings, and approached by a newel staircase. It is a very curious and very satisfactory little building, its entire length 39 ft., and its width 18 ft. 6 in. There is a three-sided apse at either end, and one bay only between them; this central bay has projections on either side, which inside have the effect of very small transepts, and externally are treated as bay windows. The windows are all geometrical, of two lights, and very good detail. Externally, there are buttresses at the angles of the apse, which rise out of the much thicker walls of the rooms below the chapel, and do not go down to the ground. In the eastern apse there are a piscina and a locker. The old pavement still remains; it is all of red tile, arranged in large circles, with tiles generally triangular in shape and of various sizes. Unfortunately, this little chapel is full of galleries and pews.

From hence I ascended to the Ritter-Saal, a fine large groined hall, somewhat like the well known hall in the Stadt-Haus at Aix-la-Chapelle. It is divided by a row of columns down the centre, from which the groining-ribs spring, and is about 100 feet long by 42 feet wide. Each bay has a very fine four-light transomed window, and the whole is of early date. Below it, on the ground floor, is a smaller hall, the groining of which springs from a central shaft, and the windows in which are of three and five transomed lights, and of very early character.

The interest of both these halls is very great, as they are quite untouched, and of a rare date for domestic work on such a scale. The exterior of this portion of the buildings is very fine, boldly buttressed, with great angle turrets, and occupying just the edge of the cliff.

The castle stands upon a narrow prong of hill, very precipitous on three sides, and all around its base the town clusters; on one side is the grand church of S. Elizabeth, looking most admirable in this capital bird's-eye view, and on the other a long flight of steps leads to a church which from above looks very well, but which did not repay examination, its only interesting feature being an old *Sakraments-Häuslein.*

I walked back from the castle by a roundabout path all through the old town, and reached my inn too late to get on to Frankfort by the train I had fixed on; but I was not sorry, as I had an excuse for getting some more sketches of the exterior of the cathedral, and had all the more pleasant thoughts wherewith to solace myself as I travelled through the dark night to Frankfort.

I think I have said enough to show that ecclesiologists may depend upon pleasure of no ordinary kind in visiting such churches as those of Naumburg, Erfurt, and Marburg. They are remarkable, not only for their generally fine character, but more especially for their exquisite sculpture and for the extent to which they have preserved almost untouched and undamaged their extraordinarily beautiful furniture and fittings; and are, therefore, of especial value to us, who have so little of the same kind of thing left in our own churches.

IV

MÜNSTER AND SOEST

In the course of the autumn of last year, I spent a short holiday, not unprofitably, I hope, in the examination of some of the old towns in the north of Germany; and, as the interest of the architectural remains in this district is very great, and our acquaintance with them too slight, I cannot help thinking that a mere transcript of my diary during the time that I was examining them may be of some use and interest. I have already printed notices, drawn up from the same journal, of the churches of Lübeck, and the cathedral at Marburg; and I shall now employ myself in giving shorter descriptions of the other chief features of this journey.

Crossing by Calais, and taking hurried glances only at S. Omer, with its noble cathedral, and the fine relic of the abbey of S. Bertin, remarkable among great French churches for its *single* western tower, I went on to Lille, — a town whose interest to architects just now is rather in the future than in the past, but whose church of S. Maurice is a striking example of the difference in the conception of a town church on the Continent and in this country in the Middle Ages. It has two aisles on each side of the nave and choir, and is groined throughout. Here we should look on such a church almost in the light of a cathedral; there, on the contrary, it is a not very remarkable parish church. Some old brick work at the back of the Hotel de Ville is the only other old feature which I remember in Lille; but its streets and market-place are busy and picturesque.

From Lille, passing by Courtrai, I reached Ypres in time to spend the afternoon in sketching and studying what is perhaps the noblest example of the domestic work of Germany. Les Halles, as this great pile of building is called, seems to have been a great covered mart, rather than a mere town hall; and when I was there, a fair was being held within its walls, and, filled with picturesque groups of people, and stalls for the sale of every conceivable kind of merchandise, the grandeur of its size and design was well seen. The main portion of the building is of uniform early middle-pointed date, and forms an immense and rather irregular parallelogram, enclosing some long and narrow courts. The principal front towards the market place is, by a rough measurement which I made, about 375 feet in length; very uniform in its design, but broken in the centre by a fine lofty engaged tower, surmounted with a spire, finishing in a sort of louvre, of modern character. The whole effect of the building is inconceivably grand, leaving behind it in point of general effect even (I am bold in saying it) the Ducal Palace at Venice. In elevation the main building is divided into three stages. The ground stage consists of a succession of openings with square heads, trefoiled; the next of a long series of two-light windows with quatrefoils in the head, the openings in which are square, the tracery not being pierced; and the third stage has again an immense succession of traceried openings alternately glazed and blank. The whole is surmounted by a lofty traceried parapet corbelled out, and the steep and original timber roof is surmounted with a ridge-crest of stone, of more delicate character than I have ever seen elsewhere. The front is finished at the angles with immense octangular pinnacles, corbelling out at their base from the wall, and the tower, which rises two stages above the ridge of the roof, has also at its angles similar pinnacles. The general *motif* of the entire front is continued happily in the steeple, the faces of which are occupied with rows of lofty windows of two lights. From the belfry, and from within another corbelled parapet, springs the spire, which, at first square, becomes, below the tourelle on its summit, an octagon.

Immediately behind Les Halles, stands the cathedral. This has a fine western tower, built *circa* A.D. 1380, and remarkable for the triple buttresses at its angles. The west door is double, and set within an enclosing arch with the west window, in a common German fashion. The interior is lofty and spacious, with cylindrical shafts, whose capitals have simple foliage of the thirteenth century. The triforium is good, and some of the clerestory (e.g. that in the south transept) is also early and good; but the whole church is not by any means of the first order. The south transept has recently been very creditably restored, the new carving being executed with much spirit. The east end is remarkable externally for its tall buttresses, without weatherings, and for the deep arches under which the windows are set, and which give the building too much of a skeleton effect to be pleasing. A rather graceful turret (of Renaissance character) surmounts the crossing.

The cathedral and Les Halles, though close together, are not absolutely parallel, but the combination of the two buildings, with their towers and turrets, and two other towers, is very good, and gives an imposing effect to the general views of the old city.

It is to be observed, that though in Les Halles the pointed arch and the very best window-tracery are everywhere used, there is no possibility of mistaking it for a church, or even for a religious building.

There are many old houses in the town, generally of the sixteenth century, with stepped gables, and four-centred window-heads with carved tympana; but their effect generally is not satisfactory.

Between Ypres and Courtrai (whither I next journeyed) are some large churches, of which that at Comines would, I think, repay examination. Courtrai has not much to call for remark; though its market place is quaint, picturesque, and irregularly grouped, with a clock-tower, turreted at the angles and with a spire-like capping, rising suddenly out from among its houses, out of whose windows sound forth constantly those cheery chimes which give so much colour to the recollection of all the towns in this chime-loving part of the world. At the back of the market place a fine middle-pointed church tower rises, capped with a most picturesque slated tourelle. The church to which it is attached is the largest in Courtrai, but not remarkable. It has an apsidal projecting chapel in the second bay from the west, noticeable in that the axis of the apse is north and south. The other churches are of little value, and much mutilated. Notre Dame has a western tower, and a chapel added on the south side of the choir which has pinnacles, and a bell-turret on the gable, of very good character.

Perhaps the most interesting building in the town is the town-hall. It is of late date, and the tracery of the windows, and the figures which once adorned the front between the windows, are all destroyed. The doors are original, and an old staircase with panelled sides, and partly old metal balustrade, leads to the hall on the first floor. This has a fine simple open roof of timber, with double collar-beams and arched braces: this, I fear, is no longer visible, as, when I was there, workmen were just about to begin the erection of a ceiling under it, to make the room fit for the reception of the King of the Belgians. In two side rooms there are very remarkable fire-places, one of which is well known by Haghe's drawing. The finer of the two is adorned with a profusion of sculptures representing the Vices and Virtues and very striking in their treatment.

From Courtrai, a short journey by railway brought me to Tournai — a town not, I think, so well known as it ought to be for its magnificent cathedral — doubtless the finest, by very far, in Belgium. The nave and transepts are Romanesque. In the former, there is that quadruple division in height so frequent in the thirteenth century churches in the neighbouring part of France. The transepts are very noble, and ended with grand apses, and both they and the choir are very much more lofty than the nave. They owe much of their grandeur to the number of detached shafts of great size, and to the fact that the aisle, triforium, and clerestory, are all carried round the apses. The choir is all of the thirteenth century, and very lofty and light in its proportions. The windows are being carefully restored; but some bad stained glass has been recently put up. In the sacristy there is a little old plate, of which I may mention a fine monstrance, and two shrines; one of which, of the thirteenth century, is one of the most exquisite I have ever seen, being adorned with a great deal of enamelling and silversmith's work, of most delicate character. There is also here a fine cope-chest; but I found only one old vestment, — the orphrey of a chasuble, with figures of saints; date about A.D. 1450; the rest were modern, and generally very tawdry. But they possess here, in addition to these vestments, an altar frontal, of great interest; it is embroidered on a white silk ground, with a tree of Jesse: the figures are well executed in high relief, and the effect of the whole, with the stiff conventional arms of the tree encircling the figures, is very striking. The embroidery is executed in the same way as our old English work; but I never saw any figures worked with so much spirit or so much character in their faces. The old fringe of red silk over gold thread remains.

The external view of the cathedral presents one of the most singular, and, at the same time, most grand assemblages of steeples I have ever seen. There are two tall towers, richly arcaded and capped with square slated spires, to each transept, and over the crossing a much lower though larger lantern also capped with a spire. These five spires are well seen from the market place, and with a tall campanile at its upper end, of the thirteenth century, combine in a very grand group. I should have mentioned that the central spire is octagonal with four square slated turrets at the angles. The east end of the cathedral deserves notice; its scale is great, and its flying buttresses and detail generally very good. Chapels are formed between the buttresses and roofed with gables running back to the aisle walls.

The Maison de Ville was formerly a convent and still retains a few old portions built up in the more modern additions.

In the market place is a small church, the entrance to which is at the east, and the altar at the west end. Over the east door are two triplets, quite first-pointed in their character. There are round turrets at the west angles and to the transepts, and a picturesque slated spire over the crossing; the whole is groined, and reminded me of the style of the transepts of the cathedral, though it is not very effective.

Another church on the way to the railway station has an eastern apse, and a tower and slated spire over the crossing. The nave has a continuous clerestory, with two or three windows in each bay; the effect of which is satisfactory. Across the nave, one bay west of the choir, there is an arch with a kind of triforium gallery across it, pierced on each side, and serving apparently for a passage-way only. It is not continued up to the groining.

THE GREAT S. MARTIN, COLOGNE

Nearer the railway there is another large church with a continuous clerestory and large unfinished-looking tower at the south-west angle.

There are some other churches, but not, I think, of great interest. This, however, is amply afforded by the magnificent cathedral towering so grandly over the town, whose only defect in the distant view is the low height of the nave as compared with the choir and transepts.

A sluggish train took me in five or six hours to Namur to sleep, and thence early the next morning by a strikingly beautiful line of railway along the banks of the Meuse; and passing by the picturesque old town of Huy, with its fine church and castle, I found my way to Liège.

The churches here are really too often visited and too well known to require any description from me. I think the little church of S. Croix, with its gabled aisles (the gables running back into the main roof), pleased me as much as anything; it is just the kind of special town church which we want to see more in fashion in our own large towns, adapting itself boldly to every variation in the boundary of the land on which it is built, and giving a very considerable effect of height without extravagant expense.

The metal font in the church of S. Bartholomew is a very admirable work of art, and most interesting in every way.

In the cathedral is a new pulpit, by Geefs, much praised in guide books, but not a favourable specimen of his powers, I trust.

S. Jacques, S. Martin, and other churches in Liège are remarkable for the richness of their internal polychromatic decorations. They are all, however, of very late date, quite Renaissance in their design and colouring, and very tawdry in effect and in detail. The east end of S. Jacques is, however, very impressive owing to the rich colour of the glass in the windows, which carries the decoration down from the roof to the floor, whilst elsewhere, the roof only being painted, and the whole of the walls left in the coldest white, the effect is heavy and unsatisfactory. We have, in short, here a good practical proof — worth a thousand arguments — that colour to be successful must be generally diffused and not confined to one part of a building.

From Liège to Aix-la-Chapelle, of which too I shall say but little. The choir of the cathedral, which had been entirely despoiled of its tracery, is being gradually and well restored. It is both a noble and a very peculiar church, and perhaps the best view of it is to be obtained from the staircase in the old Rathhaus. How striking is the immense height of the choir as compared to its length, and how thoroughly fine and picturesque is the kind of dome, surrounded at its base with gables, which crowns the polygonal nave.

No one who visits Aix should omit to see the treasures in the sacristy of the cathedral. I have never seen anywhere so fine a gathering of mediaeval goldsmith's work, and a little study of these old remains would immensely improve the work of the few men who are attempting to revive the old glory of their craft.

The Rathhaus contains in its upper stage a fine large groined hall, called the Kaiser-Saal, divided down the centre by columns and arches; it is approached by a good groined staircase, and is now being restored and decorated in fresco, by a Düsseldorf artist, with subjects from the life of Charlemagne.

Near the cathedral is a valuable remnant of good domestic work; it has windows with plate tracery, and above them a row of niches or arcading, the divisions of the arcade being filled in with figures of kings in a very effective manner. It reminded me of the famous Maison des Musiciens, at Rheims.

At Aix I was too near Cologne to omit the pleasure of spending another day among its crowd of architectural treasures, and so, instead of going to Düsseldorf direct, I gave myself a holyday, and renewed all my old recollections of its many glories.

I cannot think that the new works at the cathedral are so satisfactory as they are generally said to be. When I was there the scaffolding had just been removed from the south transept, and the effect was very far from good; there was a degree of poverty in the execution which is not felt in the old work; it looks thin, "liney" and attenuated, and makes me doubt very much, first, whether it is a fair reproduction of the old design; and next, whether the following out of an old design drawn to a small scale is possible without very great powers of designing. So much depends upon detail.

I believe that the building in Cologne which above all others ought most to be studied, is that wonderful church of S. Gereon, the interior of which is so fine, and so unlike what we ever think of doing in our new work. Its nave consists of an irregular decagon, entered from a western narthex, and surrounded by chapels, from the east of which runs a long and spacious choir, approached by a great flight of steps. This nave is about 65 feet from east to west, and slightly more from north to south; forming a very grand unbroken area, all within easy reach of any one voice, and, from its height and rich character, very impressive. The choir is of considerable length, and raised on a crypt. A large modern altar placed on the steps leading to it from the nave, completely conceals it in the general view, and much mars the whole effect.

The filth of the church when I was there was extreme, and the noble crypt which extends under the whole length of the choir was thoroughly desecrated. I noticed an original altar in a side chapel

In the crypt, used as a receptacle for candle-ends! The sacristy of S. Gereon is a noble middle-pointed addition, fitted with old presses, and with some very beautiful glass in the windows. This, in the tracery, is very light in colour, spotted with ruby.

Next in grandeur, perhaps, to this church, is the east end of S. Martin's. Seen from the street below the east end, its great height, and the combination of the apsidal transepts and choir with the fine central steeple produce very great effect. It is worthy of notice, how completely similar all these apsidal terminations are in Cologne, and how like those of the same date in the north of Italy. The apses here, for instance, are almost exactly like that of the choir of S. Maria Maggiore at Bergamo.

Cologne is rich in metal-work and early stalls. In S. Cunibert is a fine brass standard for lights, with a crucifix; in the choirs of S. Pantaleon and S. Andrew, some good thirteenth century stalls; S. Gereon has also some old candlesticks, and some woodwork worth notice, as also have some of the other churches.

Perhaps the best example of later work in the city is the fine church of the Minorites, a good fourteenth century building, with a lofty and elegant lead turret rising out of the centre of the roof.

I found in several of the Cologne churches services in the morning, attended exclusively by children. They had no seats, but a succession of boards, with small kneeling-stools at regular intervals, were provided for them. The singing was uncommonly good and hearty, and after one of the services (at S. Maria in Capitolio), I asked the children about it, and they told me that they went every day before school. I looked at some of their school-books, and found that they had a rather full Scripture history abridgment; and among other books one full of songs and hymns, which seemed to be particularly good and spirited — hearty, merry songs, which would be sure to take with children. We should do well if we could have such a service and such books for our English children.

There was an exhibition of early German pictures of considerable interest in the old hall called the Gurzenich. I found that it was organized by a Christian Art Society, which has a large number of members, and seems to be very actively at work. In the great hall of the Gurzenich is a magnificent fire-place, of late middle-pointed date, and much like the Courtrai fire-place in general idea; there are some very spirited figures in armour in its niches. This building is well known on the exterior by its general ancient character, and particularly by the lead canopies over the figures in its lowest stage.

But Cologne is too well known to make any more of my notes (which might be extended to tenfold length) palatable; and I shall, therefore, hurry on to what is, I believe, newer ground to most ecclesiologists than are its time-honoured and well known buildings.

From Deutz (the bridge to which place from Cologne affords the best general view of the city) a few hours of railway took me to Hamm, and thence by a branch I reached Münster. The country here is cheerful and English-looking; though rather flat, it is woody and well cultivated, and thickly populated, — at least, so I gathered by the multitude of passengers who swarmed at every station, all in blue smocks, and all smoking vehemently.

The churches and domestic buildings at Münster are almost equally interesting. Of the latter, the Rathhaus is the most remarkable. It is very elaborate and beautiful in all its details, but (like most of the house-fronts here) boasts of a regular show front. The ground stage consists of four open arches; the next, of four richly-traceried windows, divided by figures in niches, carved with great spirit; and above this is an immense stepped gable-end, divided into seven panels in width, and rising to about twice the height of the real roof. It is pinnacled, and filled with open traceries, which, being pierced above the roof, show the sky through their openings. The lower part of the building is of the best middle-pointed, but in the gable some of the tracery is ogee and poor.

This front was followed in Münster throughout the rest of the Middle Ages, as also by the Renaissance school, so that the whole town is full of arcaded streets, like an Italian town, and all the houses have more or less exaggerated fronts, stepped and pinnacled high above the roof-line. The *tout ensemble* of such a town, it may be imagined, is picturesque in the extreme, though not so valuable as at first sight it seems likely to prove to the architectural traveller. The endless repetition of the same — and that a bad — idea, is very tiresome, and so, beautiful as is the Rathhaus in some of its detail, and striking as it certainly is in its general effect, I have not forgiven it as being the first example with which I am acquainted of a long series of barbarisms.

The only old apartment in this building, so far as I could discover, is a room called the Frieden-Saal. It is a low council-chamber, of late date, which has been most elaborately restored, and renovated with much rich colour. There are some very good hinges and locks on a series of closets here.

Of the churches, there are some five or six old, besides some modern. The cathedral is very curious. Its plan shows two western towers, then a transept; a nave of two (!) very wide bays; transept again; and an apsidal choir, with several apsidal chapels round its aisle. The internal effect of the nave is singular. It is very simple, but from the great width of the bays rather bold-looking. The most notable things here are, — a very noble brass font; a brass corona in the choir; a stand for eleven candles, also in the choir; a magnificent stone rood-screen of late date; a very good *Sakraments-Häuslein*, and some niches for relics, etc., with their old doors; another stand for lights, something like that at S. Cunibert, Cologne; and some stalls of the seventeenth century, founded very closely upon mediaeval examples. The brass font is circular, supported upon five lions, the two eastern of which are standing, the others recumbent. The stem is covered with tracery and moulding, and the bowl has five large quatrefoiled circles, the eastern containing the Baptism of our Lord, and the other four the emblems of the four Evangelists, with scrolls and inscriptions in red letters; above them, a trefoiled arcade contains half-figures of the twelve Apostles. The corona is large, containing fifty candles in one row; but it is of late date, and frittered away in elaborate tracery and crocketing. The rood-screen has two doorways — one on each side of an altar in the centre of its west front. This altar still remains, with a sculpture of the Crucifixion at its back, but is not used now, a modern altar having been put up in front of it. Two very light open staircases on the eastern side of the screen lead to the Gospel and Epistle sides of the loft. There is also a very fine and large crucifix against one of the nave piers.

The main entrance to the cathedral is through a sort of Galilee of Romanesque date adorned with a number of fine statues; this is at the south-west of the church, whilst on its north side are some fair middle-pointed cloisters.

Next to the cathedral in importance is the Oberwasser-Kirche, a late middle-pointed building; it has a large south-west tower very much of the same type as the great tower at Ypres, having four windows of two lights in each stage, and four stages all exactly alike, and above them an octagonal belfry stage of later date. The first example of this kind of design is seen in the four belfry windows of the cathedral at Soest, and still more remarkably in the steeple of Paderborn cathedral, but here it is developed into even greater regularity. This design, however, is poor in kind, and only respectable when characterized as at Soest and Paderborn by massive simplicity. The south door of the Oberwasser-Kirche is good, being double with square openings within an arched head. Internally the church is very lofty and light, but of no great length, and has an eastern apse, and some traces of old wall painting. A very good brass water vat hung from a small crane by the north door and served as a stoup for holy water; this is a common plan in the Münster churches.[1]

This church was being scraped of paint and whitewash; so also

---

[1] I have given a drawing of this vat in the *Instrumenta Ecclesiastica*.

In the cathedral they were removing some trumpery work of the last century, and indeed generally in this district a good deal is being done to the finer churches, and in most of them a box is provided for offerings for the restoration of the fabric: in most, I should say, which are not "evangelical":— for in these, save where the government is repairing the stone work, they seem to be satisfied to put up pews and galleries, to keep the doors well locked, and to make their interiors look as cold, miserable, and repulsive as possible. Happily, however, the "evangelical" church is not very actively mischievous in architectural matters, and so one sees altars and reredoses still standing with candles and crucifixes, and curtains of white muslin or silk on each side, sometimes, as in the Petri-Kirche at Soest, double, first, on each side of the altar, and then the same height as the altar, and coming forward the full width of the footpace![1] In the old altars, there are always arrangements for closets — generally at one end — whilst in the middle of the back of the altar is often an opening, which I fancied might have been made for the reception of relics, but which seldom seems carefully enough fastened; the ends of the super-altars have also, very frequently, closets; generally speaking, the altars in this district are solid masses of masonry with a projecting and moulded mensa. This, however, is a digression, and I must now say somewhat of the Lamberti-Kirche, which is next to the cathedral the best church in Münster. Externally it has a western tower [2] of considerable dimensions dwarfed in appearance by the immense size of the roof which covers both nave and aisles; this is a not uncommon arrangement in this district, and has a parallel, as will be remembered, in the noble choir of S. Laurence at Nuremberg. Its main result is the great internal effect of height in the aisles and the opportunity it affords of obtaining what Germans were so fond of — an immense length of window opening. The entrance to S. Lambert on the south side is by a very beautiful doorway; the doorway itself is not very large but its jamb mould runs up to a great height and encloses a fine sculptured tree of Jesse; the branches of the tree form a series of medallions, in each of which is a half figure; the whole is very rich in its effect, and the sculpture quite exquisite. Internally the only remarkable piece of furniture I noted was a very fine rood. The proportions and arrangements of the church are very similar to

---

[1] It must be understood that these are not the original curtains; but that the Lutherans have here preserved an old arrangement is very evident.

[2] On the south side of this steeple still hang the iron cages in which John of Leyden and his confrères were suspended before their execution.

those of the famous Wiesen-Kirche, at Soest, which I shall have presently to describe, and mainly noticeable for the great effect of unbroken space, owing to the large span and great height of the arches, and the small number of piers supporting the roof.

Two other churches near this afforded little worth notice. One of them was Protestant, and as a consequence, was elaborately pewed and galleried; it was seven or eight bays in length, and groined throughout, and entered by a good double door. The other was very similar, and had a curious kind of narthex under the western tower.

The Ludgeri-Kirche is of more interest, having a fine octagonal belfry of late date; this was undergoing repair, as was also the church, whose nave is of simple Romanesque with a good middle-pointed apse. There is another church of small size with an eastern apse, and a very low gabled tower at the north-west angle. This is near the railway station.

For two things besides her domestic buildings Münster is certainly to be remembered: these are the brass work and the sculpture; the latter is generally remarkably good, and I think I have seldom seen more spirited figures than I saw there.

In a silversmith's shop, opposite the Lamberti-Kirche, I found a magnificent old monstrance, of the fourteenth century, and of very elaborate detail; it belonged to a church some miles distant, the name of which I have forgotten; this man was making church plate in very fair fashion, copying old examples with some care and with a good deal of feeling and enthusiasm; I need hardly say that such men are as rare on the Continent as they are here.

From Münster I returned to Hamm, and thence by another branch railway to Soest, travelling through a country without any feature by which to remember it save its interminable rows of poplars.

The first view of Soest from the railway is striking; several steeples, of which that of the cathedral is the grandest, stand up well behind a bank of trees, and a great extent of picturesque and half-ruined old town walls.

The town itself is very curious, much more like some large Swiss village, such as one remembers in the Upper Valais or the Hasli-Thal, than any other cathedral town that I know in northern Europe. The streets are all absurdly irregular, bending and twisting about in every possible direction, and full of half-timbered houses, which are all corbelled forward and seem generally to be very ancient. I think, indeed, that I have never seen more picturesque grouping of old buildings, but it is difficult to imagine how they can have preserved their old character so intact; there is absolutely, I believe, not one shop with a shop front or display of its wares of any kind, and hardly more than one modernized house, and this is a smart little inn with a nice garden, and a large Speise-Saal whose walls were literally covered with English prints, many of them old and very good. The population of the place consists nevertheless of some seven or eight thousand persons.

The churches have some very remarkable features, of which the most singular is a kind of narthex at the west end, not forming part of the fabric, but built within the churches, the main groining extending on over it to the west end, and a large gallery being formed above it. The best example of this is in S. Peter's, and I shall leave, for the present, a detailed description of it.

The cathedral is a great, rude, desolate-looking church with but few remains of any interest, save at the west end, out of the centre of which rises a fine simple Romanesque steeple. This has five single-light windows in the stage above the roof, and four three-light windows above them. Then above this belfry-stage is on each face a steep gable, filled in with openings of varied shapes — on one side, a large circular window, with three other small openings, and on another side three large windows of three lights, and a very small circular window. These gables are not the full width of the tower, and from the angles between them rise four tall and massive pinnacles, slightly ornamented with corbel tables under the eaves, and covered with steep pyramidal metal roofs. The spire is of metal, octagonal in section, — the angles of the octagon springing from the apices of the four gables, and from the internal angles of the four pinnacles. The size and solidity of this remarkable tower give great grandeur to it, and whilst in the treatment of its lower part we see the type of so many of the towers of later date in this district, in that of the spire we see the precursor of those noble spires rising from simple gabled towers which are the glory of Lüneburg and Lübeck.

In addition to an internal narthex, the cathedral has, in front of its tower, another groined sort of passage-way, opening to the west with six arches, and to the north and south with one arch. There is a second stage above these arches, and then from behind this mass rises the steeple. The whole of this part of the building is Romanesque, as, indeed, is the substance of the entire church though it has been much mutilated by modern additions and alterations. The interior is painfully neglected and dirty, though it is, I believe, the only Catholic church in the place. The eastern apse has upon its groining some painting, which seems to be ancient and very good, having figures of saints etc., on a large scale, but it is very much hidden by an odious modern reredos. There is a good wooden crucifix against one of the piers, and some fine very early glass in the transepts windows. Early in the morning, when I went again into the cathedral I found it full of people singing well and very heartily.

The church of S. Peter stands close to the cathedral; and its choir and aisles, ending with three apses and steep slated roofs, its windows filled with middle-pointed traceries, with the old steeple at the west end capped with a modern bulbous spire, group very picturesquely with the stern and grand steeple of the cathedral. In plan it consists of a nave and aisles, of four primary bays (each bay being subdivided by two arches opening into the aisles), transepts, choir and apsidal choir-aisles, opening into the transepts. The two western bays of the nave are again subdivided into three divisions north and south, and four divisions east and west; all this space being groined over at a low level, and having a floor above, forming a gallery level with the triforium, which also is large and spacious. The internal effect of this low, dark entrance-way is most peculiar. In S. Peter's, its length from east to west is nearly 46 feet — just half the whole length of the nave! The architecture of the church generally is not otherwise very interesting; though the east end is good, and has some fragments of fair glass still remaining. I have already mentioned the curious arrangement of the curtains on each side of the Lutheran altar here.

S. Paul's is another church of precisely the same type. It has a good western steeple, with a very steep square roof, or rather, I should say, a low spire. The stages of the tower are repetitions of each other. Both this church and S. Peter's are disfigured by a wonderful accumulation of pews and galleries; there is still, however, in the sacristy, a very good press, of three divisions in width and two in height.

I come, last, to the Wiesen-Kirche, a most remarkable building, of whose history, I am sorry to say, I know absolutely nothing. It appears, however, to have been all erected at one period — in the first half of the fourteenth century, — and its scale is so fine, and its character throughout so good, that it is certainly one of the most noticeable churches in the north of Germany. Moreover, in internal effect, I think I know no church of the same size which can vie with it for exquisite grace and elegance and, at the same time, boldness and grandeur of conception.

The plan may be described as a nave and aisles, of only three bays in length, about 76 feet in width, and 100 feet in length; the nave and aisles each terminating in an apse at the east, whilst at the west end there is an unfinished front, which seems to have been intended to have two towers. It is difficult to conceive how such a west front could ever have been suitable for a building which was in no other respect more than a mere chapel. It was never, however, at all nearly completed; and now a tall slated spire finishes one of the stunted towers in a fashion which is picturesque in the distant view, but very unsatisfactory when seen close at hand. The nave and aisles are covered with one great roof, and groined at the same level. The four nave columns are very lofty, and without any capitals; the mouldings being continuous to the groining; there being no more than four points of support in a square of about 76 by 120 feet, it may be imagined that from every point the whole interior is visible. The windows are of immense height, but judiciously treated, as in the clerestory windows at Cologne, by the arrangement of colour in the glass; besides which, a kind of transom of quatrefoils runs through all the windows at about one-fourth of the whole height. Below this transom, the glass is very rich and dark in colour; above the transom, for about half its height, there are figures under canopies, also dark with colour, and then a long sweep of beautiful grisaille runs up to the head of the windows, the patterns being all geometrical, and defined by delicate lines of colour: the whole is very jewelly and brilliant, and fortunately a good deal remains. This is, indeed, just one of those buildings which depends very much for its proper effect upon all its windows being filled with coloured glass. All the old altars remain, though the church is Protestant. There is one in each apse, and one against the west side of the two easternmost of the nave columns. All the altars have closets in their ends, and the one against the south-east column of the nave has a portion of a very good middle-pointed stone reredos and is itself richly panelled below the mensa. Behind another altar in the north-eastern apse, there is the remnant of a very fine middle-pointed rood of wood, which is now nailed up behind a late triptych. There is a very good early *Sakraments-Häuslein* in the north wall, and a good locker in the south wall of the principal apse, both with old iron doors. On two side altars in the nave, there have been erected some very fine pieces of late tabernacle-work. They have been brought from elsewhere; and I saw no place in the church from which they can have been taken. Another similar piece of stone work has been set up in the midst of the choir, and a door pierced through it leads into a pulpit, which grows out of and rests on the Lutheran altar! The north and south doorways are very fine; the latter having a window above it within the same arch, in the common German fashion. The whole church has an open parapet and lofty buttresses, with rather small pinnacles. The view from the east is certainly very striking; and though the idea is completely that of a chapel, rather than of a more ambitious church, it is certainly one of the finest chapels of its size that I have ever seen. The whole building is being restored at the expense of the King of Prussia, and at, I should think, very great cost, as it had suffered much from decay.

V
GERMAN POINTED ARCHITECTURE

Some apology is necessary for venturing to attempt to grapple with so large a subject as is that of pointed architecture in Germany. My only excuse for making such an attempt must be the vivid recollection of the journeys I have at different times made in that country, and the desire to help cordially in explaining to those who have still the journey before them, the features which characterize its architecture.

I have unfortunately been unable to hear what Mr. Parker has told you of pointed architecture in France; but no doubt he has dilated with sufficient enthusiasm upon the exquisite art there seen, upon the skill in the disposition of the ground plans — never equalled elsewhere — upon the beauty and vigour of the sculpture, and upon the nervous manliness and at the same time delicacy of the art in nearly all the buildings of the best period, at least in the old Île-de-France, in Picardy, and in Normandy. I grieve to say that I shall be able to give no such commendation to German architecture, and that, delightful as the recollections of what I have seen there are, I cannot nevertheless shut my eyes to the fact that in most respects it is entirely inferior to the development of the same style in France and England.

There are at the same time some peculiarities in the dates of old German work which are rather striking in comparison with English and French works.

You have, then, first of all, a few buildings, such as the convent at Lörsch, which are said to be and perhaps are of Roman design. Then next there is an immense group of churches of which those of Cologne and the Rhineland are the most distinguished examples, which, whilst it is entirely unlike anything in the rest of northern Europe, has a most remarkable affinity to the Lombard churches in the north of Italy, at Pavia, Bergamo, and elsewhere. These churches date from the early part or the middle of the twelfth century and continue with but little alteration of importance down to the end of the thirteenth, when the strange spectacle is seen of a style almost completely Romanesque in its character suddenly supplanted by another style which, so far as I can see, in no way grew out of it, and which is distinguished from the first by peculiarities of a most marked kind, and by the perfect and complete form which it at once assumed. Then after this style, which again in its turn retained its hold longer than our styles ever did, and which to a late period is altered only slightly in its detail, you will find another essentially German style answering in point of date to our later third-pointed and to French flamboyant. The Germans have therefore less natural growth to show in their architecture than we have. Instead of our beautiful gradations from Romanesque to third-pointed in which the germ of each development is to be discovered in the antecedent work, you have there a series of breaks or gaps in the chain which it is very difficult to account for, and which make the study of the style highly interesting, and at the same time somewhat perplexing.

The question seems naturally to arise whether each of these new styles, thus wanting in evidence of natural growth one out of the other, is to be looked at as a German invention in the true sense of the word, or as the result of the sudden conversion of a slow and sluggish people to the beauties of foreign work, and then their resolute and hearty earnestness in the attempt to make the style their own by some infusion of national peculiarities.

I incline to this last opinion because I believe that no style was ever invented. Architecture has always grown gradually and systematically, and it is quite possible to imagine that Germany may have refused to follow the lead of France and England in art until their superiority was so great as to make it an absolute matter of necessity, and that then an attempt would be made to give a national character to what they had in the first place borrowed.

A slight comparison of dates of a few buildings will explain my grounds for speaking as I do of German architecture.

Of the Rhine churches the most remarkable are the work of the thirteenth century. S. Gereon at Cologne was commenced A.D. 1200 and vaulted in A.D. 1227. S. Cunibert was in building from A.D. 1205 to A.D. 1248, when it was consecrated. Naumburg has a nave of A.D. 1200. Limburg is early in the thirteenth century; and Bamberg the same; whilst Gelnhausen was in building from A.D. 1250 to A.D. 1370. Now all these churches are of such a character that were we to see them in France we should at once put them down as the work of the end of the twelfth century, and we should look for another class to fill up the period between A.D. 1200 and A.D. 1270, when Cologne was commenced or the nave of Strasburg completed. You will see how important these dates are when you consider that at the same time that S. Gereon and S. Cunibert at Cologne, the choir of Magdeburg, and Gelnhausen, were being built, Amiens cathedral, S. Denis and other churches of the same kind were rising throughout France, whilst in England Westminster and a host of other churches of late first-pointed were built at the same time. I do not mean to say absolutely that no transitional buildings are to be found, but only that they were of extraordinary rarity and do not afford the same evidence of natural growth that our own do.

Of work really similar to our own first-pointed I can hardly give you more than one example, and that at Lübeck in the north porch of the cathedral, where — to say the least — the paternity of the work may well be doubtful. Of a later style and almost unique in its character, is the fine church of S. Elizabeth, at Marburg, a church whose date is well known (A.D. 1235 to A.D. 1283), and which affords us one of the few German examples of a style intermediate between the work at S. Gereon and that of Cologne cathedral. This will be seen by the sketches[1] which I have here, in which, however, it is to be observed that the design of the nave and apsidal terminations of the choir and transepts are the early portions of the work, and that the fittings and west front date nearer the end of the century. In the still beautiful reredos I think we may see the traces of an incipient departure from the style of the earlier work, and an approach to identity with what I must consider as the inferior art of the thorough German Gothic, as it is seen in its perfection in the cathedral at Cologne.

The aisles of the nave of Magdeburg cathedral seem also to me to be vastly superior to any other German work of the date that I know, whilst the western rood-screen and some of the details of the western choir at Naumburg are also of a degree of beauty which it would be very difficult to surpass elsewhere. The aisles of Paderborn cathedral, too, are of a peculiar but exceedingly good character. But these are, as I think, only exceptions which serve to prove the rule, and cannot in any degree be taken as evidence of the same kind of growth and gradual development that we trace with so much interest in every church and building of the Middle Ages in England. It was an architecture of fits and starts and conceits, not of growth, and full therefore of the contradictions and eccentricities which such a condition necessarily involves. And now having so far paved the way by a short statement of what is really the great peculiarity of German architecture, I will go on to consider and describe the several varieties of the style rather more in detail.

And first of all, as to the ground-plan. It is a curious fact, that each national style of pointed architecture has been distinguished by its adherence to some peculiarity of ground-plan, as well as by

---

[1] This paper was read before the Oxford Architectural Society, in 1857.— G. G. K.

other distinctive features. In England, we all know how great was the love for the square east end, and how strong the desire to extend the length of the nave to a sometimes almost unreasonable extent. In France, you know how steadily the apsidal termination was adhered to, and how completely it was the rule to have an aisle and chapels round the apse, making, in some of the finer French churches, an approach to absolute perfection of effect. You know, too, how very rare the square east end was in France, and yet how equally rare was any but a square end to the transepts. In Italy, again, there are peculiarities. Either you have immense halls, wide and long beyond all other examples, and borrowed, no doubt, from the ancient basilica; or apsidal churches, in which the aisles do not extend round the apse, and a series of apsidal chapels are sometimes added to the east of the transepts.

In Germany, as I shall show, we have an equally distinct class of ground-plans. The apsidal termination, though most general, does not altogether supplant the square end; but it is remarkable, that unlike the beautiful chevets of the French churches, the German apses are rarely surrounded with aisles or chapels. They are either simply apsidal, or parallel triapsidal, or transverse triapsidal, and the main difference between early and late examples, is to be found in the introduction of that angularity which gradually became the great feature of all German work. The early apsidal terminations were all circular: as, for instance, in the Apostles' church, at Cologne; whilst in Marburg, and later, in the little chapel of S. Werner, at Bacharach, though the transverse triapsidal plan is identical in other respects, it differs in that the apses are polygonal, instead of circular. At Bonn, the eastern apse is circular, the transeptal apse polygonal; and you may always take this as one of the certain evidences of later date, in works which may otherwise very nearly correspond.

Of parallel triapsidal churches, the church at Laach, and S. James at Ratisbon, are early examples; whilst Ratisbon cathedral, S. Catherine, Lübeck, the Marien-Kirche at Muhlhausen, and the Wiesen-Kirche at Soest, are examples of the same plan angularized at a later day. And you should note, that this parallel triapsidal plan is by far the most common of German plans in all ages, and is, moreover, one of which scarcely any examples exist out of Germany.[1]

Sometimes, as in S. Nicholas, Lemgo, whilst the choir is apsidal, the east end of the aisles is square; but this is a rather rare and very bad plan. In all these varieties of arrangement, there is no

---

[1] Street was not yet familiar with the Spanish churches, in which it is the dominant native form. Cf. *Gothic Architecture in Spain*, new edition, I, 58. — G. G. K.

comparison for a minute with the beauty of the French chevet; but it is right to observe, that there are some examples of imitation of this better type.

One of the earliest and most interesting, is the church of S. Godehard, at Hildesheim, in which we have the aisle round the apse, with three apsidal chapels, as well as apsidal chapels east of the transepts. This plan was imitated in the grand parish church of S. James, also at Hildesheim, at a much later date. The apse of Magdeburg cathedral is very much like that of S. Godehard, but of rather later date, and remarkable for the profusion of dogtooth in its cornices. In both, it is to be observed that the small chapels round the apse are mere excrescences, and finish with stone roofs below the parapet of the aisle. The Marien-Kirche at Lübeck is a later example of a chevet, whilst at Cologne cathedral, in emulation of Amiens, a plan of the best kind was adopted, and again wrought out on a smaller scale at Altenberg. There can be little doubt that it was not only in emulation but also in imitation of a French church, that this plan was designed. Scarcely another German church is at all like it, whereas its plan was the common one in France. In the Marien-Kirche at Lübeck, where there is an aisle round the apse, it is formed in the most clumsy manner, by enlarging the chapels; whilst S. Giles, at Brunswick, illustrates another and unsuccessful plan, viz., an apse, with the surrounding aisle, but no chapels.

I believe one of the reasons for this difference between French and German plans is to be found in the very remarkable objection which the Germans always exhibited to any departure from correct orientation of any of their altars. In the French chevet, it is impossible to attend to this; and hence, in a country where the feeling was strong on the point, it would be felt to be an unsuitable form. I believe that it was so felt in England, where, to the present day, the prejudice in favour of strict orientation is stronger than in any other country in Europe.

In Germany, we have most remarkable evidence of the feeling. At Magdeburg, for example, the altars in the apse of the cathedral are all placed with their fronts facing due west, and cutting, therefore, in the strangest way across all the main architectural lines of the building. It was for this reason that the parallel triapsidal plan was so popular.

But there is another most curious arrangement of plan, to which I must refer; that, namely, of which Laach, Bamberg, Worms, Mayence, S. Sebald, Nuremberg, and Naumburg, are remarkable examples, in which both east and west ends have apsidal choirs. The object of these western choirs is not very intelligible; but in that at Naumburg, we have most curious evidence of what I have before referred to: for the original altar in the western apse faces west, and has its back, therefore, towards the nave, so that the face of the priest at the altar would be seen by the congregation in the nave.

I ought to have observed, in speaking of some examples of apses with aisles, that even in these, the treatment was essentially German. The two churches at Nuremberg are examples which, as the aisles are of the same height as the choir, and the whole roofed over with one immense roof, present the appearance on the exterior of immense apses without aisles. And certainly there is great grandeur of effect in such a termination, though less structural truth, and less internal variety and beauty. Still, they are admirable departures from ordinary rules. The churches at Münster, S. Stephen at Vienna, Munich cathedral, Landshut, and the Wiesen-Kirche at Soest, are examples of the same kind of design. They have a very fine effect of simple unbroken height, but the absence of the triforium and clerestory is not forgiven, whilst the plan helped to develop that German extravagance of proportion in the length of the window monials which we so often have to deplore.

And here I must not forget to tell you of the cathedral at Aix-la-Chapelle, and the church of S. Gereon, at Cologne, in which the naves are circular and decagonal, of great size and grand effect, with long choirs running out to the east.

In the earlier churches western transepts are also not uncommon, as at S. Cunibert, S. Andrew, and S. Pantaleon at Cologne, S. Paul at Worms, Mayence, and many other examples; whilst towers of small size were commonly placed in the re-entering angles, between the nave, and choir, and transepts, as well as over their intersections.

Lastly, there is a plan of common occurrence, especially among smaller churches, in which the main building is a large and lofty parallelogram, with a small apse tacked on at the end, without any regard to proportion. There are two or three of these churches in Nuremberg, and many elsewhere.

I have detained you for a long time on the subject of ground-plans, but it is one of importance to the right understanding of any style of church architecture, and it was not possible therefore to pass it over.

I will now ask you to consider, a little in detail, the characteristics of the early German work. I do not intend to go thoroughly into the question of pure Romanesque work, for which I have no time. I am dealing with pointed architecture, and must confine myself as much as possible to it only. We may take the early churches at Cologne, and along the banks of the Rhine, as examples of the kind of work which is perhaps the most interesting, and very thoroughly German in all its characteristics. It was derived, as I have no doubt, from the churches in Lombardy, with which it has very many features absolutely identical. The churches at Pavia are beyond all question the prototypes of those at Cologne; but it is to be observed that their scale is smaller, and, their effect certainly not so fine.

S. Castor at Coblentz, at the end of the twelfth century, Andernach a little later, Zinzig, S. Gereon and S. Cunibert, Cologne, at the beginning of the thirteenth century, give us a fairly complete evidence of the succession of styles. After these we have Limburg and Gelnhausen, taking us on to the time at which the German complete Gothic was in other places in full perfection.

In the early churches there are many features worthy of remark:—

First, the curiously early development of a kind of heavy cusping, of which Worms, Zinzig, Boppart, Andernach, and S. Gereon at Cologne, are good examples. It is essentially German, and I know nothing like it out of the Rhine district.

Secondly, the treatment of the apsidal terminations is very remarkable. S. Castor at Coblentz, e. g., at the end of the twelfth century, has three stages in its apse, whereof that next the ground has a trefoiled arcade, the next is pierced with round-headed windows, whilst under the eaves is a recessed arcade and a cornice, which, in one form or other, was almost the invariable finish of these early apses. Zinzig has the same kind of apse, but it is polygonal, and each side is gabled. The eaves-cornice has a row of square sunk panels below it; and this singular feature we see reproduced very often, as at S. Gereon. The apse at Andernach is nearly identical with that at Coblentz, as also is that of Bonn. The fine cathedral at Worms has a very singular arrangement. The apse is polygonal, with the eaves-cornice and ground arcade as at Coblentz, but in the intermediate stage it has circular windows, filled in with quatrefoils and sexfoils. The apse and steeple of S. Martin, at Cologne, are extremely noble examples of these portions of the early German churches. Generally speaking, these early apsidal terminations are most remarkable for their similarity of design, but their external effect is, nevertheless, always striking.

The third and chief feature of the early German churches is the treatment of their steeples. They are square or octangular in plan, without buttresses, arcaded or pierced with windows pretty regularly all over their surface, and roofed in the most varied manner. You are all, no doubt, familiar with some examples of these really striking towers, and you will feel, I think, that in their whole composition they generally look too much like turrets, and are often too uniform in their height to be perfectly satisfactory. The towers were often gabled, and had square spires rising from the points of the gables; or, as in the fine example at Soest, they had octagonal spires. This Soest example has great interest: it is the first perfect example, so far as I know, of a long series of very remarkable steeples. At Paderborn, indeed, there is no doubt that the tower had a spire; but it is destroyed, and Soest is therefore the more interesting. At a later date, this kind of steeple was reproduced at Lüneburg and Lübeck, in the steeples which adorn their churches.

The variety of ornamental moulding is less, I think, in Germany than in either England or France; but there are some fine examples of carving in capitals and string-courses of early date at Naumburg and Magdeburg.

The groining of early German churches is generally simple. The lanterns, where central, are covered in with a plain kind of domical vault; and the apses have generally hemispherical groining, sometimes marked with ribs. The vaulting is first of all plain waggon-vaulting, then simple quadripartite, and sometimes — especially where (as is often the case in Germany) one bay of the groining covers two bays of the nave — it is sexpartite, and generally then very much raised in the centre.

Doorways are almost invariably square-headed, under pointed arches. In the north porch of Lübeck cathedral, as also at Andernach, and at S. Cunibert, and again at S. Gereon, Cologne, is a very peculiar doorhead, formed by two straight lines sloping to the centre at a very obtuse angle.

The windows are generally of a very simple and rude kind. There was no approach in their treatment to that delicacy which is such an especial characteristic of our English first-pointed; and this mainly because the science of mouldings was never worked out thoroughly by the early German school. It is true that no school of architects has ever rivalled the English in this particular; and one reason, perhaps, for this is to be found in the resolute way in which foreigners resisted any modification of the square abacus, whose only fault was, no doubt, the limitation it imposed upon the outline of mouldings.

One other feature of these churches must not be forgotten, viz., the great size of their triforia. This was usual all over Europe in Romanesque buildings; but in Germany in this, as in other things, the early tradition was long adhered to, and you have nowhere else such elaborate constructional galleries as theirs. Even in works of the latest date they are found, — as, for instance, in the curious church of S. Andrew, at Frankfort, where the outer aisles are galleried all round with a triforium, the arches in front of which are about twice the height of the main arches below them. The interior of Andernach cathedral will explain how grand the treatment of this feature was in the earliest buildings.

I trust I have said enough now to show you, at any rate, the general characteristics of early German work. Its great marks of distinction from French and English work are to be seen mainly in its planning, the treatment and number of its towers and spires, and in the peculiarly Italian character of its apsidal terminations; and, as I have said, this style prevailed, with but little modification, up to the very time at which the completely developed German middle-pointed made its appearance.

I suppose the characteristics of this later work must be known to most of you. Cologne cathedral is in fact so competely an embodiment of nearly all the essential features of the style, and is so well known to most people that I suspect less description is required of it than of any other foreign style. It has been often said — and that by no mean authorities — that the German middle-pointed was identical with our own, and indeed that this one style prevailed for a time all over Europe. The theory would be pretty if it were true: the gradual working up to the same point in various ways, and the gradual divergence of art again in different directions, would certainly be a strong ground for giving in our adhesion to this one perfect and universal style. But I confess that though there is something of a *similarity*, I have not been able to trace anything like an identity between German and French and English work at any time. I am thankful for this because, with all its beauty, the best German middle-pointed style is not a great style, and has many and obvious defects. From the very first is conspicuous that *love of lines* which is so marked and so unpleasant a peculiarity in German art, and that desire to play with geometrical figures — I know not how else to express what I mean — which in time degenerated into work as pitiful and contemptible as any of which mediaeval architects were ever guilty.

I have here a large collection (which should have been larger had I had time to select all the examples which I have scattered through my sketch-books) of German window traceries, which will enable you to judge whether I am too severe in my opinion of their demerits. And you may observe, by the way, that whilst in the earlier styles we have very many points for consideration in studying the characteristics of the style, in this work there is a sacrifice of almost everything else to the desire to introduce in every direction specimens of new and ingenious combinations of tracery. The windows at Paderborn are some of the finest and purest examples of early tracery. They are genuine and noble examples, and quite free from any tinge of the faults of later examples, and worthy of comparison with the best of our own early traceries. The mouldings of these windows are simple, but composed mainly of a succession of bold rolls, and so entirely free from any *lininess*. In the cupola of S. Gereon at Cologne, and a little later in its sacristy are also some good early traceries, whilst most of the windows at Marburg are also examples of the same character. So too are the traceries in one of the Brunswick west fronts, and in the apse of the church of S. Giles in the same city. From these look to the windows of S. Mary, Lemgo, and you have the commencement of the new style, though these are fine windows, boldly and simply conceived and carried out. Next to these come the marvellous series of traceries in Minden cathedral; a series, I suppose, quite unmatched for variety, and indeed, I must own, for a certain grandeur of effect, by those in any church in Europe. You will be struck, I think, by the curious desire for variety of arrangement which these traceries evidence. They are a series of aisle windows, placed side by side in a cathedral church of very modest pretensions. S. Martin in the same town has a great variety of traceries of a later type — good examples of the kind of tracery which henceforward is to be found for a long time predominant throughout nearly the whole of Germany, in which, whilst one admires and wonders at the ingenuity which has devised so many combinations of spherical triangles and circles, one is tempted to think that the men who excelled in this sort of work would have been admirably fitted for designing children's toys and puzzles, but had much better have been kept away from church windows. Among the other sketches of traceries, those from Ratisbon are of the best kind, whilst those from the cloister at Constance (essentially German work) are almost as interesting as the Paderborn examples in their ingenious variety of form. They show too, occasionally, a tendency to ogee lines in the tracery, which leads me to say a few words on the curious fact, that whereas in England the ogee line was always seen in the later middle-pointed work, this was by no means the case in Germany. The tracery in the staircase to the Rathhaus at Ratisbon, though of late date, is noticeable for the almost entire absence of any but pure geometrical figures, but then these are thrown about in a confused and irregular manner, and are entirely wanting in due subordination of parts. When, however, the ogee line does show itself in German work, it is always a certain evidence of debasement.

But to leave the question of traceries and to justify my denial of the virtues of German pointed architecture, let me ask you to compare the effect of French and German work side by side in some of these most valuable evidences of facts which photography so liberally affords us. You have here side by side a west door from Amiens and from Cologne; and again here, some door-jamb sculpture from Amiens between similar works from Strasburg. Now striking as these German examples are, do you not see how entirely the Germans sacrifice all nobility and simplicity of expression, all that we call repose, to the vain desire to arrest attention by some tricky arrangement of a drapery and some quaint speckiness or lininess of detail?

The German love of tracery is evidenced by the fondness for such spires as that of Freiburg, which, striking as it is, is not altogether a legitimate kind of thing, and is certainly inferior in its effect to the much simpler spires of which we are so justly proud.

I can only say a few words as to the plans of German complete Gothic, and this only to repeat what I have before said as to the extent to which they contrived to build on the same plans as in earlier days. The parallel and transverse triapsidal plans were as popular in Germany in the fourteenth and fifteenth centuries as they were in the twelfth and thirteenth, of which the little chapel in the castle at Marburg is a curious example. It is apsidal at the east and west ends, and the bay between has the window-splay so contrived as to make another apse north and south. It was in detail more than in plan that the later architects developed.

But I feel that time will not allow me to go into the features of the style with more minuteness, or to do more than direct your attention to the strange eccentricity which characterizes the last phase of German Gothic, of which the design for the spire of Ulm (never carried out) is one of the most curious examples. In the short time that still remains to me, I would rather prefer to call your attention to the local peculiarities which you will meet with in different districts of this great country — a part of my subject which would, if I had time for it, be of more value perhaps to those who are going to explore German churches for themselves than any other.

I have said so much about the churches of Cologne and the Rhine, that I need say no more than that they are very much a class by themselves. You have there the best specimens of early churches; whilst in Cologne cathedral, in Altenberg abbey, in the church of the Minorites at Cologne — an admirable example — in the very interesting church at Oberwesel, and in S. Werner at Bacharach, a church at Andernach, and Frankfort cathedral, you have a series of examples within a short distance of each other of the best complete German Gothic.

Then leaving this district and going in a north-easterly direction, you will find a series of towns full of local peculiarities, quite unlike those of the Rhine: — Münster, for instance, with its churches of great height and without distinction between nave and aisles; or Soest, where the beautiful Wiesen-kirche affords one of the finest evidences of what Germans could do in their palmiest days: whilst in the other churches in the same little known city you would see examples of Romanesque of the most grand kind in the remarkable steeple of the cathedral, and of a very curious kind in the low groined entrances which support a continuation of the triforia round the west end of the naves. In towns like these, and Paderborn,

Lemgo, Herford, Minden, and Hildesheim, you will find a rich store of architectural matter; and then if you will venture so far, you will find at Lüneburg, and Lübeck, and Ratzeburg, abundant examples (as I have once before explained in this room) of the German mode of building in brick developed in a group of churches quite unlike any others in Germany, and most interesting in every point of view. Then again there are those curious churches at Brunswick and Halberstadt, Magdeburg and Burg, whose west fronts, contrived apparently solely for the sake of obtaining space for the display of immense window traceries, are so completely local and so thoroughly, I suppose I may say, an invention! Here too you will see the churches almost invariably with gabled aisles, — sometimes, as in the cathedral at Lemgo, so gabled at the sides that one doubts which is the side and which the end, and sometimes, as in a church at Brunswick, filled with tracery and panelling of extreme beauty. Then again at Halberstadt, Erfurt, Naumburg, and Marburg, you may see some of the most excellent work in all Germany of the best period. And if you go further south, to where Nuremberg takes you back in almost all externals to the sixteenth century, or where Ratisbon to the thirteenth, you will find yourselves again in the neighbourhood of brick churches, at Landshut and Munich: and lastly at Freiburg you may see one of the very best of German churches, eclipsed though it undoubtedly is by the unequalled (in Germany) nave of the thoroughly German cathedral of Strasburg.

I can but give you a hurried list of names, but not without a warm recommendation to you to go and see for yourselves how very much is to be learnt in all these churches, not only in architectural matters, but even much more in ecclesiological. Germany is the one part of Europe in which the furniture of the Middle Ages still remains. There where in Protestant Nuremberg every altar still stands with its white cloth, and candles, and crucifix; where the great rood still hangs aloft in the churches; where in one church, as at Brandenburg, one may see some thirty or forty mediaeval vestments still hanging untouched in their old presses; where you may see screens of every date, from early Romanesque to the latest pointed; where coronae, and all kinds of metal furniture and ancient work of a date far earlier than any other country in Europe can show are still preserved; where, as in the choirs of Halberstadt and Hildesheim, the old illuminated office books still rest upon the old choir desk; where hangings of quaint and gorgeous patterns still hang round the choirs, and where triptychs and carved retables are so common that one forgets to take note of them; — there it is, I say, that you must go if you would wish to study and to understand fully the ecclesiology of the Middle Ages. It is indeed a country full of the most wonderful interest to the ecclesiologist in all ways, and I am anxious to say that though I have been asked by your committee to give a second paper on Italian architecture, I feel very strongly that I should be doing their work much better by telling you somewhat of all those things to which I have just referred. In the first place, I have said my say on Italy, and have nothing new to tell you; and secondly, I have been obliged to avoid saying one word either on the furniture or glass of German churches, or on the domestic architecture in which the country is so rich, — and on all these points I should be only too glad at some future day to give you some notes of what I have seen.

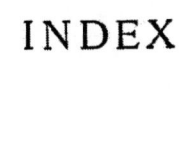

INDEX

INDEX

INDEX

Abbeville, 33.
Abbot Odalric of Conques, 242.
Abbot Peter de Wesencourt of S. Germer, 156.
Abécédaire, 155, 158, 220.
acanthus, 95.
Aesthetic Movement, 13, 32.
Agnolino of Orvieto, 94.
Ainay, church of, 35, 39, 207, 228, 247; *v.* Lyon.
Aix-la-Chapelle, 302, 307, 322.
Album Photographique de l'Archéologie Réligeuse, 215, 223, 224.
Alcalá, 43.
Alençon, 33.
All Saints, Clifton, 30.
Alps, 36, 49, 65, 89.
Altamira, Rafael, 48.
Altenberg, 321, 327.
Amalfi, 51, 53.
American attitude, 32, 33.
Amiens, 16, 32, 33, 129, 131, 151, 158, 163, 195, 206, 318, 321, 326.
Ancona, 50.
Andalusia, 42.
Andernach, 175, 323, 324, 327.
Angelico, Fra, 8, 9, 52.
Angers, 134.
Angevine type, 45, 128.
Angoulême, 231, 236.
Anjou, 128, 129.
Antiquité Expliquée, L', 223
Apengeter, Hans, of Lübeck, 277.
Apennines, 76, 82, 86.
apsidal choirs, 19, 89, 137, 176, 320, 325.

Aragon, kings of, 42.
Arbellot, Abbé, cited, 211.
Archaeologia Cantiana, 255.
Archbishop Maurice of Rouen, 133, 135.
architect, the same, at Ainay and Le Puy, 207 sqq.; Bayeux and Norrey, 123; Châlons-sur-Marne and Rouen, 193; Orcival and Issoire and Brioude, 240; Rouen and Genoa, 133; S. Germer and Paris, 156; S. Mary Stone, and Westminster, 255, 264, 267; Soissons and Noyon, 165.
architects, mediaeval, 23, 32, 73, 131, 136, 149, 151, 293, 296, 297.
architects, modern, 21, 26, 28, 40, 41, 54, 57, 100, 294, 303.
architecture, the experience, 28, 29; growth slow, 318; regular, 40; height first requisite, 18, 142; mouldings the test, 99; sculpture, 99, 264.
Architecture Civile et Domestique, 161, 184.
Arezzo, 76, 80.
Arles, 128.
Arnold, Matthew, 8, 49.
Arts Somptuaires, Les, 153.
Arundel church, 158, 265.
Assisi, 51, 76, 77 sqq., 224.
Asti, 51, 65.
Astorga, 44.
Asturias, 42.
Athens, 249.

Auvergne, dates, 241; type, 39, 201, 211, 231 sqq., 238, 244.
Auvergne au Moyen Age, L', 205, 232.
Auxerre, 34, 35, 249.
Avranche, 124.
Avila, 44, 45, 46.
Aymard, M., cited, 215, 223, 224, 225, 226, 230.

Bacharach, 320, 327.
Baedecker, 37.
Bamberg, 175, 318, 321.
baptistery, 210, 272; at Cremona, 272; Pisa, 66, 272; Pistoja, 84; Siena, 72.
Barcelona, 38, 43, 44.
Bardonnecchia, 90.
Barnstaple, 4.
Basle, 277.
Bayeux, 43, 122, 163.
Bayonne, 43, 44.
Beauvais, cathedral, 16, 17, 33, 131, 144, 150 sqq.; S. Étienne, 152 sq.; bishop's palace, 153; Bishop F. de la Rochefoucauld, 152.
Belgian towns, 34, 48, 303-307.
Bell Scott, William, 57.
Benavente, 40, 44.
Bénévent, 231.
Benevento, 50.
Bergamo, 309, 317.
Berlin, 48, 290.
Bernese Oberland, 39, 48.
Bertaux, Émile, 51.
Bideford, 4.
Bingen, John and Nicholas of, 222.
Biscay, Bay of, 42.
Biscovey, 6.
Bishop Arnaud of Périgueux, 211.
Bishop Burchard von Serken of Lübeck, 273.

Bishop Evodius of Le Puy, 203.
Bishop F. de la Rochefoucauld of Beauvais, 152.
Bishop Garnier of Laon, 181.
Bishop Gerald of Poitiers, 211.
Bishop Gerold of Oldenburg, 272.
Bishop Guy II of Le Puy, 228.
Bishop Henry of Lübeck, 272.
Bishop Henry Bockholt of Lübeck, 278.
Bishop Hughes de la Tour of Clermont, 231.
Bishop Jean de Bourbon of Le Puy, 214, 215.
Bishop Johan von Mull of Lübeck, 273.
Bishop Namacius of Clermont, 232.
Bishop Peter of Le Puy, 220.
Bishop Stephen II of Le Puy, 220.
Bishop Theodulf of Orleans, 224.
Bishop of Beauvais, 161.
Bishop of Gibraltar, 96.
Bishop of Oxford, 7, 23.
Boletin de la Sociedad Castellana de Excursiones, 47.
Bologna, 86; S. Petronio, 86 sq., 230; S. Francesco, 87.
Bonn, 320, 323.
Bonport, 138.
Boppart, 323.
Botticelli, 29.
Bourges, cathedral, 137, 163, 176, 201, 212, 244; S. Pierre, 244.
Bourgtheroulde, 118.
Boyce, George, 57.
Branche, Dominique, cited, 205, 232.
Brandenburg, 285, 328.
brasses, 6, 38, 274.
Brenner, 51.
Bretteville l'Orgueilleuse, 120.
Breuzeville, 131.

brick building, 30, 37, 38, 46, 72, 86, 270, 284, 285, 286, 328.
Brick and Marble in the Middle Ages, 21, 27, 32, 34, 36, 46, 49 sq., 88.
Brioude, 39, 201, 212, 215, 231, 234, 235, 237, 238, 240, 247.
Bristol cathedral, 27, 30.
Brown, Madox, 57.
Browning, Robert, 2, 52.
Brunswick, 274, 283, 321, 326, 328.
Buckinghamshire, 25.
Bulletin Archéologique, 223.
Bulletin de la Société Archéologique et Historique du Limousin, 211.
Bulletin Monumental, 207, 220, 230.
Burg, 327.
Burgos, 43, 44, 118.
Burgundian March, 34; style, 128.
Burne-Jones, Edward, 13-18, 33, 57.
Burne-Jones, Lady, 14, 17.
Butler, Dr., 7.
Butterfield, 15, 28.
Byzantine influences, 84, 132, 135, 194, 202, 243, 245.

Caen, 33, 119 sqq.; Abbaye aux Hommes, 246; S. Pierre, 119, 120, 121.
Calvados, 16.
Cambridgeshire, 5.
campanile at Assisi, 80; Bologna, 87; Erfurt, 294; Florence, 82; Lucca, 70; Pistoja, 83; Siena, 72; Siena cathedral, 73; Susa, 64; Verona, 72.
Carlisle, 54, 55.
carvers, 132, 135, 168, 300-01.
carvings, 186, 199, 303, 313, 317.
Castile, 42.

Castilian, 47.
Catalonia, 30, 45, 47.
Caudebec, 16.
Caumont, de, cited, *Abécédaire*, 155, 158, 220; *Bulletin Monumental*, 207.
Cavallini, 78.
Chaise-Dieu, La, 251.
Châlons-sur-Marne, Notre Dame, 134, 175, 188, 190; cathedral, 190, 194; S. Alpin, 195; the curé, 144, 191.
Chalvour, 171.
Chamallières, 220.
Chambéry, 50, 63, 89.
Champagne, style, 188.
Champagne, village on the Oise, 144-5.
Champenois, M., 191.
Chantilly, 100, 149.
Chartres, cathedral, 16, 19, 29, 33, 52, 114, 129, 130, 134, 163, 176, 185, 195, 212, 244.
Les Chases, S. Marie, 205, 227.
Chauriat, 231.
Chichester, 5, 281.
Chinon, 220.
Christian Year, The, 20, 31.
Church of England, 1, 11, 21.
Church of Rome, 11, 21.
Churches in Kent, Surrey, and Sussex, Some, 268.
Churches in Northern Germany, 270.
Churches of Lübeck, The, 270.
Churches of Velay, The, 39, 201.
Cimabue, 78, 79.
Cino da Pistoja, 83.
Clermont-Ferrand, 39, 128, 201; cathedral, 231, 251; Notre-Dame-du-Port, 212, 217, 231, 233-242 *passim*, 245, 249; Bishop Hughes de la Tour, 231; Bishop Namacius, 232.
Clifford, W. K., 49.

Clovelly, 5.
Cluny, 45, 231.
Coblentz, 175, 323.
Cock, Reimar, 278.
Cologne, 34, 151, 308, sqq., 319, 322, 327; cathedral, 173, 197 sqq., 316, 321, 326, 327; SS. Apostles, 320; S. Cunibert, 309, 311, 318, 323; S. Gereon, 308, 318 sq., 323, 324, 325; S. Martin, 309, 323; S. Mary in the Capitol, 309; others, 322.
Como, lake of, 36.
Compiègne, 159; S. Antoine, 160; cloister, 159; Hôtel-Dieu, 161; Hôtel de Ville, 161.
Compostela, Santiago de, 43, 44, 45.
Compton, near Guildford, 278.
Conques, 231, 242, 245; Abbot Odalric, 242.
Constance, 33, 294, 326; lake of, 36.
Constantinople, 30, Crimean Memorial, 22; S. Sophia, 243, 245; SS. Sergius and Bacchus, 247.
Corneto, 94.
Cornwall, 6, 79, 128, 268.
Cortona, 75.
Coruña, La, 44.
Coucy-le-Château, 162, 171.
de Coucy, Robert, 58, 184, 188.
Coudray, 158.
Courtrai, 303, 305 sqq.
Coutances, 124, 163.
Cram, R. A., cited, 28.
Cremona, 38, 272, 284.
Crépy, 107.
Crimean Memorial, 22, 30.
Cuddesden, 7, 21, 22.
Cuenca, 42.
Culoz, 62, 89.

Dalmatia, 32.
Dance of Death, 277.

Dante, 3, 83.
Devonshire, 128.
Dictionnaire de l'Architecture, 174, 212, 231.
Didron, cited, 229, 233.
Dijon, 34, 88, 277.
Divine Comedy, 3.
domestic architecture, 105, 106, 107, 110, 119, 124, 138, 158, 170, 183; Romanesque, 124, 153, 228; Gothic, 92, 96, 139, 153, 167, 170, 181, 186, 190, 230; north German, 281, 283, 294, 308, 310; *v.* also Gothic, domestic.
Donatello, 52, 87.
Dorat, 231.
Douce, Francis, cited, 277.
Dresden, 48.
Dublin, 27.
Duguesclin, 230.
Durham, 5.

East Grinstead, 22.
East Meon, 160.
Eastern influence, 212, 220, 223, 243, 247; course along the Rhone, 247; *v.* also Byzantine.
Ecclesiologist, The, 32, 37, 38, 127, 268.
Edinburgh, 54.
Egypt, 58.
Elizabeth of Hungary, S., 295.
embroidery and vestments, 6, 8, 152, 220, 280, 306, 328-9.
Emperor of the French restoring, 143, 145.
Empoli, 91.
Engadine, 48.
England, 3, 10, 32, 42, 55.
English, 1, 10, 11, 21, 32, 45, 54; influence, 128, 130, 136; stone, 30; work, 122.
Enlart, Camille, 41.
Ennezat, 230, 238.

[336]

entasis at Pisa, 67; at Le Puy, 213.
Erfurt, 292, 328; architects, 293;
Bärfüsser-Kirche, 292; cathedral, 293; Prediger-Kirche, 294; Stadt-Kirche, 292; S. Severus, 294; others, 295.
Erfurt and Marburg, 292.
de la Escosura, Patricio, 46.
España Artística y Monumental, 46.
Essai sur les Églises Romanes et Romano-Byzantines du département du Puy-de-Dome, 241.
Estoire de S. Eduard le Rey, 204.
Estella, 206.
Estremadura, 42.
Étampes, 244.
Eunate, 229.
Evreux, cathedral, 116; S. Taurin, 116.
Exeter, 4, 12.

Fergusson, J., cited, 245.
Fiesole, 82.
Florence, 51, 52, 82, 83, 276; Or S. Michele, 52, 83; S. Miniato, 84.
Foggia, 50.
Fontevrault, 231.
Fonthill, 151.
fonts, 84, 161, 274, 276, 277, 281, 310.
Ford, Richard, 41.
fortified churches, 215.
Fountains Abbey, 32, 279.
France, 3, 30; landscape and architecture, 88; Spain's debt to, 47; Italy's, 51; *v.* also Gothic, French, and painting, early French.
Francia, 52.
Francis of Assisi, S., 76.
Franco-Prussian war, 21, 48, 120.
Frankfort, 33, 324, 327.
Freiburg, 33, 328.

French towns, 33, 34, 39, 131; cathedrals, 163.
Furka pass, 36.

Galicia, 40, 42.
Gassiecourt, 142.
Gaulfredus, 220.
Gelnhausen, 318, 323.
Geneva, 89.
Genoa, 65, 67, 76, 90, 91, 133 sq., 200, 220; English church, 30, 90.
German Gothic, 174, 175, 190, 192, 196, 199, 200, 283, 326; influence, 128, 174, 182, 192, sqq., 195, 196; *v.* also Gothic, German; Painting, early German.
German Pointed Architecture, 317.
Germer, S., legend, 158.
Gerona, 43.
Gimbert, François, 225.
Giotto, 52, 78, 83, 274.
Giulianuova, 51.
glass, early, 79, 94, 101, 109, 116, 139, 142, 152, 180, 195, 196, 251, 276, 291, 293, 294, 298, 300, 309, 314, 315, 329.
Glastonbury, 154.
Gloucester, 55.
Gothic, 46, 176; revival of, 1, 13, 28, 31, 248; study of, 6, 37, 244; lectures on, 27, 201, 317; power of, 3, 4, 23, 55; modern, 8, 13, 22, 54, 55.
Gothic, domestic, 139, 183, 283, 303; at Aix, 308; at Beauvais, 153; in Belgium, 303 sqq.; at Erfurt, 294; at Genoa, 91; at Laon, 112; at Lisieux, 119; at Meaux, 115; at Monferrand, 251; at Münster, 310; at Pisa, 68; at Le Puy, 230; at Rheims, 190; at Siena, 68, 72; at Trèves, 197; at Ypres, 305.

[337]

Gothic, English, 3, 21, 130, 131, 160, 255, 320, 324; styles, 45, 128; comparison with, 122, 128, 129, 159, 165.
Gothic, French, 18, 21, 30, 32, 45, 47, 51, 79, 127, 176, 192, 244; styles, 39, 40, 128, 167, 231 sqq.; sources, 202, 244; in Italy, 77–8.
Gothic, German, 32, 174, 190, 195 sq., 200, 270 sqq., 289, 292, 304, 317, 319, 323; influence of, 128, 174, 175, 182, 194, 195; judgement on, 196, 199, 200, 317, 319.
Gothic, Italian, 30, 32, 51, 66, 70, 72, 78, 91, 207, 309, 320; influence of, 131, 133, 175; characteristic plan, 207, 309; Lombard, 32, 275, 322.
Gothic, Savoyard, 63, 65.
Gothic, Spanish, 32, 37, 39, 40, 43, 46 sqq., 320; in Catalonia, 38, 45.
Government restoring, 143, 145, 312, 316.
Granson, on Lake of Neufchâtel, 245.
Grauenfels, 36.
Greece, 32.
Gregorian music, 18, 119.
Gregory of Tours, cited, 232.
Grisons, the, 36.
groining, 74, 130, 222.
ground-plans, 130, 136, 195, 205, 207, 229, 230, 244, 309, 317, 319, 327.
Guadalajara, 44.
Guardian, The, 129.
Guercino, 52.
Guido da Como, 84.

Halberstadt, 278, 288, 301, 328.
Hamburg, 33.
Hambye, 124.
Hanover, 48.
Havre, 16.
Heidelberg, 33,
height an element of Gothic, 18, 142, 150, 197.
Heir of Redclyffe, The, 13.
Henry the Lion, 272.
Herford, 328.
Hesse, Synsingus, 283.
Hewlett, Maurice, 45, 83.
Higham Ferrers, 281.
Hildesheim, 274, 278, 321, 328.
Histoire de l'Église Angélique de Notre Dame du Puy, 228.
Historia de la Arquitectura Española Cristiana, 41.
Holland, Jessie, (Mrs. G. E. Street), 10, 53, 57, 88.
Holmbury S. Mary, 28, 30, 55.
Homer, 3.
Howells, William Dean, 49.
Hucher, M., cited, 220.
Hueffer, Ford Madox, 57.
Huelgas, Las, 45, 118.
Huesca, 44.
Hunt, Holman, 46, 57.
Hutton, Edward, 45, 49.
Huxley, Thomas, 23.
Huy, 307.

Iffley, 32.
Île-de-France, 45, 128, 194, 317.
Iliad, 3.
Inchbold, J. W., 57.
Inland Voyage, An, 39.
l'Isle Adam, 144.
Issoire, 201, 217, 231, 233, 235, 236, 237, 238, 240.
Italian influence, 131, 133, 175, 230; arcades, 310; gables, 273; workman, 276.
Italy, 22, 34, 38, 48, 49, 50, 51, 65, 80, 89, 176.

Jaca, 42.
Jean and Nicholas of Bingen, 222.

Jervaulx, 5.
Joanna the Mad, 46.

Keats, John, 2.
Keble, John, 13, 31.
Kent, 255, 260, 268.
Kneller, Sir Godfrey, 281.

Laach, 197, 320, 321.
Lagny, 113.
Lake Country, 5.
Landshut, 322, 328.
Lanercost, 20, 52, 142.
Lampérez y Romea, Vicente, 40 sqq., 48.
Laon, 38, 108 sqq., 129, 131, 162, 163, 172 sqq., 186, 188; S. Martin, 112, 172, 182; Templars' church, 183, 229; Bishop Garnier, 181.
Latin-Byzantine style, 42.
Lausanne, Anglican church, 30.
Lavoulte-Chilhac, 220.
Law-Courts, London, 27, 46, 55.
lay vocation, 2; fraternity, 12, 15.
Lemgo, 320, 326, 328.
Leon, 42, 44.
Leonardo, 29.
Lérida, 43, 44.
Liberal Arts, 39, 216.
Liège, 307.
Lille, 21, 38, 112, 303.
Limay, 142.
Limburg, 318, 323.
Limoges, 206, 211, 231, 248.
Lincoln, 31, 129, 172, 189.
Lincolnshire, 5.
Lisieux, 118; S. Jacques, 119.
Livi, Dominic, of Ghambasso, his son, 276.
Lombard churches, in Italy, 317; on the Rhine, 275, 322.
Lombardy, 32.
London, 2, 5, 6, 17, 21, 24, 26, 27, 54, 67.

Longpont, 162, 170.
Lons-le-Bourg, 64, 90.
Louis IX, S., 170, 206.
Louis XI, 216, 217, 225.
Louviers, 117.
Lörsh, 317.
Lübeck, 37, 38; 270, 286, 314, 319, 324; Burg-Kloster, 272, 276, 278, 280; cathedral, 272; S. Giles, 272, 281; S. James, 272, 281; S. Katharine, 272, 276, 278; S. Mary, 275, 321; S. Peter, 272, 281; Burg-Thor, 271, 272; Heiligen-Geist-Spital, 272, 281; Holsteiner-Thor, 271, 272, 284; Rathhaus, 283; Bishop Burchard von Serken, 273; Bishop Johann von Mull, 273; Bishop Henry, 272; Bishop Henry Bockholt, 278; Hans Apengeter, 277.
Luca della Robbia, 85.
Lucca, 69, 76; campanile, 70; cathedral 69; S. Giovanni, 71; S. Maria della Rosa, 71; S. Michele, 69.
Lucera, 50.
Lucerne, lake of, 36.
Lugo, 44.
Lüneburg, S. John, 276, 314, 324, 328.
Luther, 275.
Lynn, 274.
Lyon, 201, 212; S. Martin d'Ainay, 207, 228, 247; Manécanterie, 228.

Mâcon, 62, 88.
Madrid, 43.
Magdeburg, 318, 319, 321, 324, 328.
Maggiore, lake, 36.
Magione, 76.
Mallay, M., cited, 218, 228, 239–41.

Mancha, La, 42.
Manresa, 44.
Mans, Le, 220.
Mantes, 131, 134, 137, 139 sqq., 147, 149.
Mantua, 284.
Marburg, S. Elizabeth, 38, 169, 296, 319, 320, 328; castle, 302, 327.
masons, mediaeval, 32, 240.
Mayence, 33, 321, 322.
Meaux, 115, 131, 162, 163, 165.
mediaeval architects, 32, 131, 136, 151, 293, 296, 297.
mediaeval workmen, 58, 156, 220, 222, 225, 234, 240, 276, 277, 308.
Memling, 274.
Memoir by A. E. Street, 6, 10, 24, 27, 30, 37, 50, 56, 57, 58.
Menat, 215, 231.
Merdogne, 228.
Meredith, George, 49.
Merimée, Prosper, cited, 210, 212, 214, 222, 229, 232, 239.
Merseburg, 287.
Metz, 195; cathedral, 196; S. Vincent, 196; Templars' church, 229.
Middle-Pointed Churches in Cornwall, On the, 268.
Minden, 277, 326, 328.
Miranda, 44.
Modern Painters, 36.
Mohammedan, 42.
Monestier, 220, 230.
Monistrol, 39, 201, 230.
Montéreau, Pierre de, 60, 156.
Montfaucon, cited, 223.
Montierender, 165.
Montmajour, 229.
Moorish, 42.
Morris, William, 3, 13–17, 21, 31, 38, 57; first abroad, 16; work under G. E. S., 17.
Moûtier, Le, near Thiers, 231.

Moustier-neuf, Poitiers, 231, 242.
Mozat, 231, 239.
Mudejar, 42, 46.
Muhlhausen, 320.
Munich, 33, 48, 322, 328.
Münster, 37, 274, 310, 312, 327; cathedral 310, Oberwasser-Kirche, 311; S. Lambert, 312; S. Lüdger, 313; Rathaus, 284, 310.
Münster and Soest, 303.
Murray, 34, 41, 49; guide, 91, 125.
Mürren, 30.

Naples, 53.
Narbonne, 231.
National Gallery, 46, 48, 54.
Naumburg, 287 sqq., 299, 318, 319, 321, 324, 328.
Naumburg Cathedral, 287.
Navarre, 42, 206, 229.
Neale, John Mason, 13.
Nevers, 35, 39, 201, 231, 241, 242, 249.
Newark, 274.
Newman, 3.
Norfolk, 5, 45, 128; middle-pointed, 45.
Normandy, 38, 128, 130, 317.
Norrey, 120, 121.
Northampton, 5.
North Mymms, 274.
northern race, 1, 10.
notebooks of G. E. S., 5, 20, 22, 32, 34, 38, 50, 53, 96.
Notes d'un Voyage en Auvergne, 210, 214.
Notes of a Tour in Central Italy, 59.
Notes on French Churches, 97.
Notre Dame de la Treille, 112.
Notre Dame du Puy, 206.
Noyon, 105, 109, 114, 131, 162, 163, 164 sqq.

Nuremberg, 33, 270, 322, 328; S. Laurence, 273, 312; S. Sebald, 321.

Odalric, Abbot of Conques, 242.
Odo de Gissey, cited, 228.
Oldenburg, Bishop Gerold of, 272.
Orcagna, 66.
Orcival, 231, 238, 240.
Orders, Holy, 2.
Order of Sir Galahad, 15.
Orense, 42.
Orleans, Theodulf, Bishop of, 224.
Or S. Michele, 52, 83.
Orvieto, 51, 73, 91, 92.
Ourscamp, 162.
Overbeck, 277, 281.
Oxford, 2, 13, 14, 18, 57, 58; Union, 14; Merton college, 15; New college, 15.
Oxford and Cambridge Magazine, The, 16.
Oxford Movement, 7, 13, 14, 31.

Paderborn, 275, 311, 319, 324, 327.
Padua, 224.
Paestum, 95.
painting, early English, 262, 263.
painting, early French, 39, 126, 136, 158, 189, 215, 216, 223 sq., 227, 234.
painting, early German, 274, 277, 279, 290, 299, 301, 309.
painting, early Italian, 53, 67, 70, 74, 78, 91, 94.
paintings, by G. E. S., 4, 8, 37.
Palencia, 43.
Palestrina, 9.
Palladio, 49.
Pamplona, 44.
Paris, 16, 33, 61; American church, 28, 30; Cluny, 33, 157; Louvre, 33; Notre Dame, 4, 33, 116, 131, 134, 137, 141, 149, 163, 200; S. Chapelle, 116, 156; S. Germain-des-Prés, 58, 156, 231.
Passion according to S. Matthew, The, 28.
Pater, 29.
Pavia, 317, 323.
Pébrac, 220.
Pennell, Joseph, 49.
Père Hyacinth, 95.
Périgueux, 212, 231, 241, 243, 245, 246, 248, 249; Bishop Arnaud, 211.
Perpignan, 43.
Perugia, 76, 80, 133, 176.
Perugino, 28, 52, 277.
photography in architecture, 35.
Picardy, 317.
Pierre de Montéreau, 58, 156.
Pierrefonds, 162.
Pisa, 66, 76, 77, 272; style of, 85, 93; baptistery, 66, 84; Campo Santo, 66-7; cathedral, 67, 69; domestic Gothic, 68; Spina chapel, 71.
Pisano, Giovanni, 68.
Pistoja, 83, 85; baptistery, 84; cathedral, 83; S. Bartolomeo, 84; S. Giovanni Evangelista, 84.
plain-song, 24, 119.
Poblet, 42, 126.
Pointed Architecture in Germany, 317.
Poitiers, 176; Moustier-neuf, 231, 242; S. Hilaire, 231, 236, 242; S. Radegonde, 231; Bishop Gerald, 211.
Poitou, 129.
Polignac, 230.
Pont de l'Arche, 139.
Porretta, La, 86.
Port Vendres, 44.
Prague, 48.
Prémontré, 171.

Pre-Raphaelite Movement, 13, 32, 46, 135.
Priests in England, mediaeval, 20; in France, modern, 121, 143, 144, 191.
Proctor, Marquita (Mrs. G. E. Street), 7, 10, 12, 13, 21, 26, 38, 45, 51, 57.
Prynne, Mr., 6.
proportion in architecture, 168, 240, 269.
Provence, 251.
Pugin, A. W. N., 292.
Pusey, Edward, 13.
Pustertal, 36.
Le Puy, 39, 201, 202 sqq., 212, 221, 246; cathedral, 205 sqq., 239; chapel, 229; S. Laurent, 230, S. Michel, 203, 226 sqq., 247; paintings, 216; Bishop Evodius, 203; Bishop Guy, 228; Bishop Jean de Bourbon, 214–16; Bishop Peter, 220; Bishop Stephen, 220; François Gimbert, 225.

Quakers, 11.

Raphael, 28, 277.
Ratisbon, 33, 320, 326, 328.
Ratzebourg, 328.
Ravello, 51.
Ravenna, 220, 243.
Rayham abbey, 125.
Recanati, 51.
religious feeling, 11, 12, 19, 20, 21, 24, 49, 54, 114.
Renaissance, 42, 49, 52, 68, 71, 73, 76, 95, 187, 216, 307.
Reni, Guido, 52.
restoration, 21, 30, 51, 54, 66, 121, 129, 140, 191, 208, 255, 265, 298; his own, 30 sq., 54.
Rheims, 58, 108, 113, 129, 131, 162, 163, 184; cathedral, 113,
184; S. Jacques, 186, 189; S. Maurice, 189; S. Remi, 134, 170, 187; archbishop's palace, 186; Maison des Musiciens, 190, 308.
Rhineland, 36, 38, 174, 176, 275, 317, 318, 322, 323, 327.
ringhiera, 86.
Riom, 231, 238, 241, 251.
Ripoll, 42.
Ripon, 55.
Robert de Coucy, 58, 184.
Robinson, H. Crabbe, 26.
Romanesque, 42, 45, 67, 70, 88, 103, 176, 187, 202, 222, 244, 245, 317, 322.
Rome, 51, 53, 95; American church, 30; English church, 30.
Rossetti, 14, 16, 46, 57.
Rouen, 16, 33, 114, 117, 132, 135, 163, 193, 209, 244; S. Ouen, 117, 173; Archbishop Maurice, 133, 135.
Royal Academy, 27, 57.
Royal Institute of British Architects, 27; *Transactions of*, 27, 201, 243.
Royat, 215, 231.
Ruskin, 36.
Russia, 32.

S. Albans, 54, 274.
S. Croix, Montmajour, 229.
S. Denis, 318.
S. Georges de Boscherville, 134, 137 sq., 156.
S. Gemignano, 91, 92.
S. Genés, 231.
S. Germer, 131, 134, 154 sqq.; Abbot Peter de Wesencourt, 156.
S. Gervais, 58.
S. Gothard, 36.
S. James the Less, Westminster, 28.

S. Jean de Maurienne, 64.
S. Leu d'Esserent, 102, 104, 131, 141, 146 sqq.
S. Lô, 124.
S. Loup, 124.
S. Margaret, Liverpool, 30.
S. Mary, Stone, 255 sqq.
S. Médard, 170.
S. Nectaire, 231, 233, 238.
S. Nicodime, Athens, 249.
S. Omer, abbey of S. Bertin, 99, 303; Notre Dame, 100 sqq., 137, 303.
S. Quentin, 106, 107, 131, 162, 188.
S. Saturnin, 231, 236, 238.
S. Sophia, 243, 245.
Saarburg, 197.
Saintes, 231.
Sakraments-Haus, 277, 302, 311, 316.
Salamanca, 44.
Salerno, 51.
Salisbury, 55, 128, 181, 189.
San Sebastian, 44.
Saragossa, 38, 44, 46.
Savona, 91.
Scala, 51.
Scott, Gilbert G., 5, 28, 31; Scott and Moffatt, 6, 59.
Scott, G., 54.
Sedding, Edmund, 21.
Séez, 163.
Segovia, 44.
Senlis, 102, sqq., 108, 116, 131, 147, 149; cathedral, 103; S. Frambourg, 104; S. Pierre, 102.
Sens, 34.
Shelley, 28, 52.
shrines, 158, 239, 306; of S. Taurin at Evreux, 116; of S. Elizabeth at Marburg, 300.
Siena, 11, 51, 71 sqq., 76, 176; Academy, 74; baptistery, 72;
campanile, 72; *Campo*, 72; cathedral, 73; hospital, 282.
Sierck, 197.
Sierra Morena, 42.
Sigüenza, 44.
Soest, 37, 275, 311, 313, 314, 323, 327; cathedral, 314; S. Paul's, 315; S. Peter's, 312, 315; Wiesen-Kirche, 312, 315 sqq., 320, 322.
Soissonnais, 38, 162, 169.
Soissons, 131, 162, 163 sqq., 188; cathedral, 164; S. Jean des Vignes, 163, 166; S. Léger, 168; S. Pierre, 169.
Some Account of Gothic Architecture in Spain, 27, 32, 37, 39, 40, 41 sqq., 46, 51, 320.
Some Account of the Church of S. Mary, Stone, near Dartford, 255.
Some Churches in Kent, Surrey, and Sussex, 268.
Some Churches of Le Puy en Velay, and Auvergne, 201.
du Sommerard, cited, 173, 179.
Soria, 42.
Southampton, 160.
Southwell, 54.
Spain, 41, 42, 43, 47, 48, 118, 206, 229.
Spain's debt to G. E. S., 45; to France, 47.
Spanish towns, 42, 44; travel, 45.
Splügen, 36.
Spoleto, 51.
square east ends, 137, 173, 176, 265, 320.
Stephen, Leslie, 49; Sir James Fitz-James, 49.
Stevenson, 39.
Stone Church, 255 sqq.
Strasburg, 33, 162, 318, 326.
Street, Arthur Edmund, 6, 24, 57.

Street, George Edmund, life: born, 2; goes to London, 5; again, 21; to Wantage, 7; to Oxford, 13; abroad, 21; to Italy, 34; to Spain, 41; married, 13, 57; died, 27; buried, 27, 57. London, 21, 24, 26; competitions, 21, 22, 46, 54; controversies, 54 sq.; commissions, 6, 7, 21, 22, 27; appointments, 7, 55; honours, 27; books, 27, 34, 41 sq., 49 sq.; papers, 32, 37, 39, 201, 268. His buildings, 28, 30; drawings, 35; note-books, 34; travel, 21, 27, 31, 32; way of life, 24; knowledge, 31, 37, 40; character, 3, 23, 25, 26; energy, 3, 8, 9, 23; enthusiasm, 13, 25; wit, 25; genius, 13, 26, 35, 41; religion, 1, 9, 24, 53, 54, 114; affections of the hearth, 9, 12, 57; friends, 26, 52, 57; relation to other architects, 10, 24, 26, 27; eye for landscape and the picturesque, 36, 62, 65, 75, 86, 88, 90, 92, 94, 108, 137, 171, 172, 292, 295, 307, 313. Family: his father, 2; mother, 9; sister, 6; brother, 4, 5, 6; son, 6, 24, 57; first wife, 7, 38, 45, 124; second wife, 10, 53, 57; father-in-law, 10, 51.
Street, Thomas, the elder, 2.
Street, Thomas, the younger, 4, 5, 6.
Suffolk, 128.
Surrey, 268.
Susa, 64, 90.
Sussex, 5, 268.
Swinburne, A. C. S., 48.
Switzerland, 36, 37, 39, 48, 245, 313.

Tarragona, 44.

Tarrazona, 44.
Templars, at Eunate, 229; at Laon, 183, 229; at Metz, 229; at Le Puy, 229; at Segovia, 229.
Thames, 7, 21, 58.
Theodore, Brother, cited, 228.
Thrasimene, 74.
Timbered houses, 118, 119, 154, 313; roofs, 118, 160, 246, 305.
tissus, 220, 224.
Toledo, 43, 45, 92.
Torcello, 226.
Toro, 42.
Torrington, 5.
Tortoir, 193.
Toscanella, 94.
Toul, 195; cathedral, 195; S. Gengoult, 195-6.
Toulouse, 38, 231.
Touraine, 129.
Tournai, 175, 305.
Tournus, 62, 246.
Tours, S. Martin, 244.
Transactions, 32; of the R. I. B. A., 39, 201, 243; of the Exeter Architectural Society, 268; of the Kent Archaeological Society, 255.
tree of Jesse, 139, 225.
Trèves, 175, 195, 196, 197, 221.
tribunes, 165.
Trinidad, 30.
Troyes, 34, 131.
Tudela, 44.
Turin, 65, 89-90.
Tuy, 42.
Tyndall, 49.
Tyrol, 36, 48.

Ulm, 33, 327.
Umbria, 51, 53, 75-81.
University, 2, 7.
Urgell, Seo de, 43.

Val d'Aosta, 48.

Val di Chiana, 75.
Valencia, 43, 44.
Valladolid, 43, 47.
Van Eyck, 274.
Vauclair, 183.
Vaux-sous-Laon, 183.
Velay, le, 39, 201, 202; *États de*, 214; archives of, 215.
Vendôme, 148.
Venice, 133, 194, 224, 248, 289, 304; S. Marco, 4, 27, 212, 242 sq., 249.
Verdier, cited, 161, 184.
Vergato, 86.
Verneilh, cited, 248.
Verona, 71, 133, 270, 279, 284.
Vevey, English church, 30.
Vézelay, 35.
Vienna, 48, 322.
Vienne, 212.
village churches, 22; French, 131, 143, 145; English, 257.
Viollet-le-Duc, cited, 144, 150, 156, 162, 173, 184, 211, 215, 231.
Viterbo, 94.
Vitoria, 43, 44.
Volvic, 231.
Vosges, 36.

Wales, 1.
Wallenstadt, lake of, 36.
Wantage, 7.
Warfield, 265.
Webbe, the elder, 13.
Webbe, Philip, 21.

Wellington, Duke of, 41.
Wells, 128.
Wensley, 274.
Westminster Abbey, 27, 32, 58, 204, 244, 255, 258, 318.
West of England, 4.
wheel of Fortune, 153.
Wilars de Honecort, 184.
Wilberforce, Samuel, 13.
Wimbourne, 279.
Winchester, 5, 9, 12, 55; font, 160.
Worcester, 2.
Wordsworth, 4.
workmen, mediaeval: masons, 240; sculptor, Gaulfredus, 220, another (Robert), 234; architects, Pierre de Montéreau, 58, 156; Robert de Coucy, 58, 184; metal-workers, 274, Hans Apengeter, 277, John and Nicholas of Bingen, 222; silversmith, 225, François Gimbert, 234; glass painter, Dominic Livi, 276.
Worms, 249, 321, 322.
Würtzburg, 33.

York, 27, 32, 55.
Yorkshire, 4, 128.
Ypres, 303 sq., 311.

Zamora, 44, 46.
Zaragoza, 44, 46, *v*. Saragossa.
Zinzig, 323.
Zurich, lake of, 36.